D1349557

EXPLORATIONS IN SOCIOLOGY

British Sociological Association conference volume series

* Published by Macmillan

Contents

List of Figures

List of Tables

Notes on Contributors

Harriet Bradley is currently a Senior Lecturer in Sociology at Sunderland Polytechnic. Her research interests include the history and sociology of work, gender inequalities and historiography, and her recent book, *Men's Work, Women's Work*, is a history of gender segregation in employment.

Brian Elliott is visiting Associate Professor in the Department of Anthropology and Sociology at the University of British Columbia. His publications include *The Petite Bourgeoisie: Comparative Studies of an Uneasy Stratum* (1981), with Frank Bechhofer; *Property and Power in a City* (1989), with David McCrone.

Ralph Fevre has researched and published studies of racism, the sociology of labour markets, and industrial organisation. His main publications are *Cheap Labour and Racial Discrimination* (Gower, 1984), and *Wales is Closed* (Spokesman, 1989).

Bob Hall is Senior Lecturer in Sociology at the University of Canterbury in Christchurch, New Zealand. He has carried out locality studies and social history in New Zealand and Muncie Indiana, and has published the results of these studies.

Cynthia Hay graduated with a BA in History, and a PhD in critical philosophy of history, and taught in the departments of sociology at Bedford College, and Brunel University. She is currently employed in the Institute of Community Studies, and researching the sociological history of patronage in science.

Rosemary Mellor is Lecturer in Sociology at the University of Manchester. Her main interests are urban sociology and analysis of contemporary British society. Relevant publications include 'The Urbanisation of Britain', *International Journal of Urban and Regional Studies* (1983); and 'Urban sociology, a trend report', *Sociology* (1989).

Suzanne Najam graduated from Cambridge College of Art and Technology, and took her PhD at Edinburgh University on Political Radicalism among Fife Miners. She is currently employed on the Scottish Coalfield Study, and has published the results of her research.

Roger Penn is Senior Lecturer in Sociology at Lancaster University, where he directs the Rochdale study into Social Change and Economic Life. He is author of *Skilled Workers in the Class Structure* (1985) and *Class, Power and Technology* (1989).

James Smyth is a Research Fellow in Economic and Social History at Edinburgh University, and previously was employed on the Social Change and Economic Life initiative at the Research Centre for Social Sciences. He has published on Scottish labour history and politics, and is a member of the editorial boards of the Scottish Labour History Society Journal, and Radical Scotland.

Charles Tilly is Distinguished Professor of Sociology and History at the New School for Social Research in New York City, where he directs the Center for Studies of Social Change. Most of his work concerns large-scale social change and popular collective action in Europe and North America. His most recent books are *Big Structures, Large Processes, Huge Comparisons* (Russell Sage Foundation, 1985), *The Contentious French* (Harvard University Press, 1986), and *Coercion, Capital, and European States* (Basil Blackwell, 1990).

Gary Wickham teaches social and political theory at Murdoch University, Perth, Australia. His publications include an edited book – *Social Theory and Legal Politics* – and articles on Foucault, power, law, and postmodernism. He is currently doing research on pluralism and democracy.

1 Introduction: Sociology and History, the Past and the Present

The Editors

In 1988 the British Sociological Association held its annual conference in Edinburgh on the theme 'Sociology and History'. Nearly a quarter of a century earlier, the historian E. H. Carr (1964) had called for an open frontier between the disciplines. This volume examines the growing traffic across this frontier and in particular, what might somewhat provocatively be called the sociological uses of history.

Carr had been confident that bridges would be built across the disciplinary frontiers of sociology and history, even though it would require sociologists giving up their tendency to deal in abstractions and generalisations about 'Society', and historians their anxious defence of history as a branch of 'humane letters'.

In the early 1960s, there seemed every likelihood that Carr would be proved correct. Historians like Carr were an advance-guard intent on creating a 'new history' which would break with the orthodoxy of narrative history as 'story telling', which would generate analytical and theoretically informed accounts of the past. In those days, sociology too was beginning to break with its orthodoxy, particularly with the highly abstract model-building of structural-functionalism. C. Wright Mills (1959) had attacked such citadels of American sociological orthodoxy, and promoted the idea that a 'sociological imagination' extended well beyond the discipline's practitioners. Mills argued that little sense could be made of human relations without fusing 'history' and 'biography', the understanding of how macro-social processes fused with and made sense of the experiences of people and their families. In Britain a new generation of sociologists emerged from 1960s onwards, a generation which seemed well placed to avoid the ahistorical analyses of both American functionalism and European metatheory. This was a generation which had been exposed to the new wave of social history, as exemplified in E. P. Thompson's *The Making of the English Working Class* (Thompson, 1963) or Christopher Smout's *A History of the Scottish People* (Smout, 1969). The essays in this volume are a small testament to the cross-fertilisation between sociology and history which has gone on in the last 25 years or so. How successful has it been?

At a minimum, there has been some swapping of concepts and techniques, as members of two self-contained professions passed useful bits and pieces over the professional walls which divided them. Radicals like the late Philip Abrams, however, wanted to demolish the walls entirely. In his collection of essays, *Historical Sociology*, Abrams said;

> In my understanding of history and sociology there can be no relationship between them, because, in terms of their functional preoccupations, history and sociology are and always have been the same thing. (Abrams, 1982, p. x).

Both seek to understand human agency, and both are impelled to understand the making of social structures as a chronological process. He argued 'Try asking serious questions about the contemporary world and see if you can do without historical answers' (1982, p. 1). The relationship of structural constraints to human action is shared by both disciplines. Abrams had little time for historians who indulged in 'how it was' studies ('tales signifying nothing'), nor for sociologists who abstracted structure, trends and processes from history, and who indulged in 'ahistorical historicism'. It followed from Abrams' radical stance that 'historical sociology' was not to be viewed as a specialist sub-division of sociology, but as the essence of the discipline. Abrams' untimely death prevented the development of this project, but it is a view championed in this volume by Charles Tilly, who has become its eminent standard-bearer.

He leads off a trio of papers which offer assessments of the sociological and historical dimensions of analysis from contrasting perspectives. In the first of these, Tilly writes as a sociologist assessing the prospects of adopting a historical perspective in sociological work. He writes that 'Social processes are path-dependent. That is why history matters'. Far from 'historical sociology' becoming a specialism defined, like survey sociology, by its methods and materials, Tilly argues that it should dissolve and permeate all aspects of sociology. Once the discipline accepts this, he argues, 'sociology will have realised its potential as history of the present'.

Cynthia Hay, on the other hand, presents a survey from the point of view of a historian of the sometimes strained relationships between traditional forms of history and newer forms of social scientific analysis. She argues that the dominant form of this relationship has been the producer-consumer view of sociology and history, which allowed historians to borrow (as 'consumers', as it were) theories from the social sciences. In doing so, historians confronted the unwillingness of sociologists to admit that social theories were themselves time-bound, reflecting the context which shaped them.

By the 1970s historians were beginning to question the apparently easy relationship between sociology and history. Historians like Lawrence Stone had grown sceptical about the claims of sociology and other social sciences to provide an explanatory model for historians to work within. He wrote:

Sociology was also trapped in a wholly static vision of society, partly by its own devotion to the survey research technique, and partly by its wholesale adoption of functionalist theory. (Stone, 1982, p. 9)

Such a characterisation of sociology might seem to its British practitioners quite unfair, even bemusing, but it reflected a not uncommon view outwith the discipline. Historians of a more radical disposition also began to question the relationship of producer-sociology to consumer-history. Stedman Jones (1976) pointed out that such a division of labour compounded the problems of both history and sociology. It was no use, he argued, historians looking to sociology to resolve what was fundamentally the problem of the scientific content and status of history; nor had it driven sociologists to give up their primitive historial categorisations such as 'industrial' society. Sociology had to give up its pretensions to be an 'already constituted science', and history had to derive its own set of explanatory models before each could contribute to a 'single ideological terrain'.

On the sociological side of the fence, new developments in the discipline seemed less favourable to the erosion of the distinction between sociology and history. Sociologists had become sensitised to the problems of meaning and understanding, to the view that explaining behaviour had to be embedded in the sets of meanings and orientations which actors brought to their actions. If these could best be explored by in-depth, qualitative interviewing, then dead people told no tales. At the same time, there was developing within sociology a strand of thinking which has led to a certain scepticism about the solidity of historical 'events'. This line of thought is given systematic expression in this volume by Gary Wickham. He presents a survey of the epistemological relationship between sociology and history which serves to warn sociologists against any easy appropriation of the past or any uncritical dealings with 'History'.

If, by the late 1970s and early 1980s, the prospects of a marriage between sociology and history had begun to fade, what had happened? We cannot ignore the effects of how disciplines have been institutionalised and professionalised in the academic world. History had established itself as an independent professional discipline much earlier (between 1870 and 1930, according to Stone); sociology had not established itself within British academia until the 1960s, and then with some difficulty. Each discipline had sought to establish itself into university departments and professional associations, setting up self-reproducing mechanisms through post-graduate training. So there emerged two sub-cultures, as it were, each with its own values, vocabulary and styles of thought, reinforced by processes of training. Once established, these institutional structures carried their own momentum and rivalries, not easily disbanded and amalgamated. At the same time, sub-disciplines, particularly within history, began to hive off, and by the 1970s, 'new history', largely social science history in the form of departments of social and/or economic history, had been formed. Considerable rivalries emerged within 'history' itself, especially between 'narrative' history of the old school, and the new history with its emphasis on quantification and explanation.

Must we concede then that the marriage of sociology and history is now unlikely to take place, or, indeed, that the period of uneasy cohabitation is coming to an end? If the optimism which Carr and Mills expressed in the early 1960s had been replaced by the more mundane realities of the 1970s and 1980s, then we should not infer that the relationship has ended. As this volume shows – indeed, the three other volumes drawn from this conference attest – the relationship continues to be one of the most fruitful in the social sciences.

The chapters in this volume represent an important stage in the development of 'historical sociology'/'sociological history'.

The first three chapters in the volume, by Tilly, Hay and Wickham, can be seen as representing a triangulation on the problematic relationship between sociology and history, and as such provide a general introduction to a parallel problem, namely, the relation between the analysis of the past and the analysis of the present. The other chapters are of a more substantive focus, and have been chosen because they shed light on facets of a more narrowly defined issue, namely, 'interpreting the past, understanding the present', the title of the book.

For an understanding of present social structures and patterns of action, an understanding of the past is not simply desirable for reasons of conceptual comprehensiveness – a meritorious optional extra, as it were, – but is rather a necessity. We are speaking here as sociologists interested in understanding the present by means of an adequate interpretation of the past. It is, in many ways, rather an instrumental attitude towards the historical perspective. We are not interested in the past for its own sake, but rather because it is a vital component in making sense of the present.

Should historians be resentful of this perspective? Perhaps, but once we define our aim as understanding the present (and even the future), there is an inevitable assymetry in the relationship between a sociological understanding of the present, and an understanding of the past. The former needs the latter in a direct sense rather more than the latter needs the former. This asymetry is to some extent reflected in the confident sense of appropriation evident in Charles Tilly's chapter compared with the more defensive, even at times forced, ways in which history has adopted approaches developed in a contemporary context, as described by Cynthia Hay.

One theme which runs through many of the chapters in this volume is that there are significant dangers in such an instrumental approach, concerned as it is with using the past to make sense of the present. Plainly, such an approach runs the risk of manipulation in the sense that we are prone to accept the understanding of the past which fits best with a preferred interpretation of the present. Here we come close to the idea of the 'mythical past', an idea running through many of the chapters in this volume, whether in terms of communities' senses of their origins (Hall), or in terms of that summoned up by the founders of the 'new industrial sociology' (Penn). Many contributors make the point that our understanding of the past is strongly conditioned by our stake in the present. There is nothing unproblematic about dipping into the past to anchor more solidly our understanding of the present.

In general terms then, our instrumental approach to the past makes it all the more important to be scrupulous about our approach to it, for our instrumentalism makes us prone to adopt a convenient rather than a valid interpretation. However, overemphasising the dangers inherent in appropriating the past in order to ground our understanding of the present can only give comfort to the sceptical view – why bother? If understanding the past to make sense of the present is an enterprise so fraught with danger, why not stick to the present?

This book seeks to answer the sceptic. Perhaps the most powerful line of response is that which centres on Charles Tilly's cogent point that 'social processes are path-dependent'. To the extent that sociological analysis has to do with teasing out the patterns of causal influence which determine current patterns of events and social processes, then in tracing these patterns of causal influence we are automatically led back into the past. However, there is no automatic cut-off point in this process of tracing back the causal influences. When this process is arbitrarily or prematurely halted, the web of causal analysis is left hanging – either over the void of 'no history' or the misleading implications of 'bad history' (to borrow the phraseology used by Ralph Fevre in this volume).

Thus, one theme which runs through many of the contributions is how to improve the process of backward anchorage, of making the web of historical determinations more comprehensive.

More generally, the eight chapters of a more specific nature which follow the surveys by Tilly, Hay and Wickham, can be seen as illustrating different facets of the problems and opportunities presented by our sociological and 'instrumental' approach to the past, by our interest in better understanding the present on the basis of a true understanding of the past. Each chapter has a different balance between pointing out the flaws of previously accepted versions of the past, making a general case for a valid rooting of the present in the past and, perhaps most importantly, illustrating how this embedding can be done and showing us the nuts and bolts of how to do it.

The chapters by Hall and Smyth introduce us straight away to some of the methodological issues and practicalities involved. After surveying some of the factors underlying 'the distortion of the past' in previous phases of the community study approach, Bob Hall offers a detailed account of the methods used, involving a blending of official data sources and oral history, in the 'historial reconstruction' of a New Zealand farming community. Jim Smyth provides insight into how a historian adjusts to working with social scientists more directly focussed on the present and highlights the problems and possibilities inherent in such an interdisciplinary approach.

The next three accounts offer a range of imaginative perspectives on how the historical dimension can be incorporated. Brian Elliott surveys the potential of the 'forensic use' of biographical materials both in an individual and a family context. In terms of our earlier discussion, such biographical or life-history techniques can shed light on the kinds of 'path-determinations' which are missed by more macro- or statistically-oriented methods.

Whereas a major theme of the contributions to this volume has been the exposure of the extent to which sociologists' interpretations of the present are influenced by accepted images of the past, Suzanne Najam's chapter presents a helpful corrective to this professional self-absorption. She addresses the issue of how actors in society are influenced by their images of the past, by their 'significant history' by showing how the immensely powerful sense of historical identity among the Fife miners both maintained them through their industrial struggles and yet had the potential to blind them to the impact of social and economic changes which were incongruent with their historical vision.

Rosemary Mellor offers an illustration of the value of the historical perspective in understanding the present at the macro-level – that of the history of urbanisation in Britain. Again the enterprise is directed towards enriching our understanding of current events by firmly embedding them in their historical context. She clarifies our (often rather unformulated) sense that a fundamental transition is occurring in the form of British urbanism by identifying and describing the current 'authoritarian liberal transition', placing it in the context of long phases of British urbanisation and in particular contrasting it with the transition to a 'state family welfare' phase of urbanisation which took place in the decades around the turn of the century.

The final three chapters in the volume can be seen as forming a subsection devoted to issues of the present and the past in the field of industrial sociology. Roger Penn sets the scene with a highly critical view of the historical grounding of some of the key texts of the 'New Industrial Sociology'. He sees much of their argument as fatally flawed because it rests on what is seen as an unproblematic version of historical development but which is in fact just one interpretation of a highly contested set of issues. Penn calls for an industrial sociology which is much more aware of the contested nature of historical evidence and is thus aware of the necessity to construct carefully its own historical foundations.

The chapters by Bradley and Fevre can be seen as careful attempts to carry out this prescription. In each case there is a refusal to allow a particular aspect of industrial social relations – in Bradley's case paternalism and in Fevre's case sub-contracting – to be assigned to a dusty pigeonhole as a particular expression of one phase of a pre-ordained logic of industrial development. As both authors show, paternalism and sub-contracting are much more complicated than that, and an understanding of their role in the present and in the past requires considerable conceptual refinement. They are as complex as the history of the industrial forms of society in which they are embedded.

The 1988 BSA Conference was a time for taking stock of the relationship between sociology and history. In the main, this stock-taking was a by-product of research which quite naturally and to a certain extent unself-consciously had adopted a combination of historical and sociological approaches. In this volume we have concentrated on one aspect of this relationship – usually quite smooth in practice but quite often stormy in principle. From an unapologetically sociological viewpoint, we have sought to highlight just what it is that we are doing when we attempt to anchor our understanding of the present in an interpretation of the past.

REFERENCES

P. Abrams, *Historical Sociology* (Shepton Mallet: Open Books, 1982).

E. H. Carr, *What is History?* (Harmondsworth: Penguin, 1964).

G. Stedman Jones, 'From historical sociology to theoretical history', *British Journal of Sociology*, 27, 3 (1976).

C. Wright Mills, *The Sociological Imagination* (Oxford: Oxford University Press, 1959).

T. C. Smout, *A History of the Scottish People* (Glasgow: Collins, 1969).

L. Stone, *The Past and the Present* (London: Routledge & Kegan Paul, 1982).

E. P. Thompson, *The Making of the English Working Class* (Harmondsworth: Penguin, 1963).

2 Future History[1]
Charles Tilly

PAST SOCIOLOGY

Sociology began its separate existence as historical speculation.
Auguste Comte, coiner of the name for the enterprise that finally
stuck, had no mean plans for his cherished sociology. He considered
its future construction as the crowning achievement of scientific
enlightenment. Just as astronomy displaced astrology and chemistry
displaced alchemy, sociology would displace theological speculation
about human affairs. Comte spoke of:

> the invariant hierarchy, at once historical, dogmatic, scientific, and
> logical, of the six fundamental sciences, mathematics, astronomy,
> physics, chemistry, biology, and sociology, of which the first
> constitutes the sole point of departure and the last the sole essential
> goal of all positive philosophy (Comte, 1963, p. 133)

Dealing with the most complex subject matter and building on all the
other sciences, according to Comte, sociology would take its place at
the head of the scientific hierarchy, immediately above biology. Thus
sociology had two equally gratifying roles to play, as analyst of the
process by which humanity progressed from Theological to Meta-
physical to Positive forms of thought, and as the very culmination of
that process.

Comte's speculation about the stages of human understanding
counts as metahistory, the effort to discern a temporal pattern in all
human experience. We can usefully distinguish metahistory from
history, which examines variation in human action as a function of
time and place, and which normally deals with much less than the
totality of human action. As history approaches universality, indeed,
it becomes metahistory. On the whole professional historians shun
metahistory, or treat it as a taste one ought to indulge outside of
regular working hours. Metahistory enjoys some of the same disre-
pute among historians that the search for a single prototype of all

9

human languages receives among linguists. In both cases, workaday practitioners do not so much doubt the possibility of such a discovery in principle as sense its vulnerability to quackery, self-deception, and wasted effort in practice.

If few of Comte's successors publicly proclaimed sociology to be queen of the sciences, many of them continued to practise it chiefly as historical speculation of one variety or another. Herbert Spencer, Oswald Spengler, Pitirim Sorokin, and many lesser souls erected metahistories as the frames for their sociologies (Spencer, 1897, Spengler, 1926–28, Sorokin, 1962). Another brand of historical inquiry, furthermore, appeared at the edge of sociology, among the followers of Karl Marx and Max Weber; both schools pursued ambitious inquiries into the actual unfolding of social processes in time and space, making arguments and achieving results that professional historians would recognise, however grudgingly, as impinging on their own enterprise.

Nevertheless, from the time of Durkheim onward, the main body of professional sociologists turned away from grand historical schemes, and from history itself. Sociology – especially American sociology – became the systematic study of the present. Sociologists became specialists in structures and processes, rather than times and places, on the presumption that currently observable uniformities in structures and processes transcend the limits of time and place.

Less so than economists but more so than political scientists, anthropologists, or geographers, sociologists built a discipline in which time and place served merely as convenient markers, not as systematic objects of analysis or ever-present bases of variation. By the time of a semi-official American review of the field in 1959, the editors could describe historical sociology as an 'important subject', but omit it from their survey 'because of limitations of space' (Merton, Broom and Cottrell, 1959, p. vi). They reached their decision despite the fact that one of the editors, Robert Merton, was making distinguished contributions to the historical study of science. The authors of articles on sociological subjects that aforesaid limitations of space did allow into the volume, furthermore, rarely mentioned historical problems and material, doing so for the most part when sketching the intellectual background to the present-day, presumably more scientific, enterprise. From the 1959 publication, one could reasonably have concluded that, with the exception of an occasional oddity such as Merton's work, sociology and history had almost nothing to do with each other.

The history and sociology of that time did, in fact, dally now and then. In the 1950s, not only Merton, but also such scholars as Reinhard Bendix, George Homans, and Barrington Moore, Jr., were pursuing historical research (Bendix, 1956, Homans, 1962, Moore, 1966). Within his metahistorical frame, Pitirim Sorokin was continuing his more specific historical inquiries into altruism (Sorokin, 1950). Scholars who maintained self-conscious contact with European social thought commonly wrote in a historical idiom. Nevertheless, these historically-oriented sociologists constituted a small remnant in a largely present-oriented discipline.

What is more, twentieth-century sociologists commonly adopted a dismissive definition of their relationship to historians. As Charles Ellwood described the division of labour in a widely-read text first published in 1910:

History is a concrete, descriptive science of society which attempts to construct a picture of the social past. Sociology, however, is an abstract, theoretical science of society concerned with the laws and principles which govern social organization and social change. In one sense, sociology is narrower than history inasmuch as it is an abstract science, and in another sense it is wider than history because it concerns itself not only with the social past but also with the social present. The facts of contemporary social life are indeed even more important to the sociologist than the facts of history, although it is impossible to construct a theory of social evolution without taking into full account all the facts available in human history, and for this reason we must consider history one of the very important methods of sociology. Upon its evolutionary or dynamic side sociology may be considered a sort of philosophy of history; at least it attempts to give a scientific theory which will explain the social changes which history describes concretely (Ellwood, 1935, p. 18).

Answering in 1964 the question 'What Is Sociology?', Alex Inkeles offered a similar contrast: 'The historian prides himself on the explicitness, the concreteness of detail which characterizes his discipline. The sociologist is more likely to abstract from concrete reality, to categorize and generalize, to be interested in what is true not only of a particular people's history but of the histories of many different peoples' (Inkeles, 1964, p. 21). For some reason sociologists did not recognise the condescension in that distinction between those who gather the facts and those who explain them, those who describe and those who analyse, those who grub and those who pluck, those who scrub and those who polish.

History Redivivus

In any case, the years since Inkeles' summary have seen a great revival of historical thinking and historical research in sociology. Perhaps 'revival' is the wrong word, for two reasons. First, the sort of historical work sociologists have undertaken over the past quarter-century has few precedents in the speculative schemata of the nineteenth century. Second, the properly historical writing of founding fathers Marx and Weber had few repercussions inside academic sociology, especially its American variant, until the 1960s. Within standard sociology, there was little history to revive. To a large degree, the expansion of historical work among sociologists marked a new departure.

Why did the new growth occur? I have no intention of tracing the intellectual history of a strongly historical sociology, or even of proposing an explanation of its expansion. As an active participant in that expansion, I hope someone else will do both. Here, in any case, is the most salient fact: out of a sustained critique of the ideas of 'development' and 'modernisation' that dominated sociological analyses of large-scale social change for two decades after World War II grew an effort to historicise such analyses – to extend backward the period over which one analysed great transformations, to seek past analogues of present changes, to try out general ideas concerning the consequences of sweeping processes on well-documented historical experiences of similar processes. At the same time a minority of historians, likewise critical of the models of large-scale change that prevailed in their own discipline, were turning to the social sciences, including sociology, for alternative ways of analysing the past (Zunz, 1985).

The turn to history could have proceeded at any of four levels, metahistorical, world-systemic, macrohistorical, or microhistorical:

metahistorical: attempting to identify temporal patterns in all human experience
world-systemic: tracing the succession of world-systems, the largest connected sets of human interaction

macrohistorical: examining large-scale structures and processes within world-systems
microhistorical: studying the experiences of individuals and well-defined groups within the limits set by large-scale structures and processes

Some of sociology's historical revival has taken place at each of these levels. Anthony Giddens and Michael Mann have, for example, started to fashion new metahistories of power and social change (Giddens, 1985, Mann, 1986). Although most of their analyses have focussed on change and variation within what they conceive as the contemporary capitalist world-system, Immanuel Wallerstein and his collaborators have at least occasionally tried to chart the movement from one world-system to another. Numerous students of family structure, communities, inequality, and population processes have pursued microhistory. Yet the bulk of sociology's new historical effort has gone into macrohistory, the examination of large-scale structures and processes within world-systems. Thus we have sustained sociological treatments of farmers' movements in the US, of the European fertility decline, of the emergence of different forms of the welfare state.

Comparisons among populations identified by national states have occupied a large (to my mind, disproportionate) share of sociologists' historical energy; analyses of the so-called transition from feudalism to capitalism have, for example, repeatedly compared entities labelled France, England, Prussia, and so on. National states have had a large weight in Western history; they occupy an important place in my own historical work. But exclusive concentration on national states fosters a series of illusions: that behind the state stands a coherent society; that a single unit such as Prussia had an integrity making it possible to assign the unit a continuous history over many centuries, using schemes involving origins, stages, or developmental paths; that the important states, and therefore the ones worthy of sustained sociological analysis, were those that survived into the twentieth century; that comparison of the experiences of the survivor states will yield or test comprehensive explanations of capitalism's development. As soon as historical analysts start taking economic regions, cities, mercantile networks, churches, linguistic blocs, and other crucial social groupings into serious account, the illusions begin to fade, and the possibility of relating the histories of national states to these other histories begins to open up.

Whether conducted at the national scale or not, most of this work partakes of historicism, asserting that how things happen depends strongly on when and where they happen. Historicism permits analysts to claim that late industrialisers followed different paths than early industrialisers, that the presence of great landlords in a region at one point in time affected the subsequent possibility of democratic politics in that region, that the state of the economy during a given birth cohort's childhood shapes its members' orientations towards childbearing, and so on. Historicism counters the old sociological faith in the generality of relationships inferred from the proper systematic analysis of contemporary social life. The various intellectual enterprises that observers group together as 'historical sociology' lean implicitly towards historicism.

Not that they have great intellectual unity. The trouble with 'historical sociology' as the name of a specialty is that it groups inquiries by their methods and materials rather than by the ideas and phenomena with which they deal. The term parallels such labels as 'survey sociology' and 'qualitative sociology' – perhaps realities as coalitions *vis-à-vis* the rest of the field, but treacherous bases for common intellectual endeavours. Historical sociology, as actually practised, includes a variety of investigations at different edges of sociology: investigations of political processes, family structure, community organisation, inequality, ideological orientations, scientific activity, economic transformation, and much more. On the whole, the ideas guiding such investigations bind the investigators to others who are studying similar phenomena much more strongly than to fellow sociologists who likewise work chiefly on the past rather than the present. Nevertheless, the disparate enterprises called historical sociology have gained greatly in popularity over the last two decades, especially in the United States.

In 1959, cutting through a great deal of criticism and counter-criticism, Kingsley Davis declared that all sociologists were really functionalists of one sort or another; 'In a way it is appropriate to speak of functional analysis as something *within* anthropology', he wrote, 'because there are branches of that field that have totally different subject-matters. A similar statement with respect to *social* anthropology or sociology, however, is tautological, for the reason that structural-functional analysis *is* sociological analysis' (Davis, 1959, p. 771).

What should a thirtieth-anniversary version of Davis' presidential address say? Are we all now really historicists? Do we all now claim that where and when social changes occur strongly influence how they occur? No: in fact, plenty of sociology is still unclear about its time and place references, and unprepared to take time and place seriously. Although I have no survey to prove it, I would say that most sociologists in the United States and elsewhere still cling to the pursuit of generalities that transcend time and space, even large blocks of time and space such as world-systems. Historical sociology still represents a minority mood among sociologists.

Fears and Hopes

What future has historical work in sociology? Let me distinguish between my fearful predictions and my cherished hopes. Fearfully, I predict the institutionalisation of historical sociology: fixing of a labelled specialty in sections of learned societies, journals, courses, a share of the job market. I fear these likely outcomes for two reasons: first, because the 'field' lacks intellectual unity and, by its very nature, will forever lack it; second, because institutionalisation may well impede the spread of historical thinking to other parts of sociology. The other parts need that thinking badly.

My cherished hopes run in a different direction. In the short run, I would be delighted if more historical sociologists would broaden their scope from national comparisons to (1) other macrohistorical investigations, taking regions, markets, modes of production, connections among capitalists, and other large structures as their units of analysis; (2) world-systemic analyses, including new attempts to examine the actual historical circumstances under which European capitalism came to dominate most of the world's economies; and (3) microhistorical studies of structures and processes that sociologists now examine chiefly in the contemporary world.

In the long run, I hope for a miracle elixir, one that will dissolve the specialty of historical sociology, and let its premises – especially its historicism – permeate all of sociology. Thus not only students of capitalism and of family change, but also demographers and survey analysts, would find themselves examining how the relationships among their favoured variables altered as a function of region and historical era. The result would be a historically-grounded sociology of far greater intellectual power than its current incarnation.

A greatly broadened historical sociology can make two major contributions to the discipline. First, it can historicise sociological analyses: anchor them in time and place. If we now have established any important non-tautological generalisations that hold across all historical eras, they have not come to my attention. I do not deny in principle that any such generalisations can exist, but insist that we are better off for the time being trying to ground all generalisations historically: specifying their time and place limits, and attaching them to other empirical generalisations that reliably characterise social life within those time and place limits.

Second, a greatly broadened historical sociology can also draw in important problems that are prominent in historical analysis and in lived history, but somehow remain neglected in sociology. Most notably, it can force sociologists to examine how the residues of action at a given time constrain subsequent action. Arthur Stinch-combe provided an important example of that sort of historicising analysis in his discussion of the way that craft organisations persisted in some industries into the era of mass production (Stinchcombe, 1965). Allan Pred, a sociologically-inclined geographer, has similarly shown how the existing connections among cities in eighteenth-century North America constrained the subsequent growth of the North American urban system (Pred, 1973). In a phrase faintly echoing Karl Marx, Pred has recently preached that 'People do not produce history and places under conditions of their own choosing, but in the context of already existing, directly encountered social and spatial structures' (Pred, 1985, p. 8).

The linking idea is simple and powerful: past social relations and their residues – material, ideological, and otherwise – constrain present social relations, and consequently their residues as well. Once an employer has established ties with a particular source of labour, those ties affect his subsequent recruitment of labour, and may well reproduce themselves. Once developers have laid down a certain structure, that structure defines the opportunities for further development. Once people adopt a certain national language, that language circumscribes the other people with whom they can easily communicate. Such processes produce connectedness within time and space that goes beyond simple temporal and spatial autocorrela-tion; every existing structure stands in the place of many theoretically possible alternative structures, and its very existence affects the probabilities that the alternatives will ever come into being. In short, social processes are path-dependent. That is why history matters.

Consider some examples. The social organisation of migration affects the subsequent welfare of migrants and their descendants, among other reasons because some forms of migration build means of capital accumulation within families and ethnic groups, while others individualise whatever accumulation occurs. The proletarianisation of one generation of workers strongly affects the opportunities of the next generation of workers to become capitalists, artisans, or peasants. The efforts of great powers to build up the military capacities of friendly Third World states shape the likelihoods that the national armed forces will take over those states. The creation of collective-action repertoires through struggles between powerholders and their challengers limits the possibilities of action for all parties in the next round of struggle. Intergroup conflicts over jobs, land, or political power create new social actors, whose presence then alters the character and outcome of conflict. In all these processes, time and place matter fundamentally; when and where they occur affects how they occur. They therefore fall into the domain of history.

Of course, some sociologists are addressing these topics, and others like them; the historical revival has made a healthy difference. But we need more, more, more – enough more to refashion sociology as a whole so that it automatically takes time and place seriously, and seriously engages the challenge of placing its regularities firmly within historical eras. If these things happen, sociology will have realised its potential as history of the present.

At that point, as Philip Abrams long since prescribed, the distinction between history and sociology will have disappeared. 'Historical sociology is not', wrote Abrams,

> a matter of imposing grand schemes of evolutionary development on the relationship of the past to the present. Nor is it merely a matter of recognising the historical background to the present. It is the attempt to understand the relationship of personal activity and experience on the one hand and social organisation on the other as something that is continuously constructed in time. (Abrams, 1982, p. 16)

Abrams barred the road back to Comte, and opened it to Marx and Weber. Ultimately, however, the road back to anywhere concerned him less than the road forward: where should the historical enterprise within sociology go? It should go on to become the foundation of all sociology.

NOTE

1. This chapter has its origins in notes from an informal talk at the annual
meeting of the Eastern Sociological Society in New York City, April 1986.
I am grateful to Kai Erikson and Charles Perrow for comments on that
talk, and to Charles Lemert for encouragement to distill the notes into a
short essay. Because I mean the chapter to state opinions and provoke
discussion rather than prove points, I have omitted the bulky documentation many of its assertions would require.

REFERENCES

Philip Abrams, *Historical Sociology* (Ithaca: Cornell University Press, 1982).
Reinhard Bendix, *Work and Authority in Industry* (New York: Wiley, 1956).
Auguste Comte, *Discours sur l'esprit positif* (Paris: Union Générale
d'Editions, 1963).
Kingsley Davis, 'The Myth of Functional Analysis in Sociology and Anthro-
pology', *American Sociological Review* 24: 757–71 (1959).
Charles A. Ellwood, *Social Problems and Sociology* (New York: American
Book Company, 1935).
Anthony Giddens, *The Nation-State and Violence* (Berkeley: University of
California Press, 1985).
George C. Homans, *Sentiments and Activities* (New York: Free Press, 1962).
Alex Inkeles, *What is Sociology?* (Englewood Cliffs: Prentice-Hall, 1964).
Michael Mann, *The Sources of Social Power I. A History of Power from the
Beginning to A.D. 1760* (Cambridge: Cambridge University Press, 1986).
Robert K. Merton, Leonard Broom and Leonard S. Cottrell, Jr. (eds),
Sociology Today (New York: Basic Books, 1959).
Barrington Moore, Jr., *Social Origins of Dictatorship and Democracy*
(Boston: Beacon, 1966).
Allan Pred, *Urban Growth and the Circulation of Information: The United
States System of Cities, 1790–1840* (Cambridge, Mass.: Harvard University
Press, 1973).
Allan Pred, 'Interpenetrating Processes: Human Agency and the Becoming
of Regional Spatial and Social Structures', *Papers of the Regional Science
Association* 57: 7–17, 1985.
Pitirim A. Sorokin, *Altruistic Love* (Boston: Beacon, 1950).
Pitirim A. Sorokin, *Social and Cultural Dynamics*, 4 vols (New York:
Bedminster, 1962).
Herbert Spencer, *The Principles of Sociology*, 2 vols (London: Appleton,
1897).
Oswald Spengler, *The Decline of the West*, 2 vols (New York: Knopf,
1926–28).

Arthur Stinchcombe, 'Social Structure and Organizations', in *Handbook of Organizations*, James G. March (ed.) (Chicago: Rand McNally, 1965).
Oliver Zunz (ed.), *Reliving the Past. The Worlds of Social History* (Chapel Hill: University of North Carolina Press, 1985).

3 What is Sociological History?
Cynthia Hay

INTRODUCTION

To begin with, an acknowledgement: my title is not wholly original. It is of course borrowed and adapted from E. H. Carr, who gave his little book, which first appeared over a quarter of a century ago, the catchy title, *What is History?* (Carr, 1961). E. H. Carr wrote in support of history both as intellectually serious – as rather more than scissors and paste applied to archives – and as politically progressive. It was in keeping with both these themes that Carr enthused about history and sociology:

> the more historical sociology becomes and the more sociological history becomes, the better. (Carr, 1961, p. 62)

Carr was by no means alone in thinking that propinquity between sociology and history was, to borrow the historiographical categories of *1066 and All That* 'a good thing' (Sellar and Yeatman, 1930). It was, and still is, a view that quite a number of people have advocated: that history can only be improved by infusions of sociology, and vice versa. Not everyone has been as sanguine; certainly not Donald MacRae, when he wrote that 'sociology is history with the hard work left out' and 'history is sociology with the brains left out' (MacRae, 1956, p. 43). The advocates of a *rapprochement* between sociology and history evoked a backlash – or a defence – of the traditional virtues of traditional history which, it was argued, would only be distorted and lost in the coarser and cruder practices drawn from the social sciences. The best-known of these defences is probably G.R. Elton's *Practice of History,* which was written in part to counter the line of argument in manifestoes such as E. H. Carr's (Elton, 1969).

Carr's advocacy of closer links between history and sociology was part of his programme for new and improved history. His sentiments may be described as worthy, but not very well developed. In this they were in keeping with the times. Early in the 1960s there was developing among some historians – a minority within the profession – a strong interest in linking history more closely with sociology in particular and the social sciences more generally. It was by no means the first instance of historians taking an interest in using sociology in their work. Karl Lamprecht, in the late nineteenth century, made use of the social sciences, but he was something of an isolated figure (Lamprecht, 1905). In 1912 James Harvey Robinson wrote a manifesto entitled *The New History*, which called for historians to become more familiar with the social sciences (Robinson, 1912). Some of the historians who considered themselves 'new' historians did try to put some of these maxims into effect; Charles Beard's *An Economic Interpretation of the Constitution of the United States* is a case in point (Beard, 1913).

But despite occasional manifestoes and individual works, there was really very little that could be called either sociological or social scientific history until the 1960s. What happened in the 1960s is that what had previously been a worthy sentiment, with the occasional isolated work for illustration, became the maxim of a movement of a minority of historians, producing a significant body of work and acquiring institutional form, for example, through the establishment of journals devoted to publishing work in this vein, such as the *Journal of Interdisciplinary History*, *Historical Methods Newsletter* (later *Historical Methods*) and *Social Science History*.

A number of factors contributed to this change: what had previously been occasional flurries of interest became established and institutionalised among a minority of historians. 'Annales' history has been one of the sources of inspiration for the various forms which sociological history has taken in the last quarter-century. Other factors have been more mundane. Higher education expanded and changed dramatically in the 1960s: money for research and researchers was available, at least in certain fields, on a much more generous scale then before. Certain fields and certain kinds of approaches had greater success in obtaining funding. History was seen as a rather fuddy-duddy discipline by comparison with the rapidly developing, well-funded and thrusting social sciences – the clichés here resonate with the public images of these disciplines. But I do not want to suggest that the development of sociological history was a matter of artful image manipulation and improvement as a means to obtaining a larger share of the cake of research funding. A minority of historians were concerned that their discipline appeared to be stagnating at a time when there seemed to be considerable scope for development and improvement. Their views as to how history should be developed and improved were influenced by the curious convergence of two lines of argument, derived from rather disparate sources: the argument for the distinction between generalising and individualising approaches in scholarly disciplines developed in the late nineteenth century German *Methodenstreit*, and the view, developed in the mid-twentieth century debate on historical explanation, that historians make use, for the most part unwittingly, of theories developed in other disciplines. These two lines of argument – opposed on the important question of whether there is a single method common to all sound knowledge – were amalgamated in what became the standard account of the relationship of history to the social sciences. The import of this account was that history was an intellectually invertebrate discipline, incomplete in the very fundamental sense that it depended on other disciplines for any kind of theoretical input or structure. History on its own, without any outside support, looked rather like a world without steel, as portrayed in a recent television advertisement where forks flop and bend when people attempt unsuccessfully to convey food from plate to mouth.

Thus, two lines of argument coalesced into what became the established view of the relationship of sociology and other social sciences to history: the view that historians cannot generate theories in their own right but must import them from other disciplines. The import of these lines of argument was independent of the difficulties and doubts that detailed analysis of them might expose. This view of the relation between history and other disciplines has been the centre-piece of discussion for the best part of a century. In a pithy phrase, which is neither a Marxist coinage nor my own invention, it is the producer-consumer view of sociology and history. To the best of my knowledge, this phrasing originated in philosophic discussions of the nature of historical explanation in the middle of this century. In a classic paper, Joynt and Rescher described the historian as

> ... interested in the particular facts regarding the past *for them-selves*, and not in an instrumental role as data for laws. Indeed, unlike the researcher in 'historical' science, the historian is not a

producer of general laws, but a *consumer* of them. His position vis-à-vis the sciences is essentially parasitic. The generalizations provided by anthropology, sociology, psychology, etc. are used by the historian in the interests of his mission of facilitating our understanding of the past.

Joynt and Rescher,1961, p. 155)

However, the doctrine that historians were indebted to other disciplines for the generalisations they used was established in the literature well before Joynt and Rescher expressed it so memorably. It was a main theme of Mandelbaum's classic work, first published in 1938 (Mandelbaum, 1938). Because the intellectual foundations of sociological history in philosophic debates have, as I shall argue, influenced its development, they both require and merit a substantial digression. The subject, moreover, is one for a sociological history: it begins in late nineteenth-century Germany.

In the late nineteenth century German *Methodenstreit*, a distinction, drawn between nomothetic and idiographic approaches, was used to argue against the view, in nineteenth-century positivism, that all knowledge was of the same kind and obtained by the methods of science. This distinction was carefully stated by Rickert as a logical distinction between generalising and particularising approaches to knowledge; Rickert saw these two approaches as polar types or extremes, between which most knowledge falls (Rickert, 1962). The objection that the idiographic position rested on an unsound epistemology, namely that an individual event was to be apprehended in its individuality, was a misunderstanding of Rickert's position; this objection had arisen, as Rickert recognised, because an earlier writer, Windelband, had been inconsistent, and shifted between two senses of idiographic, the untenable one of apprehending unique events in their uniqueness, and the tenable one of describing particular events (Rickert, 1962, Windelband, 1915).

This distinction was reincarnated as a consequence of the debate on historical explanation, which began in the 1940s. In connection with this debate on the Popper-Hempel model of explanation (also known as the hypothetico-deductive or positivist model), Popper, once the 'official opposition' to the Vienna Circle, rejected the idea of theoretical and particularising disciplines, which was incompatible with the doctrine of unity of method, and replaced it with that of theoretical and particularising lines of interest (Popper, 1962, II, p. 264). Historians have the latter line of interest and, insofar as they provide sound explanations in their line of work, make use of theories provided from beyond the discipline of history, whether from sociology or from common sense; in making tacit use of such theories, they show a remarkable lack of curiosity about, or concern with, the credentials or the soundness of the theories which they presume. Their line of interest, in particular events, becomes a kind of tunnel vision that excludes any interest in theory. Thus, in connection with this debate, the discipline of history was located on the map of knowledge as lacking any theoretical content in its own right.

This corollary of the debate was congenial to many historians who considered the debate itself to be at best unrelated to the activity of doing history. Thus, the nomothetic-idiographic distinction, originally developed in criticism of positivism, was revamped as part of the producer-consumer view of the relationship of theoretical disciplines, such as sociology, to history. The standard opening of many an article on sociology and history recapitulates the development of this distinction, while overlooking the strange alliances and curious bedfellows its development has engendered.

Historians with contrasting views of their discipline have drawn on different facets of this distinction. Traditional historians have taken comfort from the doctrine that an historian's line of interest insulates him/her from any concern with theoretical matters. These historians have been described, not unkindly, by H. J. Habbakuk, in an ecological image, as having minds like a compost heap:

> They absorbed a large number of miscellaneous facts relating to the period in which they were interested or to problems very loosely defined. Their taste was catholic and they did not accept or reject on any rigorous test of relevance to a hypothesis. They retained in their minds an accumulating stock of information, as it were a compost heap, on which in due course ideas and generalizations burgeoned, as a result of reflection, flair and intuition. (Habbakuk, 1971, p. 318)

This way of working, Habbakuk observes, is at odds with the approach required to make explicit use of theories.

Historians who advocated social scientific history used the producer-consumer view to argue for using theories produced by disciplines such as sociology. Since the discipline of history lacked theoretical resources in its own right, and needed to make use of such resources to produce soundly based work, it followed that the procedure of using theories from other disciplines should be conducted systematically and explicitly. This argument licensed the development of both quantitative and theoretical approaches to history, which are the first pair of models of sociological history that I shall consider.

QUANTITATIVE HISTORY

The quantitative techniques used to analyse historical evidence range from simple enumeration to complex equations, but the sophistication of the mathematics involved is not the distinguishing feature of kinds of quantitative history; that lies, rather, in the nature of the historical topics to which quantitative techniques have been applied and the relationship between these topics and quantitative techniques. There are a number of ways in which quantitative techniques have been used in historical work. The thin end of the wedge, for quantitative history, was in the 'new economic history' which began to develop in the late 1950s, and which is usually seen as providing the impetus for applying quantitative techniques to historical topics more generally. In France, there developed what is called 'serial history', the study of changes through time in series of data on, for the most part, prices or population. The use of serial history to study various kinds of population records has developed into the established field of historical demography, for which it is undisputed that quantitative techniques are indispensable; there is no way of depicting demographic change without counting. Historical demography has been concerned with developing accounts of past social structures which are, in the classic terms of the debates on quantitative history, not impressionistic but based on careful analysis of aggregate data. Quantitative techniques have also been used to analyse other kinds of bodies of evidence, such as business directories or criminal records; both the accuracy of recording and the contemporary categories used can be problematic in historical records of these kinds. Lastly, quantitative techniques have been applied to topics and debates of long standing among traditional historians, with the claim that dogged controversy would thus at last be laid to rest; the most famous case in hand is that of American slavery.

In the case for quantitative history there are a number of standard contentions. Advocates begin by drawing attention to what they describe as implicit quantification already present in much historical writing; for example, when historians use phrases such as 'some', 'all', or 'a few'. Explicit quantification would replace such impressionistic judgements by careful and systematic assessment of the evidence. The use of quantification would clear up the sloppy thinking to which so many historians were prone, and could also settle unresolved historical controversies that had involved generations of historians. These claims presupposed that there were significant and useful bodies of historical evidence amenable to quantification; this was seen as a prospect rather than a problem: advocates of quantitative history pointed to fields of historical evidence lying fallow because they had not yet been subjected to quantitative assessment. If history was to be social scientific, quantification was in order. The prototype of a work of quantitative history was one where a substantial amount of historical evidence was quantitatively assessed, and these assessments used to support or confute general statements about an historical topic.

Quantification became a movement. In manifestoes, some of its advocates declared that quantitative history would sweep all before it, that the future of history was quantitative (Benson, 1966, Le Roy Ladurie, 1973, p. 22). Le Roy Ladurie gave a hostage to fortune when, in 1968, he wrote that 'tomorrow's historian will either be a computer programmer, or extinct' (Le Roy Ladurie, 1973, p. 14). Others were more measured and spoke of quantification in history: that is, of quantification as one technique among others, to be used to analyse appropriate evidence (Aydelotte, 1966, 1971). Work in historical demography replaced loosely grounded statements about the social structure of early modern and modern Europe with well-supported analyses of family and social structure. Studies of social mobility in nineteenth-century American cities have demolished dominant myths about the opportunities for upward mobility and replaced them with substantiated accounts of the unsettled character of urban life (Thernstrom, 1964, Katz, 1975).

Perhaps the most celebrated use of quantitative history was in connection with the long-standing debates on American slavery which Fogel and Engermann claimed to have settled through a quantitative assessment of the evidence (Fogel and Engermann, 1974). In the debate on their work, critics developed a damning assessment of their quantitative approach as based on using evidence that appeared to be selected in support of their conclusions (David *et al.*, 1976, Gutman, 1975). This controversy about the misuses of quantitative techniques and their failure to resolve a long-standing controversy did much to squelch enthusiasm for quantitative history.

By the mid-1970s quantitative history was no longer in the vanguard of the sociological history movement. Quantitative history was securely established in fields such as historical demography, where it is accepted that quantitative techniques provide one of the main ways of analysing the available evidence to elicit past social structures. In some areas of economic history, highly technical work, comprehensible only to cognoscenti, was being developed. But quantitative history was no longer seen as the, perhaps distant, ideal to which historians should aspire for the future. There were a number of reasons for this shift. After the earlier fervour, some of the difficulties in quantifying historical evidence had become uncomfortably apparent: the historian is at the mercy of what 'fire, flood and loving daughter have left' (Murphey, 1973, p. 149), and materials of these kinds may simply be too sporadic for quantification to be appropriate. For many topics, problems and periods, there simply may not be enough suitable historical evidence for quantitative techniques to be used; ancient history is a conspicuous case in point (Hopkins, 1988, p. 53–4) but difficulties of this kind occur for most of recorded time. Sometimes, the considerable efforts involved in quantifying historical statements are out of proportion to the insignificance of the results. These are some of the negative reasons why quantitative history lost its impetus, but there were positive ones as well: quantitative approaches sometimes raised questions of interest to historians that were not susceptible to quantitative treatment. For example, historical demography established some age-specific mortality rates over time. For some historians, this raised the question of individuals' attitudes towards death at times when the loss of spouses or children was common. Although quantitative techniques were sometimes used to study attitudes, as Vovelle did in his study of baroque piety (Vovelle, 1973), other approaches were developed for questions of this order, chiefly linked with the 'anthropological turn' in history, which I shall consider after looking at theoretical history.

THEORETICAL HISTORY

In the discussions among historians about the possibility and value of theoretical history, arguments have revolved around points made in the development of the standard contrast between sociology and history as generalising and particularising disciplines that has been analysed in the introduction. For traditional historians, theoretical history is an oxymoron. Historical accounts are irreducibly detailed, and anything other than limited and carefully qualified generalisations are anathema. Broad generalisations distort the distinctive features of specific historical topics. For these historians, the standard contrast between sociology and history delineates both the modes of presentation appropriate for these disciplines and an unbridgeable gulf between them because the traditional historian's approach is the only appropriate way of presenting historical materials with due regard for their individuality.

For advocates of theoretical history, the standard contrast between sociology and history did not foreclose on the possibility of using theories in developing historical accounts. Rather, they saw the current state of history, in the mid-1960s, as one of underdevelopment, which could be remedied by recourse to some of the theoretical developments in the social sciences. The discussions in critical philosophy of history, of the grounding of historical explanations in generalisations and laws, corroborated their contentions. The traditional detailed and discursive presentation of historical accounts could be beneficially replaced by organisation and analysis of historical evidence based on theories developed in the social sciences. The producer-consumer view of the social sciences and history represented the path for improving historians' practices. History could and should become more sociological in the sense that historians should seek out and analyse historical evidence and historical problems in the light of theories developed in the social sciences; these theories should be the guiding principles around which their accounts were to be organised.

Various forms of social science history developed under the aegis of these arguments. Manuals such as David Landes and Charles Tilly's *History as a Social Science* (1971) and Robert Berkhofer's *A Behavioral Approach to Historical Analysis* (1969) outlined and recommended the approach. Studies were produced of individual lives, family history, social mobility, economic activities, and unfamiliar beliefs and practices, to name but some of the subjects explored. The range of historical investigation was both widened and deepened by work oriented to theories drawn from the social sciences. Questions were raised that historians had not previously considered, and topics were explored that historians had previously neglected.

Theoretical history in the hands of historians using theories drawn from the social sciences encountered some of the same difficulties with historical evidence as did quantitative history. Historical evidence relating to a specific topic or question can be patchy and sporadic; and historians rarely have the opportunities available to social scientists for generating evidence – only oral historians claim to produce new historical evidence that did not exist prior to their efforts, and they have had some difficulties in convincing other historians that what they obtain is historical evidence rather than, say, nostalgia. The search for historical evidence to bear upon a theoretical issue can be like looking for a needle in a haystack, as Murray Murphey has argued (Murphey, 1973, pp. 141-50). Another difficulty, peculiar to theoretical history, has to do with dogmas about what theory is and what it should be, often held by sociologists.

One of the barriers between sociologists and historians, in my view, is the insistence of many sociologists that theories developed with reference, for the most part, to nineteenth- and twentieth-century societies apply throughout time and space. Sociological theory is offered to historians on a take-it-or-leave-it basis; if these theories do not meet the needs of historians interested in developing theoretically oriented accounts, then so much the worse for historians. There are several difficulties with this position: sociologists stand fast on one of the many meanings of the equivocal term, theory, as paradigmatic, ignoring both the kinds of theoretical questions raised by historical work and the subtle and nuanced analysis of theories in historical accounts developed in the debates on historical explanation. The kinds of theories which historians use may be limited in time and space, and porous or normic, in the sense that they are not invalidated by occasional exceptions. The development of theoretical history may require modification of existing theories, rather than simply adoption and application of them to historical topics, and replacement of the producer-consumer model of sociology and history with a more interactive conception of their relations.

ANTHROPOLOGICAL HISTORY

How sociological history has changed in the last two decades can be seen in the aftermath of Le Roy Ladurie's prophecy of 1968. By 1976

Le Roy Ladurie was neither a computer programmer, nor extinct, but had written one of the most popular and widely read works of anthropological history: his study, based on inquisition records, of the ways of life of fourteenth-century Cathar heretics in a small town, Montaillou, in the Pyrenees (Le Roy Ladurie, 1976). This was less a recantation than an indication of a substantial and dramatic shift in the attitudes and ways of thought of sociological historians. The 1970s and 1980s have seen quite different forms of sociological history develop, sometimes described as anthropological history and history as discourse. Although quantitative history is still pursued by a coterie of specialists, it is no longer considered to be at the cutting edge, except of course by its aficionados. As has been noted, quantitative investigations had raised questions for which other approaches seemed more appropriate.

There was a parallel 'sea-change' in critical philosophy of history. The debate on historical explanation which had, so to speak, modernised the nomothetic-idiographic distinction had become more or less exhausted, and had lost ground to discussions of narrative as intrinsic to historical accounts. These more recent discussions of narrative have not had the impact of the previous debates, which contributed to the development of the producer-consumer view of sociology and history, but they have confirmed and amplified the development of a sophisticated account of history as narrative, far removed from the older view, disparaged by the Annales historians as 'histoire événementielle', which can be naturalised as 'blow-by-blow' history (Hayden White, 1975, Ankersmit, 1983).

The 'anthropological turn' is one which the new narrative history has taken. To a lesser extent, this has involved drawing on anthropological theories as a resource for explicating historical problems. Keith Thomas's *Religion and the Decline of Magic* (1971) is a well-known work which professes to do just this; however, I think that he uses anthropological theories and examples as analogies and comparisons, and in the last analysis gives a fairly traditional historical account of how credence in magic was lost. More central to anthropological approaches to history has been a concern with culture in something like its anthropological senses. The 'anthropological turn' is in part a polemical usage, to indicate how historians have directed their attention away from the traditional concerns of political history with the thoughts and actions of particular individuals in positions of power, to the attitudes and beliefs of people who, individually, could by no means have been thought to have influenced events. It is a form of 'history from below' strongly influenced by French work in the history of 'mentalities'.

In France the idea of a history closely linked with the social sciences was developed in the 1920s and 1930s by the founders of the 'Annales' movement, two of whom, Lucien Febvre and Marc Bloch, also wrote classic works in the history of 'mentalities' (Febvre, 1947, Bloch, 1924). Although not all practitioners of anthropological history follow the Annales approach, nonetheless this framework has influenced the development of anthropological history, in part by setting out problems and issues in the 'anthropological turn' to the past.

Basic to Annales work is Braudel's distinction between three kinds of time span: the 'long duration' of geological or structural change; the middle-range of, say, economic phenomena, in cycles from ten to 25 years; and the short time-span of specific events. Linked with this is a conceptualisation of history in terms of levels, sectors or tiers, which historical writing should try to encompass. In opposition to the monographic tradition, Annales historians sought to write total history, that is, a history which treated its subject matter comprehensively, by situating it within a variety of different relevant frameworks: geographic, economic, demographic, social and cultural. The title of a recent book by Michel Vovelle expresses this aim of total history, in an idiomatic metaphor which translates literally as history ranging 'from the wine cellar to the attic' (Vovelle, 1980). The history of mentalities is concerned with 'reconstructing the attitudes, expressions and silences which express . . . collective sensibilities' (Mandrou, 1971, vol. 8, p. 436). Mentality is not located in the attic, as in the classic conflicts of materialists and idealists; it can persist over long time spans and can shape such material factors as demographic change or the lack of it.

Some of the approaches used to elicit the history of mentalities derive from this framework, and from the nature of the subject matter. To trace the attitudes of people who left little in the way of direct written records suggests the use of socially oblique evidence. Robert Mandrou's use of eighteenth-century chapbooks as a clue to peasant mentality has been criticised on these grounds: the authors of these books sought to appeal to their audience, but may not themselves have expressed peasant attitudes and beliefs (Mandrou, 1964). Le Roy Ladurie's use of inquisition records as the major source for his study of the attitudes and ways of life of fourteenth-century Cathar heretics has the advantage of recording the words of the subjects themselves, but here a sceptic might wonder if the use of socially oblique evidence affected the balance of his account: the Montaillou villagers may have entertained the inquisitor with the details of their sexual encounters in order to direct his attention away from their religious beliefs (Le Roy Ladurie, 1976). If socially oblique evidence is all that is available, reconstructing attitudes and beliefs is not an easy option. Art and artefacts have also been used: Gaby and Michel Vovelle analysed the iconography of altarpieces in Provence from the sixteenth to the nineteenth century and argued that a steady decrease in the angel-count indicated a growing secularisation of attitudes to death (Vovelle and Vovelle, 1970).

Lastly, historians have used language, vocabulary – or lack of it – and modes of discourses as clues to mentalities. For example, Lucien Febvre, in his study of whether it was possible for Rabelais, in sixteen-century France, to be an atheist, used vocabulary, present and absent, as evidence for his argument (Febvre, 1947). Later commentators have seen Febvre as a forerunner of structuralism in this respect. H. D. Mann quotes Fevre in tandem with Foucault to bring out striking similarities and to argue that the differences are stylistic and not substantive: both are concerned with collective discourses (Mann, 1971, p. 141–3). Conversely, it has been observed more recently that Foucault's earlier works were considered to be studies in the history of mentalities by historians such as Braudel and Mandrou, who found them familiar – not strange and obscure as many readers with English as their mother tongue did (Megill, 1987). These links suggest that my second pair of models overlap, and that the differences between them may be in part a matter of emphases or intellectual affiliations.

Anthropological history, then, derives from the kinds of interests developed in the history of mentalities. It is, in part, an extension and naturalisation of much of the approach of the history of mentalities to other countries. The kind of 'total history' it sets out to provide tends to be on a small scale: a case study such as Carlo Ginzburg's study of Menocchio, a sixteenth-century miller, is a microcosm of a substantial body of ill-recorded dissent (Ginzburg, 1980). It is concerned with eliciting and making comprehensible to a twentieth-century audience the beliefs and attitudes that informed social activities in past communities. It reflects the discovery, among academics, of a kinship between historians and anthropologists, and it also refracts a recognition of the importance of non-Western societies today, evidenced in the uncovering of similarities between these societies and cultural attitudes in early modern Europe.

HISTORY AS DISCOURSE

The history of mentalities has contributed both to the development of anthropological history and to the development of history as discourse. Mandrou's definition of the history of mentalities as concerned with 'reconstructing the attitudes, expressions and silences which express . . . collective mentalities', cited above, could serve, almost equally well, as a description of some of the concerns of history as discourse. The links with the history of mentalities, of Febvre and Foucault, have also been noted. History as discourse refers to two kinds of developments. First, there has been a growing interest among historians in reconstructing past discourses, sometimes adopting methods from the history of mentalities and sometimes using other approaches as well. Second, it refers to the developing awareness among historians that the prose they write is not a transparent medium but can be shaped by complex structures that carry with them certain commitments.

Some examples can illustrate the variety of approaches of historians investigating past discourses. Jonathan Spence's study of how a sixteenth-century Jesuit missionary, Matteo Ricci, constructed a treatise on the art of memory for a Chinese audience involves decoding, in a broad sense, Matteo Ricci's choices of symbols and illustrations for his treatise (Spence, 1985). Spence is concerned with the choices Ricci made in his effort to communicate with a Chinese audience, and the implications of these choices. Spence spells out backgrounds and assumptions, and grounds Ricci's discourse in a variety of historical and social contexts. The prose Spence uses in this work, in the sense that he uses non-technical language, is, I think, accessible to a reader unfamiliar with sixteenth-century European history or Chinese history.

An interest in history as discourse has also developed among some oral historians. Oral history consists in obtaining and transcribing oral testimonies from participants in past events and ways of life. It has developed as a specialist minority interest among some historians, some of whom have become interested in eliciting the forms which their informants give to their accounts. These historians listen to their tapes and read their transcriptions less for information about disappearing or lost ways of life than for the structures through which people viewed their activities and lives.

Discussions of written history as discourse have been influenced by several factors, starting with the awareness that language is not transparent of meaning, which has developed in both philosophy and sociology, and which is part of late twentieth-century cultural awareness. Here, changes in discussions in critical philosophy of history have contributed. The classic debates which shaped the standard contrast between sociology and history were developed with reference to a philosophy of science that was in the process of being undermined by philosophers of science at the time when it was gaining acceptance among historians and social scientists as delineating sound procedures for knowledge that claimed to be scientific (Danto, 1985, Introduction). The internal difficulties of reconstructing historical accounts along the lines recommended by the positivist model of explanation also contributed to the development of discussions about history as narrative in deeper senses than simply telling stories about one event following upon another. A number of technical analyses of the different kinds of structures that inform historical accounts have contributed to the awareness of written history as discourse (White, 1975, Ankersmit, 1983, Danto, 1985). The details of these analyses, and their relation to work on discourse in other fields, require lengthy discussion rather than a brief digression. In the light of these developments, the long-standing interest on the part of historians in unpacking the preconceptions in their colleagues' works has become more sophisticated.

CONCLUSIONS

A consideration of several models of sociological history makes it well-nigh impossible to duck the question of its directions and prospects. History as applied social science, applying either or both theories and quantitative techniques drawn from the social sciences, is no longer the dominant form of sociological history but rather one specialised interest among several. The development of sophisticated forms of narrative in the 'anthropological turn', the history of mentalities, and history as discourse, has not meant that innovative history has become less sociological. Rather, these developments show parallels to approaches used in some of the many fields of sociology. The relationship between sociology and history has become much more complex than the classic contrast between sociology and history indicates.

Sociological history still arouses considerable antipathy among traditionally minded historians, such as Gertrude Himmelfarb, for whom the 'sociological historian' is a figure akin to Popper's bogeyman of the historicist (Himmelfarb, 1987, p. 49, p. 54, Popper, 1957). Probably the majority of historians, in English-speaking countries at least, will remain uninterested, indifferent, or on occasion hostile to the kinds of innovation that come under the rubric of sociological history. Sociological historians, all too often, appear to be neither fish nor fowl, concerned with topics beyond the time spans with which most sociologists deal, and using approaches and concepts that are alien to many historians. There are certain similarities to the position of social history in Britain some 30 years ago. Social history became established on the academic map as part of the expansion of higher education in the 1960s, but unfortunately there are no similar prospects on the horizon for sociological history in Britain in the near future.

REFERENCES

F. R. Ankersmit, *Narrative Logic, a Semantic Analysis of the Historian's Language* (The Hague: Martinus Nijhoff, 1983).

W. O. Aydelotte, 'Quantification in History', *American Historical Review*, vol. 71 (1966), pp. 803–24.

W. O. Aydelotte, *Quantification in History* (Reading, Mass:, Addison-Wesley, 1971).

C. Beard, *An Economic Interpretation of the Constitution of the United States* (New York: MacMillan, 1913).

L. Benson, 'Quantification, Scientific History and Scholarly Innovation', *American Historical Association Newsletter*, June 1966, p. 12.

R. Berkhofer, *A Behavioral Approach to Historical Analysis* (New York: Free Press, 1969).

M. Bloch, *Les rois thaumaturges* (Strasbourg: Istra, 1924).

E. H. Carr, *What is History?* (Harmondsworth: Penguin, 1961).

A. H. Danto, *Narration and Knowledge* (New York: Columbia University Press, 1985).

P. A. David, H. G. Gutman, R. Sutch, P. Temin and G. Wright, *Reckoning with Slavery* (Oxford: Oxford University Press, 1976).

G. R. Elton, *The Practice of History* (Glasgow: Collins, 1969).

L. Febvre, *Le problème de l'incroyance au xvie siècle; la religion de Rabelais* (Paris: A. Michel, 1947).

R. W. Fogel and S. L. Engerman, *Time on the Cross* (Boston: Little Brown, 1974).

C. Ginzburg, *The Cheese and the Worms* (London: Routledge & Kegan Paul, 1980).

H. G. Gutman, *Slavery and the Numbers Game* (Urbana: University of Illinois, 1975).

H. J. Habbakuk, 'Economic History and Economic Theory', *Daedalus*, vol. 100, 1971.

G. Himmelfarb, *The New History and the Old* (Cambridge, Mass.: Harvard University Press, 1987).

K. Hopkins, 'What is Social History', *What is History today . . .?* ed. J. Gardiner (Basingstoke: MacMillan, 1988).

C. B. Joynt and N. Rescher, 'The Problem of Uniqueness in History', *History and Theory*, vol. 1, 1961.

M. Katz, *The People of Hamilton, Canada West* (Cambridge, Mass.: Harvard, 1975).

K. Lamprecht, *What is History?* (New York: MacMillan, 1905).

D. Landes and C. Tilly, *History as a Social Science* (Englewood Cliffs, N.J.: Prentice Hall, 1971).

E. Le Roy Ladurie, *Montaillou, village occitan de 1294 à 1324* (Paris: Gallimard, 1976).

E. Le Roy Ladurie, *Le territoire de l'historien* (Paris: Gallimard, 1973).

D. G. MacRae, 'Some Sociological Prospects', Transactions of the Third World Conference of Sociology, vol. 8 (London: International Sociological Association, 1956).

M. Mandelbaum, *The Problem of Historical Knowledge* (New York: Liveright, 1938).

R. Mandrou, *De la culture populaire au xviie et xviiie siècles, la bibliothèque bleue de Troyes* (Paris: Stock, 1964).

R. Mandrou, 'L'histoire des mentalités', Encyclopedia Universalis, vol. 8 (Paris: Encyclopedia Universalis, 1971).

H. D. Mann, *Lucien Febvre, la pensée vivante d'un historien* (Paris: Armand Colin, 1971).

A. Megill, 'The Reception of Foucault by Historians', *Journal of the History of Ideas*, vol. 48, 1987, pp. 117–41.

M. G. Murphey, *Our Knowledge of the Historical Past* (Indianapolis: Bobbs-Merrill, 1973).

K. R. Popper, *The Open Society and its Enemies*, 4th edn (London: Routledge & Kegan Paul, 1962).

K. R. Popper, *The Poverty of Historicism* (London: Routledge & Kegan Paul, 1957).

H. Rickert, *Science and History* (Princeton: D. Van Nostrand, 1962).

J. H. Robinson, *The New History* (New York: MacMillan, 1912).

W. C. Sellar and R. J. Yeatman, *1066 and All That* (London: Methuen, 1930).

J. Spence, *The Memory Palace of Matteo Ricci* (London: Faber, 1985).

S. Thernstrom, *Poverty and Progress, Social Mobility in a Nineteenth Century City* (Cambridge, Mass.: Harvard, 1964).

K. Thomas, *Religion and the Decline of Magic* (Harmondsworth: Penguin, 1971).

G. Vovelle and M. Vovelle, *Vision de la mort et de l'au delà en Provence d'après les autels des âmes du purgatoire, xve–xxe siècles* (Paris: Armand Colin, 1970).

M. Vovelle, *De la cave au grenier* (Quebec: Serge Fleury, 1980).

M. Vovelle, *Piété baroque et déchristianisation en Provence au xviiie siècle* (Paris: Plon, 1973).

H. White, *Metahistory: the historical imagination in nineteenth century Europe* (Baltimore: Johns Hopkins University Press, 1975).

4 The Currency of History for Sociology
Gary Wickham

INTRODUCTION

The politics of the uses of history and sociology can be quite dramatic. Questions about the way different knowledges of social practices have been and continue to be operational in a variety of sites are crucial questions for those engaged in these sites, especially if the sites are specialised knowledge arenas like institutions of higher education. My main concern in this essay is the politics of the operation of some of these knowledges in specialised knowledge arenas.

The main players in these dramas – history and sociology – are for me more masks than characters, at least in the modern sense of character (see Hunter, 1983 and 1986). I am not interested in revealing what history and sociology are *really* about, what their *real* or *true* characters are. I hold no hope for such a project. I seek to unify history and sociology only temporarily, only to the extent that certain institutional arrangements and procedures (particularly those of higher education institutions, but also those of certain books, journals, professional associations, and so on) unify them. This is very much in line with one of Foucault's recommendations in *The Archaeology of Knowledge* (Foucault, 1974, p. 26).

By and large then the terms 'history' and 'sociology' are best thought of here as labels for the institutional unifications of different knowledge projects into two disciplinary camps. I will work with the recognition that this disciplinisation is an important condition of operation of these different knowledge projects, but I will also work on the assumption that it is a condition which should be challenged wherever possible, that interdisciplinarity should be a goal for those involved in the operation of these different projects. Interdisciplinarity is assumed here to allow greater access to certain knowledges and this is why it is assumed to be a worthwhile goal.

In this chapter I will discuss some of the arrangements and procedures used in unifying the discipline of history and I will offer a few remarks about those used in unifying sociology. But neither set of arrangements and procedures will be the main focus. Rather, I will build an argument about the making and uses of histories to show that sociology (that is, different sociological projects) should not be rushing to embrace history as a partner, whether to escape the torpor of positivism or functionalism or for any other reason, because history, in the singular, is a myth, a powerful myth which works against the objective of interdisciplinarity. My arguments will suggest that sociological projects should recognise that histories are made differently in different places and at different times and that histories operate, they are used or read, as different things in different places and at different times. My arguments will suggest that in line with these recognitions histories should be valued by sociological projects differentially, that their value should depend on their currency. It will further suggest that to avoid simply reinforcing the formal institutions that police the currency of histories, sociological projects should seek to use historical knowledges without too much regard for the tag 'historical'.

I will build my argument by examining, in the first section, some of Foucault's propositions about histories; by supplementing this examination, in the second section, with a consideration of some of the ideas on history contained in a major postmodernist text, Jean-Francois Lyotard's *The Postmodern Condition*, and by outlining, in the third section, a theory about the currency of histories. In the conclusion I will offer my suggestions about the relevance of my arguments for sociology.

Two points of clarification and/or qualification are necessary before I launch into my arguments. First, Foucault's work does not include a single, coherent piece which explains his approach to the making or the uses of histories. Scattered throughout his work, especially his interviews and essays, are many remarks on historiographical problems. In a manner which is not at all unusual for Foucault, these remarks are made more in the way of expanding the boundaries of possible approaches to problems, than in the way of directly addressing them; as he himself has said of this style, albeit in a different context, 'What I have said here is not "what I think", but often rather what I wonder whether one couldn't think' (Foucault, 1980a, p. 145). What I intend to do in the first section is gather together some of these remarks (along with one summary of Foucault's approach), so that I can reasonably construct an argument about Foucault's understanding of the making and uses of histories.

Second, in contrasting both Foucault's work and Lyotard's text to what I call 'dominant methods' of making and using histories, I mean by this term British empiricist methods of making and using histories. These methods are characterised by the central theme (a central theme which has many variations) that the past really happened, can be shown to have happened and be so shown by history. I take the continuing operation of separate history departments in institutions of higher education as partial proof of the continuing dominance of these methods. If the certainty of the past had not remained so central, many more history departments would have merged into more interdisciplinary institutional configurations than has been the case.

FOUCAULT ON HISTORIES

Jacques Donzelot, whose work is quite consistent with many of Foucault's aims, provides a succinct summary of Foucault's approach to histories. He draws an analogy between this approach, which he calls the genealogical approach, and the literary genre of the detective story (Donzelot, 1979, pp. 78–9). In summarising Foucault's approach, Donzelot signals an intervention against dominant methods of making histories. We, as makers of histories, are encouraged to avoid 'comforting serene representations' which are part of a 'search for a general causality'. In place of this technique we are encouraged to look for 'clues' to help us sort out the 'enigmatic character' of that construction of reality which has stimulated the investigation, that is, that construction of reality which is being investigated as an 'aspect of the past'.

Donzelot also signals an intervention against dominant methods of using or reading histories. We, as users of histories, are told that we should not use histories in order to discover an accurate reconstruction of the past, or to allow us to better predict the future. Rather, we should use them as knowledges which address some aspect of the present.

Foucault makes a further intervention against dominant methods of making histories, methods which assume a given unproblematic reality as their object in an important passage about history and true/false divisions (Foucault, 1981, p. 11). For such methods history making involves working on the evidence to uncover what is the 'true reality of the past' and to disregard what is false. For such methods Foucault's proposition that the true/false division is a shifting, intensely political construct rather than a direct result of the existence of a given reality has extremely threatening ramifications. This proposition suggests the need for histories which do not simply examine 'the evidence' in search of 'the truth', but which probe into what counts as evidence and what counts as truth and into the effects of having some things count as evidence and truth and others as false. And in asking what historical knowledge is possible of a history which produces the true/false distinction, Foucault is further challenging the dominance of these methods of history. He is saying these methods cannot allow us to see what is at the very heart of what they do, they cannot be turned on themselves to see how they operate and transform the true/false division because they cannot recognise within themselves such a division, except in the most simplistic, uncritical way. He is saying that as they cannot do so, we should make use of an approach which can.

In this same passage Foucault also makes a further intervention against dominant methods of using histories, methods which insist that history be used or read as 'the past', that the only thing histories have to say about the present is that it is connected to the past. Foucault is suggesting that histories be read as the present, as knowledges about present politics, knowledges with important roles in deciding, in the present, what counts as true and what counts as false.

In another passage (Foucault, 1981, pp. 13–14) Foucault says that his project 'has differed since the outset from that of the historians'. He even says that his work 'irritates' historians. It does so because he is not 'proposing a global principle for analysing society', because he is rejecting all 'schemes'. In place of any 'general theme of society' he proposes the theme of the 'discourse of true and false'. He wants to investigate the following 'circle': 'the history of the "objectification" of those elements which historians consider as objectively given'.

For Foucault the objects of histories can never be the 'given' objects used by dominant historical methods. They must be the procedures and mechanisms of true/false divisions. There is another intervention here against dominant methods of both the making and uses of historical knowledges, one closely connected to the intervention against the givenness of historical objects. Foucault is also intervening against the totalising of objects. We should be examining the procedures and mechanisms of true/false divisions, but *in their specificity*, in specific practices, in specific sites (sites of medicine, sites of schooling, sites of the family, and so on). We must resist the temptation to examine the grand object society or other great totalities, and we must avoid general frameworks or schemes which are trapped by this temptation (such as the framework or scheme built around the infrastructure/superstructure coupling, or that built around the state/civil society coupling, and the like). As such, we must be careful that our investigations of specific procedures and mechanisms of true/false divisions never become simply examinations of the grand object of society by another name, never become the basis of a new general framework or schema.

Foucault clarifies and expands his interventions against the objects of histories in several places. He urges, for example, consideration of what lies behind 'the extent and rapidity' of transformations: 'a modification in the rules of formation of statements which are accepted as scientifically true' (Foucault, 1980b, p. 112). Foucault thus reveals more about what should be the objects of histories, what I have called the procedures and mechanisms of true/false divisions.

> It is a question of what *governs* statements, and the way in which they govern each other so as to constitute a set of propositions which are scientifically acceptable and hence capable of being unified or falsified by scientific procedures. In short, there is a problem of the regime, the politics of the scientific statement. (Foucault, 1980b, p. 112, emphasis in original)

Another clarification and expansion centres on the concept of the event. He warns first that we should 'avoid trying to do for the event what was previously done with the concept of structure'. We should realise 'that there are actually a whole order of levels of different types of events differing in amplitude, chronological breadth, and capacity to produce effects'. But it is not too clear from this passage just how Foucault's 'events' serve as objects of histories. He does say 'the problem is at once to distinguish among events, to differentiate the networks and levels to which they are connected and engender one another' (Foucault, 1980b, p. 114). But we are still wondering how to construct events as objects so that we can do these things. Surely he is not suggesting we simply recognise events from the evidence, along the lines of a crude empiricism? Elsewhere he makes it plain he is not. Events are not 'real objects' for Foucault at all, they are not aspects of 'the real past'. They are tactical constructs with two particular uses. He explains these two uses in defining the term 'eventalisation' (Foucault, 1981, pp. 6–7).

To summarise his explanation, 'events' are constructs used to show that what seems to be self-evident is not and to avoid historical analysis in terms of a single cause, to avoid essentialism – to avoid 'ascribing the object [being] analysed to the most unitary, necessary, inevitable and (ultimately) extra-historical mechanism or structure available'. Foucault offers a couple of brief snippets by way of examples of events in their role as breaches of self evidence – 'it wasn't a matter of course that made people come to be regarded as mentally ill, it wasn't self-evident that the only thing to be done with a criminal was to lock him up'. It is an 'event' that each of these things was and is done, not a self-evident truth. He also offers an example of an event in its role as 'causal multiplication', an example which extends the above comment on penal incarceration to show that 'penalisation' is made up of 'already existing practices of internment', which are themselves 'vast processes' that need to be further broken down.

The final intervention we will consider here involves the relegation of the human subject from its central position in dominant methods of making histories. This intervention is neatly summed up by Foucault in a passage which explains how his genealogical method, involving an 'historical contextualisation', is much more than the 'simple relativisation of the phenomenological subject'.

> One has to dispense with the constituent subject, to get rid of the subject itself . . . to arrive at an analysis which can account for the constitution of the subject within a historical framework. And this is what I would call genealogy . . . .a form of history which can account for the constitution of knowledges, discourses, domains of objects etc, without having to make reference to a subject which is either transcendental in relation to the field of events or runs its empty sameness throughout the course of history (Foucault, 1980b, p. 117).

This is a major intervention into the dominant methods of many forms of analysis, not just those used in making histories. We are being forced to recognise that 'the subject . . . does not assume a unified form, rather social agents are fragmented and scattered across various sites . . . Not all of these are consistent with each other'

(Phillipps, 1982, p. 53). For histories this means we should be constructing objects which specify the types of agent or actor involved and their conditions and modes of operation – a police person following police procedures, a bureaucrat operating in line with the rules of a government department, a limited liability company subject to the regulations of particular legislation, and so on – rather than assuming that historical knowledges are about human beings, entities with fixed biological and psychological characteristics, who can and must be considered, who run their 'empty sameness throughout the course of history'.

One of Foucault's discussions of his history of imprisonment provides us with more details on many of his interventions including that against the dominant role of the subject. In this discussion (Foucault, 1981, p. 5), Foucault argues that a history of prisons is not a history of real phenomena with real and fixed causes featuring, sometimes as causes, real and fixed subjects. His objects are not assumed to have a self-evident, unproblematic status. His objects are the ways in which certain specific procedures and mechanisms involving certain specific types of actor or agent are used to operate and circulate what are taken to be truths about imprisonment, as a form of punishment and correction, and the effects of the operation and circulation of these truths.

I want to conclude this section with a brief criticism of Foucault. It is a criticism I have developed fully elsewhere (Wickham, 1983 and 1987) in regard to Foucault's work on power. All I want to do here is indicate its relevance to his work on histories and to explain the way I have dealt with the problem in this section.

The criticism involves Foucault's essentialism. While Foucault and his work have been central to many battles against those forms of essentialism which have dogged much critical analysis in the twentieth century – those forms where the essence involved is class, or where it is the state, or where it is the human subject – his own work has not been immune from this problem, particularly in regard to his treatment of power, where power itself, as disciplinary power, has been allowed to become an essence, that which must speak in all instances.

In his discussions on the making and uses of histories, Foucault sometimes talks about history and about knowledge as if they are unitary entities, as if histories and all knowledges could be merged into a single History and a single Knowledge and inform all investigations in these singular forms. In short, he occasionally treats history and knowledges as essences, despite his own arguments against just such mistakes.

While I regard this problem in Foucault's work as a very serious one, I obviously do not think it renders Foucault useless. In this section I have indicated the force and worth of some of his interventions against dominant methods of making and using histories despite his essentialist tendencies. In indicating this, I have tried to write his essentialist touches out – mainly by constantly pluralising the words 'history' and 'knowledge' – not at all because I think we should ignore these touches, but because I don't think they are worth pursuing vigorously here, I do not think they weaken my arguments.

SUPPLEMENTING FOUCAULT WITH LYOTARD

The Postmodern Condition contains many very useful passages for supplementing Foucault's interventions against dominant methods of making and using histories. Consider Lyotard's distinction between the modern and the postmodern:

> I will use the term *modern* to designate any science that legitimates itself with reference to a metadiscourse . . . making an explicit appeal to some grand narrative, such as the dialectics of Spirit . . . the emancipation of the rational or working subject . . . I define *postmodern* as incredulity toward metanarratives (Lyotard, 1984, pp. xxiii–xxiv, emphases in original).

This particular use of the concept postmodern provides us with a framework for opposing the totalising of the objects of historical knowledges. Many histories are made and used in the name of a grand narrative, whether one around the emancipation of the human subject, some other narrative of progress, or simply a narrative of the 'the past' as an unproblematic order. We can call the Foucaultian quest to make histories knowledges of *specific* true/false divisions a postmodern quest and use this emblem to make some connections with similar quests in regard to other knowledges, thus fostering the aim of interdisciplinarity. Of course, we must be careful, we must ensure that we use this emblem only to establish specific connections to enhance interdisciplinarity. We do not want postmodernism to become an essence, to become a general category which indiscriminately gobbles up all that it sees.

In following Lyotard's lead here, albeit cautiously, we can think of the objects of historical knowledges as small narratives, a notion developed by Lyotard throughout *The Postmodern Condition* to combat what he sees as the dominance of science, or at least the narratives of science, in contemporary Western thought. He identifies two grand narratives of science which he says are used to legitimate a huge variety of different knowledges – one to do with the people's 'right to science', the other to do with the fostering of a 'moral and spiritual training' (Lyotard, 1984, pp. 31–2).

Many histories have been made and used in the name of one or both of these grand narratives of science. 'History as the people's right to know their past' – the first grand narrative – informs all histories made and used via the liberal framework and the various 'history-from-below' frameworks grouped together as 'social history' or 'people's history'. And 'history as the path to self fulfilment and moral righteousness' – the second grand narrative – informs many of the histories made and used via the liberal framework and many of those made and used via more 'institutional' frameworks, such as religious frameworks and even the constitutionalist framework.

Lyotard's idea of the small narrative can certainly help us escape the totalising grip of grand narratives. Histories, in this way, are made and used as local knowledges, stories with specific conditions of operation and specific aims, in the manner Foucault discusses for histories of hospitals, mental asylums and prisons.

Again we must be careful with Lyotard, this time for another reason. This concerns his use of the term 'small narrative'. This is a handy tool for breaching the self-evidence of grand narratives, like Foucault's 'event', but once breached we should quickly switch to the less startling but more accurate term 'specific narrative'. The local knowledges which histories should be, need not be small– 'local' or 'specific' might well refer to knowledges (stories) with regional, national or even international conditions of operation and aims. It is the tendency to force connections, to aggregate unnecessarily, which is of concern to us, not the size of any knowledge or group of knowledges.

Let us turn now to Foucault's argument that histories should be used or read as aspects of the present, not as records of the past. Fredric Jameson argues in his Foreword to *The Postmodern Condition* that the book involves 'an unexpected modulation towards Nietzschean thematics of history' in that Lyotard's small narrative knowledges, unlike scientific, rational knowledges, serve 'as a way of *consuming* the past, a way of forgetting'. Scientific knowledges, on the other hand, serve to 'store, hoard and capitalize' the past and, he adds, the control of this 'storage hoarding and capitalization' is 'one of the crucial *political* issues of our own time' (Jameson, 1984, pp. xii–xiii, emphases in original). Lyotard himself goes on, 'The narratives' reference may seem to belong to the past, but in reality it is always, contemporaneous with the act of recitation' (Lyotard, 1984, p. 22).

It should be clear by now that my cautionary remarks about Lyotard's text add up to a similar criticism to that I levelled against Foucault in the previous section. Like Foucault, Lyotard (and Jameson) needs to have the occasional essentialist chaff extracted from the political wheat which his writing contains. As in the case of Foucault, I am trying to sort the wheat from the chaff as I go. Some pieces of chaff have obviously been allowed through – Jameson's claim about 'one of the most crucial political issues of our time', as if political issues naturally organize themselves and connect themselves into an agenda, is a prime example. But I urge the reader to see these pieces of chaff as parts of a warning to the unwary, rather than as bad sorting on my part. For the purposes of this chapter, it is not worth dwelling on them.

In making use of Lyotard's notion, slightly reworked, of specific, local narratives, we should highlight his notion that local narratives only seem to belong to the past and we should add to it that all histories only seem to belong to the past. Histories may be spoken (or written, or filmed, and so on) as the past, but they are always heard (or read or seen or used) in the present and this is what is important about them. This is where they have effects. This is a crucial intervention against dominant methods of using or reading histories. These dominant methods see historical knowledges as timeless, as part of a great tapestry of a History of the Past. They do not allow that histories are continuously consumed by specific political uses. For them histories hide, as History, behind the idea of the past, the politics of which is set in concrete and not open to contestation. I am suggesting that we should use Foucault and Lyotard to establish that histories, whether they hide behind the idea of the past or not, are important precisely because of their differential consumption (they may be consumed any number of times, being effectively different histories for each consumption) in specific political sites, as part of specific political objectives. This point is further enhanced by Lyotard's developments of the notions of language games and performativity. But before considering these, let me offer an example.

A recent newspaper report in *The Weekend Australian* captures superbly some specific political consumptions or uses of a particular history, seen both as a specific local narrative and, through the dominant methods of reading histories, as an immutable part of the grand past. The report concerns the call by the Australian Teachers' Federation for all Australian teachers to boycott school activities and curriculum programmes celebrating the bicentennary of European settlement in Australia unless they also contain Aboriginal perspectives of the 200-year period. For the teachers' union these school activities and curriculum programmes constitute the makings and uses of particular historical knowledges about the colonisation of Australia and its original inhabitants, for the specific political objective of improving the social, political and economic conditions of Australia's aborigines for the specific political objective of 'Aboriginalising' the curriculum of Australia's schools.

The report makes much of the fact that the union's call was 'attacked' by 'a prominent historian'. This historian, Professor Les Marchant, the report notes, 'described it [the union's call] as a fascist act of intellectual terrorism'. He is quoted at some length: 'Complete misconceptions could develop about this country's history if education is to be turned into propaganda. If our education system is going to be bent in such a way that we produce people who learn only dogma, then there is not much hope of Australia taking its place in a high technology future' (*The Weekend Australian*, 9–10 January 1988, p. 1). The dominant methods of using history are very much on display here. For the champion of these methods in this report, historical knowledges of Australia are part of the History of the Past of Australia. This History is untouchable, except by 'fascists and intellectual terrorists'. But Professor Marchant is clearly hiding behind the idea of the past here, trying to protect a political objective of particular 'official' historical knowledges from contestation. This political objective is the promotion of certain knowledges at the expense of others in order to achieve a place in the 'high technology' sun.

We can now wrap up our examination of the *The Postmodern Condition* by returning to Lyotard's treatment of language games and performativity. Lyotard acknowledges Wittgenstein in developing his understanding of language games. He describes a language game in the following terms – 'each of the various categories of utterance can be defined in terms of rules specifying their properties and the uses to which they can be put' (Lyotard, 1984, p. 10). He makes three 'observations' about language games:

> The first is that their rules do not carry within themselves their own legitimation but are the object of a contract, explicit or not, between players (which is not to say that the players invent the rules). The second is that if there are no rules, there is no game . . . The third remark is . . . every utterance should be thought of as a 'move' in a game (Lyotard, 1984, p. 10).

These rules, moves and the games themselves are politically saturated. Lyotard draws a military analogy in considering discussions between friends as language games: 'the interlocutors use any available ammunition, changing games from one utterance to the next: questions, requests, assertions and narratives are launched pell-mell into battle. The war is not without rules, but the rules allow and encourage the greatest possible flexibility of utterance' (Lyotard, 1984, p. 17).

The operation of historical knowledges, that is, the uses of particular histories, can be beneficially theorised via Lyotard's treatment of language games, though there is nothing to be gained, I would suggest, from using the term 'language game' itself. Different histories are made and used in different places and at different times according to different sets of rules which are the object of implicit contracts involving makers of particular histories, their users and history institutions, the institutions which police the currency of histories (a point which will be taken up in detail in the next section).

We can think of the negotiations about these histories, about the processes of them achieving a certain currency, as different moves. We can also see the politically saturated character of all these moves and of the complexities of the aspects of the 'battles' which are constituted by the different moves, by the attempts of different historical knowledges to gain a certain currency in order to achieve a certain political objective.

This is where Lyotard's treatment of the concept of performativity becomes very handy. Lyotard says that in replacing 'the definition of essences with the calculation of interactions', the 'performativity criterion . . . brings the pragmatic functions of knowledge clearly to light'. In other words, what counts about historical knowledges is how they perform, whether they do things to promote a particular objective.

THE CURRENCY OF HISTORIES

In this section I will mainly develop the proposition that histories are made differently in different places and at different times, that is, different tools with different currencies are employed in making histories differently at different times and in different places. This will provide the basis of a theory of the currency of histories. Elsewhere (Wickham, 1984) I have outlined the other half of this theory – that histories are used differently (they are effectively different histories) in different places and at different times. I will summarise my main example from that paper at the end of this section to allow a full picture of this theory of the currency of histories.

The *Concise Macquarie Dictionary* offers, *inter alia*, the following two definitions of 'currency': 'that which is current as a medium of exchange' and 'general acceptance, prevalence, vogue'. We can supplement these definitions with the following passage from the cultural theorist Stephen Greenblatt:

> In order to achieve the negotiation, artists need to create a currency that is valid for a meaningful, mutually profitable exchange . . . I should add that the society's dominant currencies, money and prestige, are invariably involved, but I am using the term 'currency' metaphorically to designate the systematic adjustments, symbolisations and lines of credit necessary to enable an exchange to take place (Greenblatt, 1987, p. 13).

For our purposes something has currency if it has general acceptance or prevalence and if it is a central part of a system in which things are exchanged, including systems where knowledges are exchanged.

Why though do some things have greater currency than others? The answer is fairly straightforward. Some things have greater currency because they are the subjects of agreements which have developed in particular communities and which are *supervised and policed* by particular institutions within those communities. In the case of coin and paper money, for example, their currency is supervised and policed in most communities by a central bank.

In applying the concept of currency to the making of histories we must first discuss some features of making histories which allow the concept to be usefully employed. While histories are made differently in different places and at different times, they are not made without rules. The dominant rules of making histories vary, but they cannot be painlessly escaped. The price paid by those histories made within the confines of rules other than those dominant at the time and place of their making is that they are not accepted as histories, though of course later changes to the dominant rules may see them brought into the fold.

Some concepts used as tools in making histories (I will discuss some shortly) are used so freely and so often that they become assumptions. They take on their status as assumptions because they operate within the confines of dominant rules of making histories. The dominant rules are supervised and policed by certain institutions of making histories within communities of making histories. These institutions are the central banks of history making. In policing and supervising the rules, they police and supervise the currency of concepts operating, mainly as assumptions, within the confines of the rules. The institutions include: higher education history departments, in both their teaching and researching capacities; history journals; publishers of history books; history conferences; and some history clubs and societies.

An examination of three historiographical pieces – Raphael Samuel's 'People's History' (1981a), his 'History and Theory' (1981b), and the first of Carr's lectures, 'The Historian and His Facts', collected in *What is History?* (1964) – will allow us to draw up a brief working list of concepts-as-assumptions used in dominant methods of making histories. The list must be headed by the concept of the past. It informs all the other concepts-as-assumptions on our list. I will discuss it in more detail shortly.

The concept of evidence, involving facts and documents, is a very widespread assumption behind thinking about making histories. According to Samuel, 'Enquiry is framed in terms of the evidence available rather than of the phenomenon to be explained . . .' (Samuel, 1981b, p. xl). He knows that 'the documents', as the main form of evidence, do not provide us with a trouble-free path to the garden of the real; they introduce us 'not to the real world of the past, but only to its system of representations' (Samuel, 1981b, p. xliv). He openly acknowledges the positive impact of structuralism in helping to problematise simplistic understandings of the role of documents (Samuel, 1981b, p. xlvi) and he warns against complacently supposing that the documents can be 'penetrated', against 'succumb[ing] to the illusion that the past has come alive' (Samuel, 1981b, p. 1).

Carr takes a critique of simplistic treatments of the concept of evidence further in discussing facts. He talks of historians worshipping 'in the temple of facts' (Carr, 1964, p. 16). He argues very strongly against the 'cult of facts' pointing out that no piece of information is self-evidently a fact for history even if it is located in 'the documents', that for a knowledge to operate as a fact it has to undergo a certain process within institutions of making histories, to be 'proposed for membership of the select club of historical facts' and then seconded and sponsored (Carr, 1964, p. 12).

Despite problematising the assumption of the certainty of evidence and facts, neither Samuel nor Carr want to take this problematising 'too far'. Samuel defends 'weighing up the worth of different kinds of evidence' as 'inevitable' (Samuel, 1981b, p. xlix). Carr warns against 'the dangers' of 'the Collingwood view of history', against 'total scepticism' (Carr, 1964, p. 26). In this chapter I am obviously arguing in favour of taking the sort of problematising Samuel and Carr pursue 'too far', that is, I am arguing against seeing any aspect of what historians do as 'inevitable'.

The concept of periodisation (involving the concept of linear temporality) is another fairly central assumption behind thinking about making histories. Samuel acknowledges the importance of 'the whole notion of stages of historical development', especially as it was used by Marx, at the heart of much periodisation (Samuel 1981a, p. xx) and he notes its role in certain forms of social history – seeking out 'a linear path' of development delving into the recesses of pre-history, and tracing the evolution of humanity through savagery and barbarism to civilisation' (Samuel, 1981a, p. xviii). He makes it clear though that periodisation is an assumption nonetheless – 'periodisation, however convincing, is always arbitrary' (Samuel, 1981a, p. xliv).

Before discussing the past as a concept-as-assumption, I must stress that I make no claim at all to exhaustiveness in compiling my list; it is, as I said, a working list for the purposes of this essay.

Samuel and Carr raise issues about the key concept of the past both explicitly and implicitly. Explicitly, they both see the nature of the past as somewhat problematic. Carr introduces his discussion of the problematic nature of the past by acknowledging the importance of philosophical problems concerned with the way we know the past (Carr, 1964, p. 10). Samuel introduces his discussion by noting that historians see themselves as 'guided by an imaginative sympathy with the past' (Samuel, 1981b, p. xl) or, in the case of certain types of social history, as 'attempting to capture the voice of the past' (Samuel, 1981a, p. xviii).

Carr argues, using Collingwood, that history cannot be about 'the past by itself', but about a combination of the past by itself and the historian's thinking about the past by itself. The past in this way is 'still living in the present' (Carr, 1964, pp. 21–2). Samuel echoes this in talking about 'bringing the experience of the present to bear upon the interpretation of the past' (Samuel, 1981a, p. xv) and about the present 'continually subverting our understanding of the past' (Samuel, 1981a, p. xlvi).

Part of Samuel's and Carr's implicit treatment of the past involves the point, made earlier, that this key assumption informs all the other assumptions on our list. As well, their implicit treatment involves the way they use the concept directly but still as an assumption. For instance, while the above passages demonstrate Samuel's and Carr's awareness of and even sympathy for attempts to make the status of the concept of the past a little less secure, they also demonstrate the limits to this awareness and sympathy. There is certainly no recognition of the possibility that the past might not *really be there* and that consequently the concept may be dispensible. This is in direct contrast to Foucault. These limits are even clearer when Samuel tells us that we should not think of the influence of the present on the past as too 'disabling' (Samuel, 1981b, p. xlv), or when he acknowledges the existence of 'the reality of the past itself' (Samuel, 1981b, p. xlix), or when Carr, warning of the dangers of Nietzsche via Collingwood, shies away from the proposition that history writing constructs and controls 'the facts of the past' (Carr, 1964, pp. 27 and 29).

Consider our working list of concepts-as-assumptions as tools used in making histories over the past 30 years or so. As these histories are being made these tools are used freely and easily, though not quite all those on our list are used in each and every case. The past is used in all of them, evidence (and documents and facts) in all of them and periodisation (and linear temporality) in nearly all of them. These concepts have currency, given to them by the central banks of history making, to the point where they must be used in at least the above proportions (definitely the past, definitely evidence, almost definitely periodisation). Histories made as undergraduate or postgraduate work at universities must use them if they are to pass as histories, if they are to gain their makers good grades and/or Master's or Doctoral degrees. Histories made for publication as journal articles or books must use them or they will not be published. And histories made for presentation at conferences or in history clubs and societies must use them or they will either not be accepted for presentation or draw scorn and ridicule for their makers when they are presented. Histories which are made not using any of the concepts-as-assumptions as tools, or even not using enough of them, will find that the concepts they do use as tools have about as much currency as a goat in a department store; their exchange value (as knowledges) is very limited.

In my earlier piece (Wickham, 1984) on the way histories are used differently in different places and at different times, I discussed in detail the example of a history of the New South Wales Builders' Labourers' Federation (a union branch famous, or notorious, in Australia in the 1970s mainly for its stand on banning jobs for environmental reasons, a branch eventually taken over by its own federal or national branch).

I considered several different likely uses of this history and tried to show how it could function as a different history, a different knowledge, in each use. In a university history department concerned with labour history, the Builders' Labourers' Federation (BLF) history could be used simply to validate the conventions of history making (periodisation, evidencing, and so on) dominant in the department, or it could be used to challenge these conventions. It could be used to argue political bias within or against the department, characterising the history as a 'left-wing history' or a 'right-wing history' rather than a 'neutral history'.

In contemporary BLF politics the history in question could be used by those who supported the take-over of the New South Wales (NSW) branch by the federal branch to justify the take-over or it could be used by those who opposed the take-over to demonstrate the folly of this action.

In industrial courts the history could be used by the current leadership of the BLF to demonstrate that the union has been much more 'responsible' since the take-over and thus deserves an improvement in pay and conditions. Or it could be used in evidence by the employers to demonstrate that the union does not deserve such an improvement. Similarly in official inquiries, like Royal Commissions, it could be used as evidence in defence of, or to condemn, the union.

What should be the consequences of this theory of histories as currency? As I hinted earlier, the main consequence should be a determination within institutions of making histories and within institutions using histories to see no aspect of the making or using of a history as fixed or inevitable. No concept should be allowed to become an assumption.

Take the central concept of the past as an example. Samuel and Carr, I pointed out earlier, do not recognise the possibility that the past might not *really be there*, that the concept might be dispensible. Of course, many other historians also do not recognise it. But, the past *does not really* exist to ground and guarantee histories. Instead the past is a concept employed as a tool alongside other tools in making histories and in using them. It is central not because it is *there*, but because its currency is successfully maintained within institutions of making histories and within institutions of using them.

This is not, I stress, in any way an argument against the use of the concept of the past or against the use of any of the other concepts on our list. Arguing for or against particular concepts is not what this chapter is about. Rather, it is an argument for greater awareness, within institutions making histories and institutions using them, of intellectual developments in wider debates. Histories are not, after all, made or used in intellectual vacuums.

In other words, the currency of histories should become a key question for those involved in making and using histories. More exactly, it should become a key calculation. Particular tools of making histories and particular histories themselves should not be assumed to be good or bad because they have been used for a long time, or because they have been validated by certain figures or institutions or for whatever reasons. Instead, careful calculations should be made in the light of the conditions of operation of each tool and/or each history at the time and place of its use, in the way discussed in the example of the BLF history and the earlier example of the histories of European settlement in Australia.

CONCLUSION – SOCIOLOGY BEWARE

Various scholars have commented in the last few years about the benefits for sociology of links with history, especially social history. Consider just two examples:

In the last two decades, Western sociological enquiry has witnessed the re-introduction of a historical perspective into the study of society. The combination of ahistorical structural-functionalism and empirical studies . . . has been gradually undermined . . . As a result, the task of conceptualising and explaining the nature of social change has begun to be restored . . . Given the rediscovery of the problem of social change it is scarcely surprising that sociologists have begun to re-open channels of communication with historians (Holton, 1981, p. 46).

There have been many attempts by sociologists and historians to bridge the gulf that separates their disciplines . . . [These attempts have led to] the intellectual project of a 'historical social science'. . . This project is . . . part of the continuing effort to understand the formation, and transformation of large-scale social units over long periods of time . . . Currently this endeavour retains its appeal as a corrective . . . to the static and a-historical constructs of structural functionalism (Alexander, 1981, p. 56).

These passages reveal a commitment to fostering links between sociology and history mainly for the purpose of gaining a 'broader', 'more complete' picture of 'society as a whole'.

The arguments I have posed in this chapter suggest that this is not an appropriate direction for sociology. As I said in my introduction this essay assumes the worth of interdisciplinarity. It also assumes that sociology is better placed than history to achieve greater interdisciplinarity. It assumes this because it assumes that those involved in making and using sociological knowledges are much more likely to make calculations about each tool of sociology and/or each sociological knowledge than are those involved in the making and uses of histories, for no other reasons than the different institutional arrangements and status of sociological knowledges. But interdisciplinarity should be about destroying disciplinary boundaries to allow greater access to particular knowledges; interdisciplinary objectives are objectives of sites of politics of knowledges. Interdisciplinarity becomes a reactionary multidisciplinarity when the main concern is to stay within the disciplinary compound and borrow from other disciplines in order to make the compound bigger, whether it is done in the name of a greater understanding of 'society'or a greater understanding of, say, 'man'. The search for 'society', as if it is the ultimate object of knowledges, is as alienating in terms of access to knowledges as searches for 'man', as if it is the ultimate object, have been shown to be by much feminist work.

In trying to achieve greater interdisciplinarity sociology should be wary of History, in the singular, because history is best seen as different knowledges with different currencies. As such, sociology, as different knowledges with different currencies, should be wary of becoming like History. In acknowledging the different currencies of different histories, sociological knowledges should be aiming to destroy both the capital H and the potential capital S, and should be aiming to make the labels 'historical' and 'sociological' redundant as qualifiers for the word 'knowledges'.

NOTE

I would like to thank Chris McConville and Debbie Tyler for their comments and suggestions on an earlier draft of this chapter and Cathy Greenfield for helping me to see the possibilities of the concept of currency.

REFERENCES

M. Alexander, 'Historical Social Science: Class Structure in the Modern World System', *The Australian and New Zealand Journal of Sociology*, Vol. 17, No. 1, 1981.

E. H. Carr, *What is History?* (Harmondsworth: Penguin, 1964).

J. Donzelot, 'The Poverty of Political Culture', *Ideology and Consciousness*, No. 5, 1979.

M. Foucault, *The Archaeology of Knowledge* (London: Tavistock, 1974).

M. Foucault, 'Power and Strategies', in C. Gordon (ed.), *Power-Knowledge* (New York: Pantheon, 1980a).

M. Foucault, 'Truth and Power', in C. Gordon (ed.), *Power-Knowledge*, ibid., 1980b.

M. Foucault, 'Questions of Method', *Ideology and Consciousness*, No. 8, 1981.

S. Greenblatt, 'Towards a Poetics of Culture', *Southern Review*, Vol. 20, No. 1, 1987.

B. Holton, 'History and Sociology in the Work of E. P. Thompson', *The Australian and New Zealand Journal of Sociology*, Vol. 17, No. 1, 1981.

I. Hunter, 'Reading Character', *Southern Review*, Vol. 16, No. 2, 1983.

I. Hunter, 'The Novel', Course Handbook, Brisbane: School of Humanities, Griffith University, 1986.

F. Jameson, 'Foreword' in J. F. Lyotard, *The Postmodern Condition: A Report on Knowledge* (Manchester: Manchester University Press, 1984).

J.-F. Lyotard, *The Postmodern Condition: A Report on Knowledge*, ibid., 1984.

R. Phillipps, 'Law Rules O.K.?' in P. Botsman (ed.), *Theoretical Strategies, Local Consumption*, Series 2/3, 1982.

R. Samuel, 'People's History', in R. Samuel (ed.), *People's History and Socialist Theory* (London: Routledge & Kegan Paul, 1981a).

R. Samuel, 'History and Theory', in R. Samuel (ed.), *People's History and Socialist Theory*, ibid., 1981b.

The Weekend Australian, 9–10 January 1988.

G. Wickham, 'Power and power analysis: beyond Foucault?', *Economy and Society*, Vol. 12, No. 4, 1983.

G. Wickham, 'The Politics of History and the New South Wales Builders' Labourers' Federation', *Local Consumption Occasional Paper*, No. 2, 1984.

G. Wickham, 'Foucault, Power, Left Politics', *Arena*, No. 78, 1987.

5 Biography, Family History and the Analysis of Social Change

Brian Elliott

In his book *Historical Sociology* Philip Abrams (1982) urged us to think about Sociology and History as essentially the same enterprise and while there are some, particularly in history, who have reservations about this, there are plainly many scholars in both disciplines who, in recent years have followed his prescription. Within History there has emerged a specialism – social history – that at its best combines the theories and methods of sociology with much of the historians' traditional craft. In Sociology a focus upon long-run changes in the development of capitalism or in the processes of state-making, a concern with momentous events like social revolutions, the desire to make temporal rather than, say, cross-cultural comparisons or simply the ambition to set the actions, beliefs and institutions of particular groups in context has given rise to a distinctive strand of writing – to historical sociology. In Britain, as Calhoun (1987) observes, much of the most interesting and exciting work which meets Abrams' objectives has been done by the historians but the Edinburgh Conference revealed that within British Sociology there is now a substantial and growing concern with history. The fruitfulness of historical sociology has certainly been well displayed in American sociology in the last decade or so with many writers like Barrington Moore, Skocpol, Hareven and Tilly exploring major processes of change, re-examining classic themes from the founding fathers of social science and bringing to bear a diverse array of techniques of investigation.

A writer like Charles Tilly has shown, both in his books and articles and in his career, that it is indeed possible to combine the two crafts of history and sociology. And from his vantage point, as someone with a foot in both camps as it were, Tilly has had occasion to reflect upon the relations between the disciplines (Tilly, 1981) and from time to time to offer recommendations for the development of social history and (if we accept that there is no substantial difference in its objectives) for historical sociology. In the special edition of *The Journal of Family History* devoted to 'Family History, Social History and Social Change', for instance, we find him discussing what he sees as the two principal purposes of social history (Tilly, 1987). These he calls Reconstitution and Connection. Reconstitution is the effort to reconstruct 'a round of life as people lived it'. Connection refers to the attempts to show the links between 'life on the small scale and large social structures and processes'. Plainly, he sees the latter task as the more important for, laudable as much of the former may be, there is always the danger that if '. . . social historians devote themselves chiefly to reconstitution they will produce many bright fragments of dubious comparability and uncertain relationship' (1987, p. 319). The search for connection is not simply a recipe for good social history; it is surely the same instruction that C. W. Mills provided three decades ago for the general encouragement of the sociological imagination and the development of the discipline of sociology within which the patterns of everyday life of social groups were to be rendered intelligible and meaningful by relating them to major historical changes and events. Now, as then, the promise of sociology can only be realised through the provision of historical understanding. But now, as then, the real task of making that desired connection is a difficult one.

Part of the difficulty, of course, is the fact that those regularities and patterns that we commonly refer to as structures are not simply external, ineluctable constraints. Tilly recognises this when, writing about the various forms of family life that have been described by social historians, he asks 'Does each coherent group create a model of social (including family) structures and then implement that? Or do people have broad operating rules for social relations which precipitate the arrangements we think of as structures?' (1987, p. 329). He favours the latter view. So, too does Abrams, who points out that:

> Historical sociology treats history as the way social action and social structure create and contain one another. Its method is necessarily dialectical reflecting the endless interplay of fact and meaning that constitutes, decomposes and reconstitutes social experience. (1982, p. 108)

If then good social history or good historical sociology involve this constant quest for connection between structures and everyday experience, and if what is required of us is real sensitivity to the ways in which the regularities, patterns, structures are continuously, subtly remade, how should we proceed? What methods and styles of research are needed? Since the task is evidently complex there can be no simple recommendation, no easy promotion, of a narrow range of methods. Recapturing the nature of the social life of peasants or nobility, tracing the impact of economic boom or slump or war or rebellion, describing the growth of states or whole socio-economic systems and the day to day adaptations of diverse populations requires all the traditional techniques at our disposal. We need to scour the documentary sources, the papers and records of individuals and institutions, the statistical data of governments, churches and businesses; we need the census and survey, the community studies and the interviews with the powerful and the powerless. From all of these we may distil an appreciation of the broad regularities and structures; from these we should be able to construct theories and hypotheses of an increasingly refined kind. But in many cases – and the problem is more acute the further back in time we go or the more we focus on the ordinary, or the poor populations who have left few records of their own making – we find it hard to capture the meanings of the decisions and choices that gave shape to people's lives, and the texture of their social existence. Exploring that 'dialectic' that Abrams referred to is extremely difficult.

However, in those cases where our interest is in relatively recent history, in the past of the last 50 or 60 years or less, then plainly we can, as sociologists or social historians take advantage of the fact that our subjects (many of them at least) are still alive. Biography and history can be connected through detailed accounts of individual, family and community life. And research in that vein has, of course, been growing in popularity. The impetus has come partly from those (and they are to be found in both history and sociology) who have been self-consciously developing *oral* history in the last few years – people like Raphael Samuel, Paul Thompson, Trevor Lummis and others in Britain; and partly from those who rediscovered the value of the life history approach pioneered by Thomas and Znaniecki and others in the 1920s – people like Norman Denzin, Tamara Hareven and Daniel Bertaux.

The advantages of the various oral and biographical styles of work are obvious. To those concerned to write 'history from below', to those who wish to ensure that the voices of ordinary men and women can be heard in the historical record, oral history is indisputably important. Among sociologists, particularly those who, during the 1970s, grew dissatisfied with conventional, positivistic styles of research and wanted to develop a more phenomenological approach, the collection of detailed life stories had much to offer. Critics of the oral history or life history approaches could, of course, challenge the validity and reliability of data collected in these ways or argue that substantial generalisations were difficult to make given the small scale, in-depth nature of most investigations. And it would be hard to deny that work in these modes has, in Tilly's terms, produced much more by way of reconstitution than connection. But it is by no means clear that these 'soft' methods can contribute little beyond description.

Reflecting upon and experimenting with the use of some of these biographical approaches suggests that they may be used very deliberately to explore the connections between major processes of change or great dislocative events and patterns of everyday life, and that they may have an important part to play in the refinement both of methods of research and our theories, hypotheses and empirical generalisations. The key is to develop what we might call their 'forensic' potential.

THE FORENSIC USES OF BIOGRAPHICAL MATERIALS

The word 'forensic' conjures up the courtroom – denotes hard questioning, vigorous cross-examination. Thinking about the collection of life history data, the gathering of family histories, the construction of what Bertaux and Bertaux-Wiame (1986) call 'social genealogies' (or using such data where they are already available), can encourage us to do just that – call into question some of our conventional methods, data, theories and hypotheses about what we like to call structural change. Of course, this is not the only basis on which we can conduct our critical appraisals: much of our work on social change can be criticised in its own terms, using essentially the same methodologies. But starting our examination from the biographical perspective can lead to more radical criticism, can help us to keep the image of social structures as 'precipitates' of social action in the centre of our field of vision and should encourage us constantly to look for the connections between big changes and the distinctive experiences of particular social milieux.

The idea of using life history materials in something like this way is not, of course, original. To take just one recent example: Lynn Jamieson (1987) in her paper 'Theories of Family Development and the Experience of Being Brought Up', uses her semi-structured interviews dealing with the early life histories of a sample of elderly men and women in Scotland to 'interrogate', as she puts it, the generalisations and theories contained in the classic accounts of the emergence of the modern family. Those classic accounts were built up with the use of diverse demographic information, census materials or survey data (some, one would have to say, were constructed with very little hard historical evidence at all). Jamieson's collection of experiential data challenges commonly held notions about the timing of changes in family form, about the varieties of class-specific characteristics of family life and, most importantly, logical links between changes in economic, occupational and other broad features of modern society and the alterations in family life that allegedly accompanied them. Her experiential data cannot, drawn as they are from a sample of less than one hundred interviews, thoroughly disprove theories about the modern family as a 'haven in a heartless world', about the supposed emotional intensity or child-centredness of the family: nor can they establish in an entirely convincing way that important changes in family form and life took place a good deal later than is frequently argued. But what they can and do achieve is a radical questioning of the conventional theories and methods, and in this way they can lead to new questions and more precise and refined hypotheses.

Biographical materials – family histories, life histories and social genealogies – are difficult ones to work with, requiring considerable skill and patience to collect and even more patience and imagination to analyse. Transcription of long, tape-recorded sessions is expensive and time-consuming and for the researcher there is often a sense of being overwhelmed by the sheer volume of material and the problems of selection and interpretation. But their potential in the writing of 'sociology as history', as Abrams calls it, is substantial, and as yet only partially realised. Among the many ways of employing such data and developing their 'forensic' qualities those below seem particularly important.

First, they can be used to trace those connections between major processes of change and the actual experience of specific social groups. There is still an enormous amount to be learned about the impact of what we can think of as the master process – the development of capitalism and capitalist relations, the growth of industrialism, the spread of urbanisation, the business of state-making. These, the central concerns of the founding fathers of social science, are not completed processes but on-going ones. To be sure, studying the early phases of these processes in Europe takes us back well beyond the experience of any who are alive now, but capitalism, industrialism, urbanism have all altered their character substantially in the old countries where they began. And is Thatcher's state the same state that the British lived in during the 1960s? Evidently not. In newer countries, in the peripheral regions of the old world, the dislocative effects of the master processes are only now being felt. And, many of the most dramatic changes *have* occurred within the life-spans of those whose personal or family histories we can collect. If, as is certainly the case, there have been major alterations in the occupational, communal and family lives of our populations, if a distinctive modern life cycle has emerged, how and when did these occur and how can we best describe and analyse them? Evidence from the official sources, the censuses and diverse enquiries of the state, evidence from the market research organisations; commercial pollsters and others, evidence from sociological surveys and case studies can teach us much, but they do not take us close into the real, lived experience and uncover the intimate dynamics of the social world. But the biographical studies can do that.

Secondly, biographical materials allow us to get beyond the cross-sectional quality of most official data and much of the survey evidence – the materials from which, in history and in sociology we construct our models of changes and our portraits of family forms, life cycles, patterns of mobility, and so forth. Generally, these data do not allow us to trace groups or individuals through time or space. We know that to study processes of change we frequently require longitudinal designs, but these are technically difficult to manage, expensive and, in consequence, rare. Biographical materials do not provide thoroughly adequate substitutes but they do take us much closer to the sequences we want to understand.

Thirdly, biographical materials allow us to overcome the overwhelmingly individualistic quality of much of the data we use by revealing the *collective* processes involved in, for instance, getting married, setting up households, getting a job or getting ahead.

Thinking about and collecting life histories and family histories leads us to question our individualistic methodology.

Fourthly, a biographical approach forces upon us a recognition of those dialectual processes that Abrams referred to, for in the recounted experiences we hear our respondents recalling not only the facts of their lives but the meaning that events or decisions had for them. We learn about the values and beliefs that guided their actions, the salient ambitions, aspirations and strategies that influenced them. And these, of course, are not simply 'their' beliefs or values but are, in most instances things derived from, shared with others in a particular milieu. Certainly we need to be cautious, sceptical and sensitive in our interpretation of these reconstructions of their lives, for frequently they will be shaped by powerful myths embedded not only in their immediate social world but in the wider culture (myths of the self-made man or of the proletarian radical are two that commonly occur) as Jean Peneff (1986) has observed. But difficulties in interpretation notwithstanding, these life stories and family histories do give us an appreciation of the ways in which culture shapes action and how the myriad actions coalesce into the regularities we call structure.

The biographical approach then is rich in possibilities. Its more extensive use can lead to reappraisal and criticism of our methods of studying social change and the models of change that we have built.

THE BIOGRAPHICAL APPROACH AND THE STUDY OF SOCIAL MOBILITY

In order to illustrate more clearly the critical uses to which a biographical approach can be put we can draw upon ideas which Daniel Bertaux and Isabelle Bertaux-Wiame have been developing and some preliminary findings from studies that they have conducted. These will be supplemented by some observations that come from essentially similar exploratory investigations that I conducted, initially with no knowledge of the Bertauxs' work, but latterly with some deliberate reference to their concerns.

Patterns of social mobility have been extensively studied in sociology and there has been a good deal of work on the same topic by historians too. Such enquiries tend to follow a well defined set of issues and employ very similar methods of investigation. The main focus is on occupational status changes. The researchers want to know about the rates of movement up and down a prestige hierarchy – sometimes the changes that occur during the course of individuals' working lives, but more often the changes that appear when we compare the occupations of sons with those of their fathers. The data are gathered from sample surveys and relate, of course, to individuals. Within sociology there is no doubt that such studies have long been regarded as important ones for they touch upon matters of profound social and political significance – the relative openness of a society and the effects of efforts to achieve greater egalitarianism. They are also admired, at least by those with a quantitative bent, for the methodological elegance and sophistication that the best of them display.

But to Daniel Bertaux (and he is one who spent his early years as a sociologist working in this particular vineyard) the conventional mobility studies are seriously flawed. Their statistical sophistication, he argues, has far outstripped their real sociological insightfulness and their resolutely individualistic methodology has concealed the fact that mobility processes are far more profoundly social and collective than these studies allow us to see. Moreover, as attempts to look at a major social process, these investigations have an enormous deficiency: they look almost exclusively at men. This criticism has, of course, been made by many writers, including as one would expect, many feminists, but from the perspective of one like Bertaux, who has spent more than a decade encouraging the development and use of biographical methods, there are really two points to be made. Not only should we pay more attention to the rates and routes of mobility for women (as a recent study by Goldthorpe [1987] does) but we need also to explore the possibility that women – mothers especially – may have far more influence on the social mobility of their children than has been supposed. To explore these matters, especially the latter, will require studies of a quite different kind: of a biographical kind.

Life histories and other biographical materials which are often rich in details about status ambitions and mobility serve then to sharpen criticism of the conventional studies and underscore their methodological and conceptual shortcomings. If we think about social mobility on the basis of our own experience or that of groups and families and individuals we know well, if we start that is, with an immediately familiar kind of biographical perspective, we are led to ask some questions which really challenge the commonplace sociological enquiries.

The Bertauxs begin by asking (Bertaux and Bertaux-Wiame, 1986) 'Who gets ahead? Individuals or whole sets of siblings?' The possibility that sets of brothers and sisters may have rather similar educations, may find themselves in occupations of broadly similar status levels, that in the marriage patterns the principle of homogamy is powerful, that a group of siblings may find themselves, in maturity, moving in rather similar social worlds – all that is intuitively appealing. Which is not to deny that we can think of counter-instances, of the cases where one of the offspring became, say, a doctor while others became routine white-collar or even manual workers. But the question is how common is it for whole sets of siblings to follow similar social trajectories? And where there are sharp differences among groups of brothers and sisters we can ask is this too patterned? Do older siblings do particularly well or badly? Are there constraints in particular milieux that might influence this? Very quickly we are led to a new curiosity about the *process* of mobility, about the complex of social factors that may come into play. The design of the usual mobility studies rules out the exploration of all but a very limited number of these.

Thinking about factors that may influence the mobility prospects of groups of siblings leads to the recognition that these are of at least two broad kinds. There are 'External' ones like the structure of job opportunities, the buoyancy or depressed nature of local, regional or national economies at particular points in time and conventional studies do, of course, pay attention to these. They do so especially when they address the question of widespread shifts in the nature of the occupational structures and seek to take out their effects when measuring rates of mobility. And no doubt the current investigations of regional economies being carried out in the several Social Change and Economic Life projects in the UK will tell us more about these kinds of 'external' factors. But there are plainly other influences that in a rather crude way we can think of as 'internal' ones. The Bertauxs suggest that there are distinctive 'microclimates' in families, cultural constellations that may encourage or inhibit social mobility or steer it along particular pathways. Certainly there seems to be major differences between families in terms of the kinds of projects and aspirations (and the specificity of these), that parents and perhaps other family members establish for the younger generation.

What we really need to know is what is transmitted to the young from within the family. Particular, describable attitudes and aspirations? Rooted in what? Religious commitments or perhaps special experiences of parents? Describing cultural transmissions is peculiarly difficult, but placed side by side the accounts that I have gathered leave no doubt that stark differences exist. Among the Canadian students who were my subjects, the persistence in some families of a restless, striving Protestant asceticism was very evident. In other families the projects and ambitions had little to do with religious commitment but much to do with deprivations and dashed hopes of the parents.

Material transmission, of course, matters enormously – the where-withall to support youngsters in their studies, money to buy private education, funds to support diverse life-styles, property and capital assets to start a business – all have substantial effects.

Cultural transmissions, material transmissions – but there is also another kind that might simply be labelled 'social'. Parents invoke social ties, sometimes those of kinship but often looser ones to acquaintances made through business or leisure, in the process of helping their offspring to find colleges to go to or jobs to take. Life history and family history accounts focussed on mobility seem to contain much that attests to the strength of those 'weak ties' that Granovetter (1973) drew to our attention.

If social mobility is really more of a family affair than we have so far shown in our sociological and historical studies what role do women play in all of this? Do mothers do more than fathers to establish the Bertauxs' microclimate of the family? Is this a feature of certain social groups – the traditional working class in the UK, Jewish immigrant communities? Literary as well as sociological accounts suggest that this issue would certainly bear systematic investigation.

And what about other family members? The Bertauxs (1988) suggest that grandparents may play important roles in ensuring the advancement or at least the maintenance of the status positions of their grandchildren. Since more and more people live to see their grandchildren grow into maturity, transmissions across three genera-tions becomes a matter of more and more interest. As yet we know little about this.

There are ties too between older and younger siblings that are important. In some families we find older siblings supporting younger ones, assisting them with funds for education and social contacts that are of value in obtaining work. Sibling bonds seem especially significant in the process of migration, with elder siblings (usually males), acting as pioneers in the move from country to town, from region to region or indeed from country to country. Once established they sponsor brothers, sisters, parents and other family members in making those moves in space that so often are the preconditions for changes, improvements, in economic and social fortunes. If we are to explore some of the links between geographical and social mobility we find in these accounts of family histories much evidence of kinship bonds as the 'auspices' of migration – to use a term employed in a paper written a good many years ago (Tilly and Brown, 1967).

Biographical materials then remind us or reveal for us, the real complexity of social mobility. They force us to think not just about upward mobility but about those lateral moves across changing occupational structures and, as the Bertauxs insist, they make us recognise that simply maintaining social status, preventing downward movement, is a matter of interest not just to individuals but to wider social groups. Not just individual, but family resources of the most diverse kind are mobilised in the struggle to offset illness, divorce, job loss and the host of eventualities that can threaten some sections or members of a family with social demotion. For most individuals, for most families, long-range mobility is rare. The common experience is a struggle to maintain respectability, to hang on to those things that guarantee a measure of comfort and security in an uncertain world.

These then are some of the issues thrown into sharp relief by accounts which describe the actual experiences of social change as they are recollected by family members. If we wish to gather biographical materials that provide useful data we can, as the Bertauxs (1986, 1988) suggest, use several slightly different methods. We can collect individual life histories; we can by talking to several family members, try to piece together a family history or we can have our respondents construct a social genealogy – that is, a family tree on which is recorded a number of salient details about, for instance, education, jobs and careers, geographical moves of individuals. In the very limited, strictly exploratory kind of investigations that I have conducted the social genealogy was the most useful device. I began by asking each student to interview his or her parents and to record information about the two sets of grandparents – the countries, regions and communities they were born in, the size and composition of the households of origin, principal occupations, geographical mobility. Similar information was then gathered for the parents – the nature of the families, economies, cultures and communities in which they grew up, and then some data on the families and households they had established and the places in which they lived. Students were also asked to look for evidence of the impact on their families' lives of major social changes – the big events like wars, revolutions, depressions and booms, or the more gradual shifts in occupational structures, patterns of educational opportunity or the growth of the welfare state. The prime purpose, of course, was to get them to explore the relationships between biography and history. Most of them seemed to enjoy this exercise and in the end it achieved its main objective admirably. Discussion of broad structural changes suddenly took on real life when they could begin to trace the ways in which their grandparents and parents were part of history, the way their lives had been affected by, say, the depression of the 1930s, a world war, revolutions in China and Southeast Asia or the new opportunities in education or jobs. Summarising data on family size and household composition revealed major changes across the generations, information about geographical moves uncovered their families' parts in the process of urbanisation. Didactically the very modest little enquiry had highly rewarding effects and small group discussions in which students described to each other their family profiles produced an interesting social effect in breaking down somewhat the anonymity and isolation of the learning experience in a class of 70.

Many weeks later I asked each student to read the Bertaux paper and consider the central hypothesis, that social mobility was not so much an individual as a family affair. They then went back to the original social genealogies and refined these by collecting more detailed information on at least two branches of their family. (Most commonly they compared their own immediate family with that established by one of the siblings of their parents.) They then wrote essays appraising the strengths and weaknesses of the Bertaux approach (comparing it with a brief summary of a conventional mobility study) and considering the validity of the main hypothesis by cautious use of their own data. The results were fascinating.

A few rejected the biographical approach and defended the conventional style of research on various methodological grounds or by reference to social genealogies which seemed to show that social mobility *was* very much an individual matter. But the great majority found reasons to support the idea that social mobility does seem to be patterned at the level of the family.

The significance of the 'external' factors, the economic and social contexts in which families lived emerged frequently and vividly as the students contrasted the educational and occupational trajectories of groups of siblings – those in the families that had stayed in the small towns of the prairies say, with those who had moved to a large and rapidly growing city like Vancouver. Many in the class came from India, China and other parts of Southeast Asia and for them the differences between their lives and those of their siblings were set against the experiences of and prospects for their cousins living still in very much less industrialised or still colonial social structures.

'Internal' factors – the cultural 'microclimates' of families were sometimes brilliantly described, as in the cases where students came from staunchly Protestant families within which strict codes of self-denial, hard work and long-term educational and occupational projects were very deliberately enjoined. Many (though certainly not all) of those from Chinese backgrounds wrote about the discipline, application and ambition that characterised their upbringing. There were discernible class-related differences in the cultural transmissions to whole sets of siblings and in a few cases the real reasons behind parental ambition for their children were revealed in moving ways. The clearest exploration of the roots, the real meaning of a family ethos was provided by a Japanese Canadian student whose construction of the social genealogy had evidently prompted lengthy discussion of the family history and the revelation of much that had rarely been disclosed before. During World War II the Canadian government interned families of Japanese descent. Canadian citizens, Japanese Canadians, were shipped off to camps remote from the main centres of population. Families were split up, many privations endured and when hostilities ceased there were government efforts to prevent these families from returning to British Columbia, from where most of them came. They were instructed to seek work 'east of the Rockies'. Worst of all, they lost all their property – their farms, fishing boats and homes. The father of the student explained his own determination not just to acquire an education, but to excel at university. Skills and qualifications were the one thing 'they couldn't take away from you'. Both mother and father in this case had experienced the internment and all the injustice that went with it. Small wonder then that in this family there was a strong emphasis on educational and occupational success!

About the role of women in the process of mobility it would be difficult to generalise with confidence from such a limited exercise, but there certainly seemed to be support for the idea that in the majority of families the mother's aspirations and ambitions for the children were more clearly articulated, more substantial than those of the fathers. The most definite exceptions to this were interesting.

They seemed to be found either in farming families or in those of the very wealthy. Both of these might be seen as instances where productive property is most evidently and exclusively in the father's hands and where, certainly in the case of farmers, it will be transmitted principally along the male line. More detailed analysis of the deviant cases might prove instructive but these should not distract us from what I think is the more important possibility: that mothers, and maybe grandmothers, for whom the family is still the principal focus of activity and responsibility, play a most important role in maintaining or advancing social status. One of the essays offered what seems like an unhoped for natural experiment on this theme. A Chinese Canadian student described her paternal grandfather, born in Shanghai in the early years of the century as a wealthy merchant and a 'very traditional' Chinaman. He was polygamous. His three wives, though none from poor families, came from somewhat different backgrounds. Each bore two or three children, and while the evidence leaves much to be desired, it appeared that the offspring of the different mothers had distinctive social trajectories. The values of each mother it seemed, patterned the lives of her children in discernible ways. (To test the propositon that mothers have more influence than fathers, hold father constant, vary wives!)

Finally, in this necessarily brief account, it is perhaps worth recording that the data gathered from the students at the University of British Columbia offered some support for a finding that Daniel Bertaux made in his early exploration of these matters which he conducted at the University of Laval in Quebec. Among his respondents there were many from farm families, and the social genealogies and family histories that they constructed suggested that birth order affected mobility patterns in a particular way. Eldest sons tended to stay home, to work on the farm (presumably with the expectation of inheriting it) rather than pursuing qualifications and seeking social mobility through a non-farm career. Younger siblings then received more education in these families and were more likely to display upward or lateral mobility. There were relatively fewer from farm backgrounds in the Vancouver group but among those who did come from such families a similar pattern was evident.

Overall, of course, these little experimental investigations cannot provide us with confident generalisations, but what one can legitimately say about them is that they do encourage us to think about an important process in new ways.

THE BIOGRAPHICAL APPROACH AND THE STUDY OF
THE MODERN LIFE CYCLE

In his paper 'The emergence of the modern life cycle in Britain'
Michael Anderson (1985) describes and analyses major changes in
the patterns of birth and death, of marriage and childbearing from
the early eighteenth century to the 1970s. Throughout he is addressing a number of key questions: 'How did the life cycle change and
when did a distinctive modern pattern appear?' 'What factors
brought about these changes?' and 'What were the wider social
implications of these changes?'

The data on mortality and fertility, on ages of marriage, ages of
men and women at the birth of first and last children, their ages when
those children first married or had offspring of their own, the
changing patterns of women's and men's working lives and the rates
of dissolution of marriages through death or divorce enable Anderson to make a series of extremely interesting general observations.

First, he is able to show that:

> . . . over a period of about 100 years, and particularly between
> 1939 and the 1970s, the whole pattern of the life cycle changed
> dramatically; the 'modern' life, cycle emerged. (Anderson, 1985,
> p. 86)

The nature of this new life cycle was such that, thanks to improved
standards of living and of health, far more of the population lived to
enjoy often lengthy periods of grandparenthood and even great-
grandparenthood. Reductions in family size, earlier ages of marriage
and the compressing of childbearing into a relatively few years in a
woman's life meant that many women were freed from what had been
protracted phases of childcare and were able to take up positions in
the labour market. The dramatic increase in the proportion of
married women who were gainfully employed was one of the most
marked features of the British, as of most modern capitalist economies during the 1960s and 1970s. And there were major changes for
men too. Compulsory retirement from their jobs and systems of state
and private pensions ensured that, generally, along with their wives,
they could expect a substantial period released from the necessity
(and maybe the satisfactions) of shifts or 9-to-5 routines.

All this leads Anderson to a second general observation about the relative certainty, security and predictability of the modern life cycle. For those who grew to maturity between, say, the late 1930s and the mid-1970s, life was not commonly punctuated by premature death and disease (though plainly World War II did cause death or disability for some of their parents or relatives); nor, for the vast majority, was it disrupted by the consequences of terrible slumps and lay-offs or impaired by the awful shortages of housing and the accompanying necessity of making a home in the kinds of insecure, overcrowded and decrepit conditions that earlier generations knew. Of course, there was a housing crisis after the war, but this was rapidly alleviated by the vast expansion both of publicly provided housing and housing for owner occupation. The urban problems of the late 1940s and early 1950s, though serious, were nothing like those that were common throughout most of the nineteenth century and the early years of this century.

Anderson was impressed too by what seemed to be the convergence of the life experiences of different groups of the population – and indeed the demographic data certainly do much to support his argument that the span over which major life cycle transitions occur has been reduced, leading to a third generalisation, to what he terms 'the homogenization of experiences'. Many of the stark, long-standing differences between the working class and the middle class sectors of society, he implies, have been eroded, and these profound structural changes have considerable implications in terms of everyday life and culture.

At the end of his paper, Anderson indulges in a little speculation. There are, he tells us, some indications that this 'modern' life cycle may be a rather fragile thing; that some of the basic demographic patterns may be changing; that the homogenisation process may be crumbling. Plainly, though he does not explore this in any detailed fashion, the modern life cycle depends in some vital ways on the state – on state intervention to manage the economy and reduce the impact of booms and slumps, or state provision of housing, welfare and health provisions. By the mid-1980s, when Anderson's paper was written, it was clear that the Thatcher government was determined to supplant the 'Keynesian consensus' with an economic and social philosophy that envisaged a much freer rein for 'market forces' and a substantial reduction in almost all state-provided resources. Would the impact of this political change reverse the 'homogenisation of experiences'? The question is not posed quite so starkly but that is the curiosity that is sparked by his concluding paragraphs.

Anderson then has provided us with an interesting and important set of findings and ideas but, like all efforts to build good, general interpretations of social change they invite, indeed, they deserve criticism and refinement. His analysis is based upon a variety of official data – censuses, Household Surveys and the like – and it is certainly possible to question and qualify his research in its own terms, using essentially similar methods and data. An obvious step would be to disaggregate the data on key variables so that we could examine more closely the patterns for different social classes and other broad groupings. In practice this is not easy to do since most of the officially produced demographic data in Britain are not presented in ways that allow this. One requires access to the original materials and then has to make a special study. If we were to try to explore Anderson's idea about the 'fragility' of the modern life cycle and assess the impact of recent changes in state policy we would confront the same problem and it would be compounded by the fact that, as part of the Conservative government's effort to reduce public expenditures, there has been some attenuation of the gathering and publication of official statistics. All of which underlines Tilly's point about the irony that in trying to examine the links between big structures and individual experience we are very often dependent upon information from those very structures – in this case the state – whose influence we want to measure (Tilly, 1987, p. 323). Those who control the state tell us what they want us to know. They do not necessarily tell us what *we* want to know and on occasion, as in recent years in Britain, they may go to some lengths to suppress information that might lead to genuinely critical appraisal of policies. With all these limitations and difficulties though, it is still possible to examine more closely Anderson's main arguments using data similar to his own.

However, if our goal is to establish the 'connections' between broad structural changes and the actual experiences of groups and individuals we could usefully approach Anderson's findings about life cycle changes not only by refining the statistical data, we could do so too by gathering and using biographical materials. Indeed, the need to do this is evident if we consider that he refers explicitly to life *experience*, yet experiential data are precisely what his account lacks. It is a deficiency which is entirely understandable where he is dealing with those who lived in the eighteenth and nineteenth centuries, but clearly it could be supplied for those who have lived through and whose experiences constitute the changes in which he is most interested: the relatively recent changes that give form to this specifically 'modern' life cycle. Family histories and social genealogies can be employed to give vital detail to those connections between aggregate birth, death, divorce and other rates and the real lives of men and women and at the same time they can be employed in a questioning, critical, 'forensic' way.

We could begin by considering the fact that while the life cycle patterns for various groups of the population may show 'convergence' they do not display synchronous change. Within the aggregate regularities we know there are some significant differences. The shift towards the modern life cycle did not occur at precisely similar times for, say, different classes. For example, the move towards two-child families occurred later for working class than for middle class groups. Kendrick *et al.* in their analysis of Scottish demographic data (1984) (and in recent times Scotland's demography has not been much different from that of England and Wales) shows this clearly. As late as the 1950s and 1960s mean family size for Social Class 1 mothers (those married to professional and managerial men) was 2 while for those in the Registrar General's Social Class V (unskilled workers) it was 3 and more detailed information on the incidence of large families (more than four children) shows wide class differences persisting into the 1960s. The move towards the small, two-child family occurred as late as the 1970s for the working class. Similarly, ages at marriage also reveal class differentiated trends. Roughly, we can say that in the 1950s and 1960s the working class led the way towards earlier marriage, while in the 1970s and 1980s middle calss women pioneered a trend towards later marriage.

The point is that the *contexts* within which these kinds of demographic changes occurred were obviously different. Family histories and social genealogies provide not only evidence of these changes, as they record the varying numbers of offspring or different ages of marriage in successive generations, but they allow us to grasp something of the social, economic and historical settings in which they occurred. Anderson's analysis tells us about aggregate patterns at particular points in time. Using biographical materials moves us closer to the kind of life course analysis outlined by Hareven (1978) and Elder (1985) in which we can compare the transitions in family form and life cycle experience across different social groups. In the family histories we learn how cumulative experiences of family life, of work, of community, shape decisions. We find ourselves once more, as with the social mobility instances, looking at external, structural constraints that help people's lives but also at cultural factors – at those aspects of the 'microclimate' of families – that help to establish conventions, plans and aspirations. This time they attach to marriage, child-bearing and child-rearing, to setting up house, to the desirability or necessity of women working outside the home, of having a career or a particular standard of living.

In his paper Anderson stressed the relative stability, predictability and regularity of the modern life cycle compared with life cycles in earlier periods. His focus is on what, on average, people can expect. But life history and family history accounts reveal how, for some sections of the population – particularly the poorer ones – life is still full of uncertainty. Family histories collected by Straw (1985), for instance, contained frequent reference to the impact of illness, injury and premature death among a working class population, reflecting both the remembered misfortunes of those in the older generations but also the continuing inequalities of health (which current medical statistics corroborate). Employment prospects and experiences too, of course, show very substantial differences across the population if we disaggregate by class, gender or ethnicity and these too are starkly displayed in life and family histories.

Biographical methods then serve to qualify in important ways Anderson's observations about the relative predictability and security of the modern life cycle. To be sure, death, particularly the death of young children, is much less common today than was the case, say, in Victorian Britain. But what we see in the experiential accounts is evidence of the fact that such security as was attained by the working class, and especially the poorest sections of that class, was reached only very recently and any trends towards more stability or predictability in the life cycle are by no means certain to continue.

Indeed, in the family histories currently being collected we shall surely see proof not just of persisting class-based differences but also *divergencies*. Anderson's speculations about the 'fragility' of the modern life cycle will be borne out as we gather more information on the many families whose members, particularly young members, have lived through the years of the late 1970s and 1980s in Britain. These were the years during which unemployment reached levels not seen since the 1930s and youth unemployment in some parts of the inner city or other deprived areas reached 60, 70 and even 80 per cent. Glen Elder wrote about the Children of the Great Depression (Elder, 1974) and while conditions in Britain in the early 80s were not so bleak, the poverty not so abject or widespread, still the effects of 'recession' will be deep and lasting and like the crises of the 30s, will mark a generation. The neo-conservative market-oriented policies, have had a profound impact on the poorer sections of the community, not only through their effects on jobs but also through the reductions in the value of state-provided benefits for those who are workless and needy. Housing policies too have created terrible problems as prices have soared and public sector house building programmes have come almost to a halt. Homelessness is once again the plight of many thousands. Homelessness, joblessness: two conditions which are bound to have consequences for the modern life cycle, for they will prevent the establishment of independent households, will mean deferred marriages and later, perhaps, smaller families. If state policies during much of the postwar period contributed a good deal to the making of a distinctive modern life cycle, those of the years since 1979 have surely done much to undermine these trends of 'convergence', 'homogenisation' and growing 'predictability'. Officially generated statistics will tell us something about that, but the fullest appreciation will come from data of another kind: from those that offer detailed experiential accounts. Family histories will give us a strong sense of what it has been like to live in a society that has become markedly more divided, more inegalitarian.

CONCLUSION

Studies of the modern life cycle then, like studies of social mobility or accounts of changing family forms, can benefit greatly from the use of biographical approaches. These techniques offer more than mere description, more indeed than their original proponents, the Chicago School sociologists, foresaw. Shaw (1945), Sutherland (1937), Thomas and Znaniecki (1918–20) and others used life histories in illuminating but still relatively conservative ways to complement investigations of urban life, of crime, of migration and other processes, investigations carried out in essentially positivistic frameworks. The biographical accounts enriched the understanding of social processes but they were not employed seriously to challenge the methods, theories and epistemology of the early sociology.

The claims made for the biographical approach by some of those who have engineered its recent revival are altogether larger. Ferrarotti, for example, describes how his early interest in collecting life histories merely as 'background' for his studies of industrialisation and technical change has developed to the point where he now sees biography as restoring a full appreciation of subjective meaning and providing 'a means of access – often the only possible one to the scientific knowledge of a social system' (1983, p. 67). Drawing upon Sartre, he argues that

. . . when we are dealing with the consideration of human practice, only dialectical reason allows us scientifically to understand an action, to reconstruct the processes which make behaviour the active synthesis of a social system, and to interpret the objectivity in a fragment of social history by starting from the non-evaded subjectivity of an individual history. Only dialectical reason allows us to attain the universal and the general (society) by emphasising the individual and the singular (man). (1983, p. 73)

The new enthusiasm for the biographical approach and the recent growth of historical sociology can be seen then as intersecting in some interesting ways. In both we find ourselves exploring the manner in which individuals simultaneously constitute and are constituted by society. In both we are encouraged constantly to move from the unique, particular experience of individuals or groups to the regularities that allow us to identify broad patterns of change. In this constant to-ing and fro-ing we must, says Ferrarotti '. . . identify the most important spaces, those which serve as pivots between structures and individuals, the social field where the singularizing practice of man and the universalizing effort of a social system confront each other most directly' (1983, p. 76).

Those 'pivots' are found in small primary groups, in peer groups at work or, in neighbourhoods – above all in the family. And if that is true, then we can extend our biographical enterprises so that we collect not just personal biographies, but collective biographies – which is, of course, precisely what the Bertaux recommend in their attempts to look afresh at social mobility processes.

The reawakened interest among sociologists in history, not only in a specialism called 'historical sociology' but more generally in writing 'sociology as history' raises inevitably all the old questions about how as sociologists or as historians we can recover the past. Paul Rock's comments (which reflect the impact of phenomenology or sociology in the 1970s) throw the familiar difficulties into sharp relief:

> As mediator and creator of order, the historian produces a particular kind of description whose coherence and plausibility flow from his techniques of reconstructing that everyday reality. He can know the past, but the content and form of any knowledge he acquires are finally shaped by his existential relationship with the dead. The dead are not available to him, he cannot converse with them: he can know them only through fragmented and partial records. He cannot survey them as he would a contemporary, observing the detail of gesture, tone, expression and position. He cannot question them. He cannot assume any community of context of experience to unite him with the dead. (Rock, 1976 p. 354)

Pressing this kind of argument to its logical conclusion Rock argues that 'subjective worlds are irrevocably inaccessible to the historian' (1976, p. 358) and therefore the whole historiographic enterprise is absurd. But to most historians and sociologists that would seem too extreme. Both historical and sociological description and explanation, as Rock suggests, rest upon assumptions that the past leaves imprints, residues, that are discoverable in the present, that between the dead and those alive today there is at least some coincidence of common-sense understandings and that there is some broad similarity of social forms. There are certainly 'great regions of experience and happenings that can never be recovered. Only a skeletal portrait of the past is possible . . .' (1976, p. 367) but with all its limitations, that portrait is worth painting.

When we reflect upon these difficulties of reconstruction and connection it is surely the case that, at least as far as the recent past is concerned, biography does offer a way of recapturing events and their meanings. Not only sociologists but historians too can interrogate men and women who have lived through periods of momentous change, whose actions and beliefs constituted (and constitute) major transformations which we need to know about. We can question them (and note all the nuances of speech, gesture and expression) and (though we still require circumspection) we can assume some community of experience with them.

There are many alive today whose lives span the greater part of the twentieth century – a period of profound change with its revolutions and wars, its periods of rapid economic growth and others of depression and recession. These years (and these people) have seen the rise and fall of empires, global processes of industrialisation and urbanisation, transformations in the position of women in many countries, major demogaphic changes and great changes in the role of the state. Even if we take only the last ten or 15 years and look, say, at what has been happening in just one country, Britain, we find much that we could usefully explore. We would be looking at a country that has experienced a rapid decline in political and economic power, a recent major recession and a government intent on transforming its economic, social and political arrangements. To examine such a country and such changes we need social history and historical sociology. And in both specialisms we require approaches that will take us close to the lived experience of all classes and generations, approaches that will enable us 'to understand how transformation at the national and local levels are experienced within families and neighbourhoods. Few foci of research are likely to be more practical or, potentially more intellectually creative' (Smith, 1982, p. 297).

REFERENCES

Philip Abrams, *Historical Sociology* (Ithaca, New York: Cornell University Press, 1982).

Michael Anderson, 'The emergence of the modern life cycle in Britain', *Social History*, 10 (1), 1985, pp. 69–87.

Daniel Bertaux, *Biography and Society* (Beverly Hills: Sage, 1981).

Daniel Bertaux and Isabelle Bertaux-Wiame, 'Families and Social Mobility', paper delivered to XIth World Congress of Sociology, New Delhi, 1986.

Daniel Bertaux and Isabelle Bertaux-Wiame, 'Le Patrimoine et sa lignée: transmissions et mobilité sociale sur cinq générations', *Life Stories/Récits de vie* 4, 1988, pp. 8–26.

C. Calhoun, 'History and Sociology in Britain', *Comparative Studies in Society and History*, 29 (3), 1987, pp. 615–25.

Norman Denzin, *The Research Act: a theoretical introduction to sociological methods* (New York: McGraw-Hill, 1978).

Glen H. Elder, Jr., *Children of the Great Depression* (Chicago: University of Chicago Press, 1974).

Glen H. Elder, Jr. (ed.), *Life Course Dynamics. Trajectories and Transitions, 1968–80* (Ithaca, New York: Cornell University Press, 1985).

Franco Ferrarotti, 'Biography and the Social Sciences', *Social Research* 50 (1), 1983, pp. 57–79.

John H. Goldthorpe, *Social Mobility and Class Structure in Britain* (Oxford: Clarendon Press, 1987).

Mark S. Granovetter, 'The Strength of Weak Ties', *American Journal of Sociology*, 78, 1973, pp. 1360–80.

Tamara Hareven, *Transitions: The Family and the Life Course in Historical Perspective* (New York: Academic Press, 1978).

Tamara Hareven, *Family Time and Industrial Time* (Cambridge: Cambridge University Press, 1982).

Lynn Jamieson, 'Theories of Family Development and the Experience of Being Brought Up', *Sociology*, 21 (4), 1987, pp. 591–607.

Steve Kendrick, Frank Bechhofer and David McCrone, 'Recent trends in Fertility Differentials in Scotland' in H. Jones (ed.), *Population Change in Contemporary Scotland* (Norwich: Geo. Books, 1984).

Barrington Moore, Jr., *Social Origins of Dictatorship and Democracy: Lord and Peasant in the Making of the Modern World* (Boston: Beacon Press, 1966).

Jean Peneff, 'Le Myth Dans L'Histoire De Vie', unpublished paper Université de Nantes, 1986.

Paul Rock, 'Some problems of interpretive historiography', *British Journal of Sociology*, 27 (3), 1976, pp. 353–69.

Clifford Shaw, *The Jackroller* (Chicago: University of Chicago Press, 1945).

Theda Skocpol, *States and Social Revolutions* (New York: Cambridge University Press, 1979).

Dennis Smith, 'Social history and sociology – more than just good friends', *Sociological Review*, 30 (2), 1982, pp. 286–308.

Patricia Straw, 'Times of their Lives: A Century of Working Class Women'. Ph.D. thesis, University of Edinburgh, 1985.

Edwin E. Sutherland, *The Professional Thief* (Chicago: Chicago University Press, 1937).

William I. Thomas and Florian Znaniecki, *The Polish Peasant in Europe and America*, Vols. 1–5 (New York: Knopf, 1918–20).

Paul Thompson, *The Voice of the Past: Oral History* (Oxford: Oxford University Press, 1980).

Paul Thompson with Tony Wailey and Trevor Lummis, *Living The Fishing* (London: Routledge & Kegan Paul, 1983).

Charles Tilly and C. Harold Brown, 'On Uprooting, Kinship and the Auspices of Migration', *International Journal of Comparative Studies* (September, 1967), pp. 139–64.

Charles Tilly with Louise Tilly and Richard Tilly, *The Rebellious Century* (Cambridge, Mass.: Harvard University Press, 1975).

Charles Tilly, *As Sociology Meets History* (New York: Academic Press, 1981).

Charles Tilly, 'Family History, Social History and Social Change', *Journal of Family History*, 12 (1–3), 1987, pp. 319–30.

6 Social Change and Economic Life in Kirkcaldy, 1891–1987: Sources and Methods, a Historical Perspective
James J. Smyth

INTRODUCTION

The current state of the relationship between sociology and history appears to be very healthy. The interest shown by historians and sociologists in each other's work and the common interests explored in that work hardly needs to be stressed. Many individual examples could be cited but the continuing success of journals such as *Past and Present* and *History Workshop Journal* testify to this, as does the recent appearance of new journals from the sociological side of the divide, *Work, Employment and Society* (issued through the BSA) and the appositely titled, *Journal of Historical Sociology*. This last-named more or less takes as a statement of principle the words of Philip Abrams (as well as the very title of his book):

> In my understanding of history and sociology there can be no relationship *between* them because, in terms of their fundamental preoccupations, history and sociology are and always have been the same thing. Both seek to understand the puzzle of human agency and both seek to do so in terms of the process of social structuring [. . .] It is the task that commands the attention and not the disciplines.

The editors of the *Journal of Historical Sociology* comment that since Abrams' book was published (posthumously in 1982), 'his sentiment has gained wider acceptance than he might have expected'. Certainly we seem to have gone far beyond the old, sterile positions of the 'diehards' (in Abrams' phrase) who denied any relationship between the disciplines at all. Yet, it would be all too easy to assume that, beyond individual efforts, a new, more integrated and unproblematical relationship between the two disciplines has emerged. There is a problem, it seems to me, in the very formulation of 'Historical Sociology' (or 'Sociological History' for that matter); Abrams essentially argues for a complete re-definition of sociology and history given that the separation between them is 'meaningless' yet, by the very act of labelling his project, it imperceptibly elides into becoming a 'field' of sociology – one amongst many and not sociology as such. This forces the realisation that while the work of individuals can cross the boundaries that separate disciplines more or less at will, they cannot break down the institutional barriers so easily.

One of the ways by which we might judge best the current relationship between sociology and history is by examining the actual experience of an interdisciplinary project, that is, where sociologists and historians work together while retaining their own, separate identities. This chapter is based on the experience, and is written from the viewpoint of a historian working with sociologists on the Social Change and Economic Life Initiative (SCEL). What is offered is intended as a contribution towards thinking through the practicalities of combining sociological and historical research. There is no attempt to present a blueprint for new interdisciplinary theory, although questions of the nature of the relationship between sociology and history will necessarily emerge even if they are not resolved.

THE PRACTICALITIES OF THE INTERDISCIPLINARY APPROACH: SOURCES AND METHODS

The first problem or worry for historians working alongside sociologists is a very basic one of working out where does the history fit in. Somehow sociology should be self-evidently central and unquestioningly in command, as it were, of the overall project. This has certainly been the case in SCEL. This initiative is a major study of six different localities in Britain by six different research teams and yet, despite being about social *change* and economic life, only one had an in-built historical dimension though, even here, it has been a 'related study'.

If history is not central to a project about change what then is its relationship? Is it there only to provide a bit of local colour, setting the scene in Chapter 1 before the real action begins? This is not just a complaint from marginalised historians but a perception shared by some sociologists as well. Gordon Marshall, writing recently in *Work, Employment and Society*, essentially asks the same question about sociology's view of history. Is it, 'simply a filing cabinet of convenient and exotic facts with which to illustrate favoured preconceptions relating to generalised theories of social systems?' (Marshall, 1988, p. 260).

The Edinburgh SCEL study has attempted from the very outset to recognise and overcome this tendency on the part of sociology. In our original proposal it was stated that, 'empirical investigations of the present' run a danger in drawing contrasts 'with an imagined past world (which is in fact no more than a mythical construction in the minds of the investigators)'. Furthermore, and as in the case of the SCEL initiative, where there are a series of related studies of different localities, it was argued that there could be a tendency to infer change 'from comparisons between the study areas ranged along some hypothetical continuum of communities at different "stages of development" '. Our basic point was not simply the need for historical accuracy *per se* but to warn against the temptation

to portray as 'new', developments in many work-related aspects of familial behaviour which nationally at least appear either to have shown considerable continuity over time or merely to be a reversion to earlier historical patterns after a short period of absence. (RCSS, 1985, pp. 38–9)

The Edinburgh team's chosen area is Kirkcaldy District (or, technically, Kirkcaldy Travel To Work Area, see below) located within Fife in the east of Scotland's central belt. We have had a particular interest in studying the relationship between the world of work (or paid employment) and the household. This is our prime concern but is not our exclusive interest. However, the main task is – how do we get to grips with the sense of *change* in this relationship over the last century (our self-defined time span). What sources and strategies are available to us?

SCEL is fuelled by surveys – the 1000 strong work attitudes/work history survey, the 300 strong household/community survey and the attached employers' survey which have been carried out for each area. Surveys are well-established tools of sociological research but have not and are not – to my knowledge – much employed by historians. From the historian's perspective there is a negative way of responding to the survey as a source – which is to regard it as fatally flawed, a false construction which has been created by the sociologist and is not a 'true' document or source. This might be a likely response from 'traditional' historians but it does point to the nature of historical research – that it is source-driven. The other side of the coin to this response may well be envy of sociologists, since they can actually create their own sources.

However, once forced into considering the use of surveys by the simple fact of being involved in such a project the historian can respond in a number of ways beyond simply ignoring the survey as the exclusive property of the sociologist. At the most straightforward level the historical dimension can be introduced to the survey by simple questions such as place of birth, occupation of parents, and suchlike which provide some factual benchmarks, and by questions concerned more with attitudes, for example, asking people of their perceptions of different periods (the 1950s or the 1930s) in comparison with today and with each other. (At a more fundamental level there is the historical nature of the surveys themselves – once collected and deposited all these questionnaires become historical documents. And that means they are ours.) In order to make the surveys more responsive to the differing conditions of each locality and to the research interests of each team, the individual and household surveys contained a team-specific element. This had the benefit for us in Edinburgh of including more historically related questions but, as we were the only team with a historical study this meant there was an in-built bias towards having such questions located in the Edinburgh team-specific component and hence out of the 'core' element of the questionnaires.

For the moment, therefore, we have to accept that the surveys are primarily contemporary documents. The task of the historian is to try to find some 'historical' sources which will complement the surveys in some way. Unfortunately, there appear to have been no market research firms operating in the Kirkcaldy area in the late nineteenth century so we have to fall back upon that old mainstay – the Census. Obviously we use the published census figures right up to 1981 for whatever information they can give us but the latest census for which we are allowed to examine the actual manuscript schedules is 1891.

And it was for this reason – primarily a question of the availability of sources – that led us to fix upon a time-span of one hundred years.

The Census schedules are very limited in the information they contain in comparison to a full survey questionnaire. They are, however, all we have got – in terms of a surrogate survey – and their detail is by no means negligible. The Census was collected by household and contains the names of each member of the household, their relation to the head of family, their married state, age, sex, profession or occupation, and whether an employer, an employee or working on own account, where born, whether a gaelic speaker, whether deaf or dumb, blind or a lunatic. From this we cannot get the detailed life and work histories that our contemporary surveys provide, nor can we glean any information on attitudes, politics, religion and so forth. Nevertheless, we are given some detail on households in 1891 as regards size, age and sex ratios, occupations and migration. Therefore, we have a (historical) benchmark for the Household with which we can compare and contrast our contemporary survey data.

At the opposite ends of our time-span we have our contemporary surveys and the 1891 census schedules, both of which provide us with definite 'hard' data which can be translated into machine-readable form. As such, however, we have not yet come into contact with our subjects, the inhabitants of Kirkcaldy District and it is face-to-face contact that is necessary if we are to further explore our interests and to investigate topics and processes about which surveys and census schedules can tell us very little. This direct contact is made through in-depth interviews of our survey respondents and by oral history interviews.

The most obvious and most fundamental difference between these two strategies is that the contemporary interviews are conducted with a selected sample of people who were part of the surveys, while it is impossible for our oral history respondents to be so directly connected with the 1891 Census. It was our original intention to trace our oral history sample through the survey respondents, that is, to seek to interview their mothers and fathers. Tempting as this exercise was, we were forced to abandon it.

Our selection of oral history respondents was actually made on the basis of the 1891 Census – not directly by tracing individual families but by using the census schedules to locate communities which by occupations and age and gender patterns, we considered could be of particular interest as regards the relationship between the household and the world of paid employment. This was one reason why we relied upon the census rather than the surveys. Another, more mundane, explanation was simply that the completion and processing of the surveys (which were carried out by a market research firm and not directly by the academic teams) and the passing of the actual interview schedules back to us took too long. This was a mechanical problem which could have been resolved if the timing of the various component parts of the study had been altered. Thus it would have been possible to link survey and oral history respondents directly had it been decided upon at the very beginning. Yet this mechanical problem becomes, in turn, a conceptual issue since to have made this link would have implications about the prominence given to the historical component. However, more seriously given the overall approach adopted, was the growing realisation that we would be wrong to try and tag the oral history component of our study onto the surveys and the survey methodology.

Had we located oral history respondents through the surveys we would have found ourselves being drawn out of our study area, since many of the survey respondents are migrants into the area whose parents would still be living in different parts of Scotland or elsewhere. This approach may have made more sense in terms of following actual migration patterns but, apart from the difficulties of tracing individuals, it would be hard to resolve such a strategy with what was designed as a locality-based study. Another approach would have been not to relate people directly through the surveys but, like the survey, go for a representative sample of respondents from the whole locality. This would have been a relatively straightforward task but we decided against it and in favour of a more specific community-based approach which would yield greater depth of information rather than breadth of coverage. It is not a perfect solution – for instance, we necessarily 'lose' those people who have emigrated from the area – but, following Paul Thompson (Thompson, 1978), we regarded the community-study as the best and most rewarding method for our purposes.

Our four main sources can be divided into different sets of pairs. At one level the surveys and in-depth interviews represent the 'sociological' sources while the census schedules and the oral testimonies represent the 'historical'. Looked at another way, the surveys and census schedules represent quantitative data while the in-depth interviews and oral testimonies represent qualitative data. In this latter respect there is no rigid dividing line between the sources as the property of one or other discipline. It is clear that, at the very least, the sources all cross-reference to different extents but that does not make them part of a seamless whole. As our discussion of the oral history part of the study indicates, each source – while related to the others – demands its own particular strategy of investigation if it is to be utilised properly. Having decided on our sources and appropriate methods we, nevertheless, had to face a fundamental problem when dealing with any study over time; how far can our study area be said to represent the same place in 1987 as it did in 1891?

THE PROBLEM OF SPACE AND TIME

The choice of SCEL localities was based on there being Travel To Work Areas (TTWA). The Kirkcaldy TTWA, as defined by the Department of Employment, is coterminous, largely, with Kirkcaldy District. The only difference is that Kirkcaldy TTWA comprises all of Kirkcaldy District plus a small part of North East Fife District, Largo Ward. There was good reason for us to jettison the TTWA approach and make Kirkcaldy District our official study area but the use of TTWAs was meant to allow comparison between all six study areas. However, the close match between Kirkcaldy District and Kirkcaldy TTWA and the fact that Largo Ward only accounts for 2.4 per cent of the total population has made it impossible for us to visualise practically our area as anything other than Kirkcaldy District. Nevertheless, in terms of the mechanics of the contemporary study, this contingent demarcation of TTWA does work broadly in that it enables us to match characteristics of the population (through the individual and household surveys) with characteristics of employers (through the employers survey). However, this linkage does not apply historically. There is not the data, the boundaries do not 'fit' and there is the problem of how the concept of a TTWA would translate into the conditions of the nineteenth century or even the 1920s.

The most obvious point to make about our chosen locality is that Kirkcaldy District as such only dates back to 1974 when it was created as part of the reorganisation of Scottish local government. The effect of this reform was to replace the old system of Burgh (Town) Councils and County Councils with a new division of District and Regional Councils. Since in comparison to the rest of Scotland, Fife had 'a disproportionate, not to say excessive, number of local authorities' (Smith, 1952, p. 67) this was a significant development and makes locating Kirkcaldy District historically by no means a straightforward task. A basic level of continuity does exist, however, at the 'higher' tier of local government, between the old Fife County Council and the new Fife Regional Council, both of which cover the same geographic area. The County Council was sub-divided into four local government Districts and, at this level, there is no straightforward continuity with the present three District Councils which make up Fife Region. Kirkcaldy District Council comprises elements of three of the old local government Districts – Kirkcaldy, Wemyss and Lochgelly. The most significant element of the old structure, however, had been the independent Burghs and their disappearance in 1974 was the major change introduced by reorganisation.

Seven Burghs in all were incorporated into Kirkcaldy District – Kirkcaldy (by far the largest), Markinch, Burntisland, Leslie, Kinghorn, Buckhaven & Methil, and Leven; plus, of course, Glenrothes New Town. These seven Burghs contained *c.* 70 per cent of the total population in the area that became Kirkcaldy District in 1891, a proportion that remained much the same by 1951.

Beyond simple numbers and percentages and the careful (re)drawing of spatial boundaries we have to ask whether there is any historical integrity to Kirkcaldy District. Partly it is a question of government boundaries but it is more a matter of the social and occupational structure of the area. As a TTWA Kirkcaldy has a fairly self-contained labour market, but the designation of being a TTWA is simply an economist's designation; it does not refer to the type of employment in the area or the nature of the local workforce. Despite the 'compact' nature of the Kirkcaldy TTWA we can still distinguish certain divisions within it. The most salient contemporary contrast is that between Kirkcaldy and the other older towns with the vestiges of 'traditional' industry and the New Town of Glenrothes with its 'sunrise' micro-electronics industry; the remaining area being largely rural and sparsely populated. The further back we go, however, the more pronounced becomes the internal differentiation, and the more the area appears as a multiplicity of local labour markets with particular localities being dominated by a particular industry and, in many cases, by a single firm.

In this respect the history of our area is simply the agglomeration of the histories of a multiplicity of areas. However, this problem of 'place', even if heightened in our case, would have to be encountered in any such study. Even an area which seems clearly defined over a long period of time, as with any large town or city, has a history not simply of growth from a centre outwards over virgin territory, but also of the incorporation of pre-existing townships and communities. The Burgh of Kirkcaldy has developed in both these ways, the last of the neighbouring localities it incorporated being the Burgh of Dysart in 1930. And even today many people feel their primary attachment is to Dysart and older people bemoan that, 'the worse thing that ever happened to Dysart' was being joined to Kirkcaldy. This simple example illustrates the point made by Doreen Massey, 'Most people still live their lives locally, their consciousness is formed in a distinct geographical place' (Massey, 1984, p. 117).

Massey's book, *Spatial Divisions of Labour*, was of value in helping to conceptualise the problem of place and time. Massey's insistence, as a geographer, on 'The uniqueness of place', and that differences between localities do 'matter' (Massey, 1984, p. 117) is one that most historians would agree with and is in tune with a locality-based initiative. So much is straightforward but Massey develops this recognition of simple 'geographic variation' to include the time-dimension. As befits a geographer, Massey talks in terms of the stratification of economic (and other) activities. But it is not the case that there is a linear 'layering' of different structures as each, in succession, gives way to the new.

> . . . local areas rarely bear the marks of only one form of economic structure. They are products of long and varied histories. Different activities and forms of social organisation have come and gone, established their dominance, lingered on and later died away. (Massey, 1984, p. 117)

It is the combined and uneven nature of this 'layering' that produces the structure of the locality.

> local changes and characteristics are not just some simple 'reflection' of broader processes; local areas are not just in passive receipt of changes handed down from some higher national or international level. The vast variety of conditions already existing at local level also affects how those processes themselves operate. (Massey, 1984, p. 119)

This concentration on the specific and recognition of the multiplicity of local characteristics reintroduces the old problem of straightforward empirical history, that is, the sheer scale and complexity of the actual historical process will always escape any theoretical straitjacket imposed upon it. However, unless we are prepared to surrender before empiricism (and we would agree with Abrams that there is always a theoretical assumption operating in historical work, no matter how well-hidden) then we have to accept and indeed welcome this necessary tension between the general and the specific. As regards the remit of the SCEL initiative we would argue that our use of distinctive yet interrelated sources does offer a way of working through the problems.

As indicated above, our attention was drawn to the existence of particular local labour markets within our study area and the significance of particular industries and firms. Once we began to examine these phenomena we were forced to revise our initial assumptions about the broad patterns of social change in our area. Two issues have proven to be of special interest: female employment in the textile industry; and employer provision of housing.

1. Women in Linen

Many of the industries and firms we examined historically had very definite 'gender biases' as regards their demand for labour. The most obvious example of this was mining, in which there were 324 women employed in the whole of Fife in 1891 (3.11 per cent of the total mining labour force), and no women employed at all within Kirkcaldy Burgh. There was no industry that was so overwhelmingly dominated by women but in textiles (mainly linen) female labour represented *c.* 74 per cent of the labour force in both Fife and Kirkcaldy Burgh. The significance of linen to the Fife economy is rarely alluded to, yet even as late as 1891 the textile industry was still the biggest employer in Fife, and remained so in Kirkcaldy Burgh until World War I.

One of the prime interests of the SCEL initiative is women's participation in the labour market – an area where use of 'change' and 'the new' have to be treated with caution. This was a trap that we partly dug for ourselves. Our initial and necessarily cursory, examination of employment in Kirkcaldy District focussed upon the apparent contrast between the 'new' patterns of employment associated with the micro-electronics industry and the demand for a younger, largely female workforce and the 'traditional', heavily masculine world of employment associated mainly with coal mining; in 1951 25 per cent

TABLE 6.1 *Women Employed in Flax and Linen in 1891 by Age*

Figures given are for The County of Fife and Kirkcaldy Municipal Burgh
and for ages below 19, 20–24 and below 25

COUNTY OF FIFE

Total women employed	under 20	20–24	under 25
27537	10483 (38.32)	5548 (20.28)	16031 (58.60)

Women employed in Flax and Linen			
7566	3403 (44.98)	1609 (21.27)	5012 (66.24)

BURGH OF KIRKCALDY

Total women employed	under 20	20–24	under 25
4175	1678 (40.19)	924 (22.13)	2602 (62.32)

Women employed in Flax and Linen			
1571	713 (45.39)	360 (22.92)	1073 (68.30)

SOURCE *Census of Scotland 1891.*

of all employed males in Fife worked in mining. Yet, if we go back to our base year of 1891 we can see that not only was the manufacture of flax and linen dominated by women but primarily by younger women, as Table 6.1 makes clear.

This is not to say that there has been no change in employment and specifically female employment patterns or to minimise the effects of what change there has been, but to emphasise that detailed historical knowledge is necessary for a full understanding of the (complex) forces of social change. The history of an area cannot be assumed to exist in an easily-available and published form but has to be looked for. This is also a good example of the value – indeed necessity – of collecting oral evidence since, given the lack of published material, there is no other way of getting to know about the experience of female textile workers in Fife.

Unless this effort is constantly made we run the risk of constructing too neat and tidy periods or compartments of stages of development which, for all their theoretical rigour, are only partial and do not register the actual process and lived experience. Even Massey falls victim to reading developments as always 'new'. Massey discusses the creation of new jobs in the old mining districts – jobs which are mainly low-paid, involve little sense of control and which employ women in the main. These are contrasted to the traditional skills and solidarity of the (male) miners. This process has taken place in our locality of Kirkcaldy District which contains part of the Fife coalfield and Glenrothes New Town. According to a *Financial Times* survey, quoted by Massey, Glenrothes has 'an almost uncanny strike-free record' (Massey 1984, p. 217). Uncanny, that is, in contrast to the *Militant Miners* (MacDougall, 1981, MacIntyre, 1980). Massey relates this contrast, in part to the lack of female experience of waged labour and the exclusion of women from public and political activity. Yet in Fife it was not so clear-cut. Mining communities co-existed with villages and towns dominated by industries – most notably linen but also paper-making – which had a high demand for female labour, part of the supply for which came from young women of the pit-villages.

2. Employers and Housing

Another area where our initial perceptions of the past and of change within the locality had to be subsequently widened was housing. The change in housing tenure – generally speaking from private-rented to publicly rented – is everywhere assumed to be of social and political significance. In Scotland, with its historically greater proportion of Council housing than England, its worse housing conditions (Smout, 1986) and a tradition of direct political action over housing (Melling, 1983), this change is seen as of crucial importance. Our original view of the housing market was, broadly, of a two-fold change – from private-rented to public-rented – occurring from the 1930s on, and the more recent development from public-rented to privately-owned. Again, the reality of these changes cannot be denied but our historical researches discovered an extra element of employer-provided housing. We already knew of its existence within the mining communities but we did not expect to encounter it as such a widespread phenomenon operating in other industries such as linen, paper and linoleum.

We are able to quantify this type of housing tenure through documentary sources such as Valuation Rolls and the Register of

Sasines, with which Scotland is well-endowed, and then further examine the nature of the relationship through our oral evidence. As well as provoking an interest in new areas and issues, this experience of a form of 'tied' housing provided us with a very concrete link between the household and employment. For instance, even as late as the 1940s we were informed of the case of an employer providing householders with a 'missive' to sign stating that their children would be made available to work in the Mill. This same employer, at the end of World War II, attempted to force the return of women workers who had left due to the exigencies of war work back into the Mill on the threat of their or their families losing their houses.

Our examination of employer-provided housing led us into the wider issue of paternalism. What we discovered – and, again, this was contrary to our initial assumptions – was that paternalism (identified with medium and large family-owned businesses) was a conscious and highly successful strategy practised by employers over a long period. The success of paternalism as an employer strategy can be gauged by the fact that in the case of two of the firms we studied in depth (both of which were in operation for well over a century) one experienced only two recorded instances of strike action and the other provides no evidence of industrial disputes whatever. It should be noted that our studies of these firms did not rely upon 'officially' produced company histories but included oral testimonies of the workforce.

The efficacy of paternalism in securing both industrial and political quietude appears to contradict the militant tradition of the Fife miners. Fife is one of the few parts of Britain to have returned a Communist MP to Westminster, Willie Gallacher, who held West Fife (which includes part of our study area) from 1936 to 1951. While the Communist Party also enjoyed some success at local government level, areas of left-wing influence were bordered by areas where local employers effectively 'ran' the Council. This refers back to the discussion of the lack of militancy among the workforce in Glenrothes New Town and the existing tradition of female employment, though the relationship between the two is not a simple one of cause and effect. However, to reiterate, it is not a question of one tradition supplanting another but of both co-existing. Paternalism was also practised within the mining industry, though with less success than in linen, paper and linoleum.

The concept of paternalism allowed us to grasp much of the long-term nature of changes in industrial relations or, rather, the social relations attendant upon industrialisation, since paternalism involved not only the individual worker but also the employee's household and the wider community. Paternalism can be identified at the very beginning of industrialisation in our area and, while it can be seen to operate still in particular companies today, our view is that as a system of dominant locally-owned and controlled family businesses effectively it came to an end in the 1960s (Morris and Smyth, 1989).

CONCLUSION: HISTORY AS BACKGROUND OR HISTORICAL ANALYSIS?

Our two examples have attempted to show the value of detailed historical investigation. All studies will make certain assumptions about the history of an area but, even where these assumptions are broadly accurate, there remains the likelihood that they will be partial accounts and leave out particular items and even whole areas that are interesting for themselves and, perhaps, crucial to any thorough understanding of change. A common (and still justified) criticism historians have of sociologists is the expectation that 'the history' somehow is always there, simply waiting to be picked up. The attraction of the approach adopted by Massey, that is, the view of the 'layering' of historical experience and its combined effects, is that it recognises that there is no monolithic sense of the past or of 'tradition', and attempts to structure an understanding of the present through the varied experiences and influences of the past. Even so, a subtle theoretical approach is not enough on its own. As our discussion of women's employment in linen, paternalism and Glenrothes New Town illustrates, the empirical investigation of the past needs still to be accomplished.

The question being posed here is how is this to be accomplished within the confines of an interdisciplinary project such as the SCEL initiative. Even where sociologists are sympathetic to a historical perspective there remains the problem of time and space. SCEL is survey-driven. The questions that appear in the surveys are what matter at the end of the day since they provide the building blocks for later analysis. This is not the place to make complaints about the lack of historically related questions within the SCEL questionnaires; everyone involved in SCEL could make similar complaints about favourite topics they were forced to abandon or reduce. (Even such large questionnaires as those employed by SCEL cannot hope to cover everything.) It is rather to point out that the structure of SCEL did not encourage a historical dimension. Despite being locality-based there is an in-built dynamic to the SCEL initiative (with its six study areas) to move from the local to the national. Since none of the other study areas had a specific historical input there have been no direct or national contrasts and comparisons to be made. Further-more, and even with the best will in the world, where only one team has a definite historically related study there is an in-built tendency to relegate the 'history' to that team and to its team-specific part of the questionnaires.

This relative isolation of history in a large-scale multidisciplinary initiative should make social scientists ponder upon not only how to accommodate history as another element in a study but upon the process of change itself and how we understand that process. Patrick Joyce has commented upon the need for, 'a synthesis of social theory and the fullness of the historical process' but added the warning that:

> In the present state of sociology and social history this synthesis is likely to be an unsatisfactory one: until the theory of society is subject not merely to the qualification of the historical example but to the wholesale re-ordering of the force of historical change the way ahead will not be easy. (Joyce, 1980, xxiv)

Once we begin to think through this problem of synthesis we are impelled to question the validity of the separation of our 'rival' disciplines. We are back to the issue raised by Philip Abrams, that 'it is the task that commands the attention and not the disciplines'. Yet this separation cannot be ignored since it is where the disciplines meet in the academic world of institutions and not simply in our own heads that the problem lies. It is for this reason that the resolution of the conflict between disciplines must be a collective effort. Individual master-plans are fine for individual research but are unlikely to prove satisfactory where a truly collaborative multidisciplinary project is being planned. The French historian, Jean Chesneaux, has warned against an interdisciplinary practice where, 'each specialist continues to function in terms of his own rhetoric . . . and the results are stuck together end to end' (Chesneaux, 1978, p. 131).

There is, perhaps, a tendency for interdisciplinary studies to break down into their constituent parts. There is no easy solution to this problem but there is, surely, the desire to produce something more than the sum of these parts. The SCEL initiative and others will provide guidelines for future research but not blueprints. From a historian's perspective I would argue the value of a longer time-span of study. The most obvious model is the *longue durée* of Braudel and the Annales School. This is not suggested as a means of constructing a paradigm for a 'super project' which would place history as the leading discipline. Though with history's monopoly of the time dimension in the study of human society it is easy to see the logic and attraction (for historians) in such an approach. It is as well to remember Marc Bloch's warning against the historian's 'obsession with origins', the false search for a beginning that is also an explanation (Bloch, 1979, p. 29).

Without going back further and further into the past in an endless pursuit of the 'origins', it is possible to consider in-depth locality-based studies covering the beginnings of industrialisation up to more or less the present day. I believe the strategy towards sources and methods adopted by the Edinburgh SCEL team could be further extended by using earlier nineteenth-century census material. In Scotland we are fortunate in also having the Old and the New Statistical Accounts but careful work among early Parliamentary Papers and local collections can reveal a surprising amount of detail. Existing pressures on time, money and the demand for 'interim deliverables' cannot be ignored and it would be naive in the extreme to believe that extra resources are likely to be released to meet the demands of such an approach. However, these pressures cannot be allowed to dictate what we study and the ways we believe our common interests should be studied. It may be that interdisciplinary projects would have to be longer both in gestation and in the time taken to complete them. Though it may be that the timing of the different component parts of such projects could be altered, for example, the bulk of historical research could be completed before the contemporary fieldwork was undertaken.

However the practicalities are finally worked out, the value of the long–term approach is that it offers potentially the richest and most productive means of examining continuity and change, and by doing so best allows sociology and history to work in tandem on the task in hand rather than one merely 'informing' the other.

NOTE

1. The research to which this chapter refers was carried out as part of the ESRC's Social Change and Economic Life Initiative. I am grateful to Stuart Campbell, David McCrone, R. J. Morris and the other members of the Edinburgh team. I would like to thank Stephen Kendrick in particular for all his help and advice.

BIBLIOGRAPHY

P. Abrams, *Historical Sociology* (Shepton Mallet: Open Books, 1982).
Marc Bloch, *The Historian's Craft* (Manchester: Manchester University Press, 1979).
J. Chesneaux, *Pasts and Futures or What is History For?* (London: Thames & Hudson, 1978).
Journal of Historical Sociology, Vol. 1, No. 1, 1988.
P. Joyce, *Work, Society and Politics: the culture of the factory in later Victorian England* (Brighton: Harvester Press, 1980).
I. MacDougall, *Militant Miners* (Edinburgh: EUSPB, 1981).
S. MacIntyre, *Little Moscows: Communism and Working Class Militancy in Inter-War Britain* (London: Croom Helm, 1980).
D.Massey, *Spatial Divisions of Labour: Social Structures and the Geography Production* (London and Basingstoke: MacMillan, 1984).
J. Melling, *Rent Strikes: People's Struggle for Housing in West Scotland 1890–1906* (Edinburgh: Polygon, 1983).
R. J. Morris and J. Smyth, *Paternalism as an employer Strategy* (SCEL Working Papers Series, forthcoming).
R. Pahl, *Divisions of Labour* (Oxford: Basil Blackwell, 1984).
Research Centre for Social Sciences, University of Edinburgh. 'Proposal– Research Initiative on Social Change and Economic Life', 1985.
A. Smith, *Third Statistical Account of Scotland; County of Fife* (Edinburgh: Oliver & Boyd, 1952).
T. C. Smout, *A Century of the Scottish People 1830–1950* (London: Collins, 1986).
P. Thompson, *The Voice of the Past* (Oxford: Oxford University Press, 1978).

7 The Historical Reconstruction of Rural Localities: A New Zealand Case Study

Bob Hall

The field of community studies is one that has undergone much change and redefinition in recent years. In the 1950s it was subjected to criticism on both methodological and theoretical grounds (see Reiss, 1954). Methodologically, its essentially qualitative approach was considered to lack the rigour of more quantitative counterparts, whilst theoretically its static, structural-functional theoretical underpinnings were held to lack the relevance of more dynamic theoretical frameworks. As a result, its holistic approach fell out of favour as sociologists became more specialised in their research foci. Another factor to be considered here was the disillusionment with the field that followed in the wake of a long but largely unproductive debate on the meaning of community (see Hillery, 1955 and 1959, Parsons, 1959, Sutton and Kolaja, 1960, Martindale, 1964, Simpson, 1965). These criticisms were then added to through the 1960s and into the early 1970s. In this period, community studies were seen as being ahistorical, non-cumulative, overly descriptive, idiosyncratic and non-comparative (see Glass, 1966, Stacey, 1969, and Bell and Newby, 1971).

Whilst it would be wrong to present these criticisms as though they were totally accepted – the method did retain adherents and supporters – it would be true to say that as far as mainstream sociology was concerned, the community study was taken to be representative of a past era in sociological work. Thus the method that had provided so many of the early sociological classics appeared to have been eclipsed.

Against this background it is of some significance that the approach has re-emerged out of seeming oblivion with a vitality that belies the earlier criticisms levelled at it.[1] This re-emergence is largely attributable to the fact that the field has been significantly reconstructed. Community, as such, has ceased to be The *object* of study and the approach has come increasingly to be viewed as a *method* of study by which sociological issues can be explored within a local setting. This has been accompanied by a new awareness of the need to take into account the influence of the extra-local on the local. There has also been a greater appreciation of the need to integrate locality research with such mainstream theoretical issues as social change, social class, power, mobility and inequalities (see Wild, 1974 and 1983, Newby *et al.*, 1978, Pearson, 1980, Williams, 1981, Hall *et al.*, 1983, and Pahl, 1984).

With these developments there has also come a more explicit recognition of the need to understand the historical evolution of the locality as a means of understanding its contemporary social structure. Work in this new vein has thus sought to demonstrate the utility of historically-grounded locality research for understanding processes of social change within the wider society.[2] The timing of this has paralleled similar developments within the discipline of history itself.

COMMUNITY STUDIES AND THE SOCIO-HISTORICAL NEXUS

In 1962 E. H. Carr commented '. . . the more sociological history becomes, and the more historical sociology becomes, the better for both' (1962, p. 84). This may be seen as a commendable ideal, but, as Stephan Thernstrom subsequently remarked, the 'mutually enriching dialogue' has been a long time coming (Thernstrom, 1965, p. 234).

Thernstrom's comment was made in the context of an article in which he took to task Lloyd Warner's 'Yankee City' series (Warner and Lunt, 1941 and 1947) for its lack of a critical awareness of what constituted 'historical evidence'. According to Thernstrom, the record of the past that appeared in the 'Yankee City' volumes was the record of a 'mythical past', compiled by the researchers from an uncritical acceptance of local mythology and informed by their own ideological preconceptions. Thernstrom referred to this as 'implicit history' and argued that in order to get at the 'actual past', the researcher had to aim for 'explicit history' based on a careful examination of the sources:

> The distortions that pervade the Yankee City volumes suggest that the student of modern society is not free to take . . . history or leave it alone. Interpretations of the present require a host of assumptions about the past. The real choice is between *explicit* history, based on a careful examination of the sources, and *implicit* history, rooted in ideological preconceptions and uncritical acceptance of local mythology. (1965, p. 240, emphasis mine)

It is noteworthy that among the classics of the community studies tradition, 'Yankee City' has not been alone in being subjected to such attention. What Thernstrom did for 'Yankee City', Peter Gibbon (1973) repeated for the Arensberg and Kimball study of County Clare in Ireland (1940). In a similar fashion the Middletown III project (see Bahr and Bracken, 1983) criticised the Lynd's studies of Muncie, Indiana (1929, 1937). In each case, a distorted view of the past was the focus of the critique since the researchers were deemed to have relied on 'implicit' history rather than 'explicit' history. It is understandable, therefore, that traditional community studies have often been criticised for lacking an adequate historical perspective. In the words of one commentator, many community studies have viewed history as 'nothing more than an introductory appendage' (Pearson, 1980, p. 14).

To the extent that this was the case, community studies mirrored an inadequate appreciation of history within the wider discipline of sociology. Sztompka (1986) traced the roots of this inadequacy to a 'double genealogy' within the discipline – one European and the other American. According to Sztompka, the European root is to be found in the *a priori* developmental theories of such writers as Spencer, Comte, Durkheim and Toennies who tended to treat history mechanistically as 'an autonomous domain . . . from which human actors were strangely absent' and whose direction was 'predetermined, fatalistic, independent of human efforts' (1986, p. 324). Sztompka referred to this heritage as 'sociology above history'.

By way of contrast, the American root of sociological ahistoricism was to be found in the 'melioristic, presentist, empirical and micro-sociological' concerns of twentieth-century American sociology (1986, p. 327). Sztompka concluded that indigenous American theoretical orientations such as social behaviourism, symbolic interactionism, exchange theory and structural functionalism all 'self-consciously' abstracted from 'the historical dimension of social reality' (1986, p. 327). This, combined with the uncriticalness of 'narrow empiricism' and 'pragmatic presentism' in the research context, contributed to the ahistorical bias in American sociology. Sztompka referred to this heritage as 'sociology without history'.

The net effect of the heritage of both roots of this 'double genealogy' was that an ahistorical orientation reigned in sociology for the major part of the twentieth century. During this time, sociologists tended to hold a 'heavily distorted' stereotype of history as being an 'ideographic', 'individualising' and 'purely descriptive' enterprise that focussed on 'concrete events' and the conduct of 'outstanding, great individuals' (Sztompka, 1986, p. 322).[3]

Though dominant, however, the ahistorical tendency was not exclusive and Sztompka singled out as exemplars of 'truly historical sociology' the work of Karl Marx, Alexis de Tocqueville and Max Weber (1986, p. 326). According to Sztompka the rebirth of historical sociology since the mid-1970s can be traced to their 'authentically historical work' (ibid).

In 1984 Theda Skocpol proclaimed 'a golden period of historical sociology' and concluded 'by now . . . a stream of historical sociology has deepened into a river and spread out into eddies running through all parts of the sociological enterprise' (1984, pp. xii and 356). The field of community studies did not remain immune from this and part of the galvanising influence here was the work of Max Weber. It is of some significance that Weber's discussion of community formation and closure (Neuwirth, 1969) has provided the analytic framework for a number of recent Australasian locality studies (Pearson, 1980, Wild, 1983, Hall *et al.*, 1983). Such a Weberian processual emphasis has been an important element in redefining the community study approach and placing it much more firmly within the historical tradition.

Appreciating the necessity for an adequate historical perspective has therefore been an important beginning point in transforming the community studies approach, but there are still practical methodological problems to be overcome. Bahr and Bracken (1983), for example, indicate that historical research based on oral histories often suffers from three sorts of bias – memory, nostalgic and idiosyncratic. First, memory is a very unreliable research tool because of its fallibility. Second, recollections of the past tend to be tinged with a nostalgia for what were taken to be better days. Third, old timers who are used for oral histories are unrepresentative by definition, since they have survived and remained. Bahr and Bracken sum the problem up in the following manner:

> Descriptions of historical context and the attendant implications about change that community researchers construct from their interviews with old-timer informants should generally be viewed with caution, unless the descriptions are buttressed in empirical data which date from the period being described . . . (1983, p. 132)

And yet, documentary records also suffer from their own particular biases. First, there is the bias that results from selectivity in the editing, deposit and survival of documentary records (Webb *et al.*, 1971, pp. 53–7). Second, there can be bias in content with written sources tending to be the products of, and relating to the activities of, an élite rather than ordinary men and women. Bahr and Bracken (1983) refer to this as élitist bias.

A key problem is therefore how to reconstruct historically the social structure of a locality in such a way that it will go beyond mere reminiscences, will counter the difficulties caused by informants' faulty memories and idealisations of the past and yet will also avoid the inherent biases in documentary analysis. These were some of the problems that were faced when the task was begun of exploring the process of community formation and change in the Kurow district of New Zealand's South Island (see map).[4] The resolution of the problems involved blending sociological fieldwork and historical analysis in a manner that allowed for a synthesis of oral histories and documentary analysis.

THE CASE STUDY

The fieldwork for the project was carried out between December 1977 and December 1982.[5] The research strategy involved carrying out a *diachronic* analysis of the district's historical development by working around fairly detailed reconstructions of aspects of the local social structure at particular points in time. The dates for these *synchronic* reconstructions were selected to represent, as far as possible, significant periods not only in the history of the district but also of the wider society. These dates were 1890, 1905, 1920, 1935,

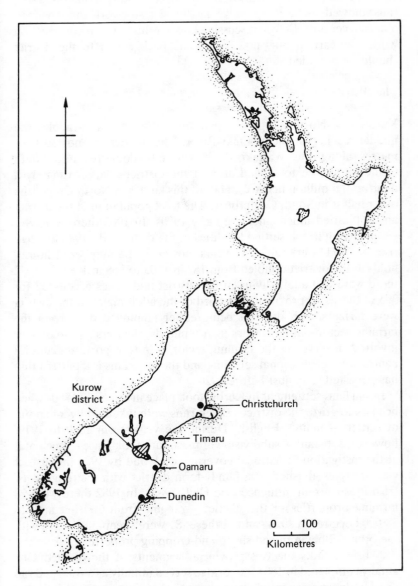

FIGURE 7.1 *Location of Kurow district, New Zealand*

1950 and 1965.[6] The inclusion of the contemporary situation, 1982, thus allowed for a comparative historical framework that spanned almost a century. Before discussing how this historical reconstruction work was carried out, however, some background to the district should be provided.

The District

Kurow is a North Otago sheep farming district that straddles the middle reaches of the Waitaki River. The district extends 30 kilometres along the Waitaki River and 60 kilometres into South Canterbury. The total land area of the district is approximately a quarter of a million hectares. Half of this land is in North Otago, the other half is in South Canterbury. The total population of the district has not varied much since the early 1900s. In 1905 there were 897 people living in the settled localities in the district. By 1982 this had risen to 1171. Between these years, however, the number of households in the district doubled from 187 in 1905 to 368 in 1982. In 1982 there were 760 adults living in the district and males accounted for 395 of these. Approximately a third of the adult males in the district were farmers with the rest being either employed directly in the farming sector – as farm workers, shepherds, shearers and so on – or involved in servicing the farming sector – in transport, agricultural contracting, professional servicing and the like. This is a pattern that has persisted since just before 1920.

Initial land settlement in Kurow took place in the early 1850s when licenses to graze the district's sheep runs were taken up by a handful of settlers – mainly English. During the years from 1880 to 1910, however, substantial subdivision of these runs took place – much of it at the instigation of national governments – and by 1920 the district was firmly established as a family-farm district with a strong Scots/ Irish Presbyterian influence (see Hall, 1985). In 1982 there were 98 farming properties in the district – ranging from 100 hectares to 38 000 hectares in size – and of these, 81 were sheep properties with the other 17 being mixed sheep-and-cropping properties.

A bridge links the two provincial segments of the district. Originally completed in 1881, the bridge served initially as a road and rail link. Following repeated flood damage, however, the rail link was discontinued in the 1930s and today it serves merely as a road link. On either side of the bridge are to be found the district's two permanent settlements – Kurow Township in North Otago and

Hakataramea Township in South Canterbury. Both were settled in the early 1880s but Kurow Township has always been the larger of the two. Between 1905 and 1982, the population of Kurow Township increased from 209 to 421 while, in the same period, the population of Hakataramea Township declined from 109 to 56. Since the early 1900s just over a third of the district's population has lived in these two settlements with the rest being spread over the district's nine rural localities.

Kurow Township is the district's service centre. The commercial facilities in the township represent the normal range that one would expect to find in a New Zealand rural service centre. Along the main street are three stores, two hotels, a bank, a butcher's shop, a hair-dressing shop, an electrician's shop, a craft shop, two petrol stations, three stock-and-station agencies, two cafes, a motel, a motor camp and a transport firm. The township also has a railway station, a high school with approximately 200 pupils, a post office, a stock inspector's office, a catchment commission, a golf course, a bowling club, a recreational domain, a race track and three churches.[7]

HISTORICAL RECONSTRUCTION

In beginning the task of reconstructing the historical development of this district, a first priority was to review methodological strategies used overseas. Here it became obvious that census material and street directories had featured prominently. A first step, therefore, was to assess the usefulness of these sources in New Zealand.

Census Material

Historical reconstruction work done in localities in North America and in Britain has relied heavily on information from original census schedules (see Curti, 1959, Katz, 1975, Conzen, 1976, Griffen and Griffen 1978, and MacFarlane, 1977). A limitation on the use of such material, of course, has been the 100-year access restriction. This has meant that researchers have been able to work with census schedules only from the period prior to 1880. Nevertheless, the work that has been done has been extremely fruitful not only in providing accurate local historical detail, but also in successfully dispelling myths held about localities in the periods in question (see Thernstrom, 1965, and Bahr and Bracken, 1983). The census has therefore been an extremely significant source of data in historical reconstructions carried out in localities in North America and in Britain.

No such possibility was found to exist in New Zealand where, apart from 1976 onwards, the administrative problems of storing census schedules and ensuring confidentiality were resolved by wilful destruction. Although some material would have been lost anyway in subsequent fires, it does appear that government officers decided early to destroy systematically the original census schedules. One New Zealand social scientist has commented:

> Rightly or wrongly, successive New Zealand governments have placed individual privacy above the retention of a national heritage, so innumerable valuable documents, most notably Census records, have been consigned to the furnace. (Pearson, 1980, p.185)

A similar fate befell many non-governmental records also. In this way, a substantial amount of historical documentation has been destroyed in New Zealand, and social scientists therefore do not have the same potential data base from which to work as their counterparts in the northern hemisphere. This is regrettable.

Even with regard to published New Zealand census material, however, there are still serious limitations when it comes to historical locality research. Unfortunately, the available census material is frustratingly unresponsive to the needs of the social scientist who is attempting to work on the historical reconstruction of localities. For one thing, the administrative boundaries used from census to census have seldom remained fixed and almost never correspond with social boundaries that would be recognised by local people. This is compounded by the fact that, below the level of county or borough, the census provides only total population figures for localities, that is, no detail is provided whatsoever on the occupational, marital, age and, at times, even sex structure of a locality's population. In New Zealand, therefore, the census is of little help in the task of historically reconstructing localities.

Street Directories

Another potential source of information to aid historical reconstruction are street directories. These have been used quite extensively in North America, particularly in researching the issues of transience and mobility within urban localities (see Thernstrom, 1964, and Katz, 1975). Similar use has been made of such directories in New Zealand. For example, David Pearson in his study of Johnsonville (a suburb of Wellington) used *Wise's* and *Stone's* street directories in his reconstruction of the occupational structure of the suburb for the period 1875 to 1955 (see Pearson, 1980). It must be appreciated, however, that such street directories provide information only on nominated heads of households and that they do not necessarily include all households. In reviewing the usefulness of this data-source, Pearson therefore warned that they suffered from 'omissions and inaccuracies' (1980, p. 186).

It is difficult to know whether directories such as these are likely to be more or less accurate in rural areas than in urban areas. On the one hand, urban street names and numbered addresses give the urban lists a seemingly greater potential for accuracy. This has to be offset, however, against the fact that the population in rural localities is likely to be smaller and more stable than its urban counterpart. One might think, then, that these directories would provide more accurate information for rural than for urban areas. Initial work with the Kurow information, however, revealed that the data source was not as accurate as had been expected. Cross-checking directory information with material drawn from other documentary sources – school registers, marriage records, minute books and so on – revealed that Pearson's warnings were pertinent. There were, indeed, 'omissions and inaccuracies'. Bearing in mind that these directories were providing information only on nominated heads of household anyway, it was obvious that this was another data source that was not going to bear the expected fruit. An alternative approach was needed, and this was found when the significance of land records was finally appreciated.[8]

Land Records

A key insight that helped resolve many of these methodological problems lay in gaining an appreciation of the potential of the Torrens system of land registration used in New Zealand (see Hall *et al.*, 1982). Following the implementation of the Torrens system in South Australia in 1858, and its subsequent adoption elsewhere in Australia and the British Commonwealth, it was finally introduced in New Zealand by the Land Transfer Act of 1870. Under this system, land ownership was to be legally established and transferred on the basis of government certification and registration.

The *certificate of title* issued by the government is the only acceptable device for attesting ownership and transferring property rights – the only legal determinant of ownership of land. A principal feature of the Torrens system is the registration and guarantee of land title by the state. This means that data available from the certificates of title are reasonably accurate and comprehensive. While these documents have been recognised as the 'definitive source' of data on land ownership in New Zealand (Strachan, 1979, p. 91), as yet little systematic use has been made of them by historians.[9]

There are two further features of the Torrens system, however, that have particular significance for social scientists interested in historical reconstruction. First, private title to land is a matter of public record. This means that land ownership data are readily available in New Zealand unlike other countries where equivalent information is private and can be obtained only with the permission of the registered owner. Second, the system is property oriented. This is in contrast to other, more conventional land registration systems which are owner-oriented. The focus of the Torrens system is thus a particular piece of land and the certificate of title records the transfer of property rights to that land from person to person. This gives the Torrens system unique possibilities when it comes to researching land ownership in New Zealand.

THE RESEARCH PROCESS

The obvious significance of land records for historical reconstruction research is that land ownership can be used as a beginning point for determining who was in a locality at any point in time Achieving this in the Kurow study required a blending of documentary research and informant interviewing.

Documentary Research

The beginning point was to obtain information on district landholding from the relevant certificates of title. The legal description for every section of land in the district was established using government survey maps. These legal descriptions were then used to obtain the reference number for the current certificates of title for each section.

This was done using indexes held in the Lands and Deeds department. The current certificates were then searched and photocopied. When copies of all of these current certificates had been obtained, it was simply a matter of tracing the prior certificates and copying them also. In this way, a copy was obtained of all the current and cancelled certificates of title for the whole district. In most cases, the earliest cancelled certificates of title were dated around 1880. All told, this exercise produced some 1700 documents, each one containing details on anything from one to 30 separate land transactions.

Processing this amount of material would have been impossible without the computer. A method for coding the data was devised so that the computer could be used to reconstruct the pattern of landholding in the district for any designated day in the century from 1880 to 1980 (see Hall *et al.*, 1982). The date that was used was 25 December since there were no land transfers on that day and hence there was no possibility of double-counting on ownership. Thus, to get information for the years 1890, 1905, 1920, 1935, 1950 and 1965, it was simply a case of using the computer to print out for the designated date a list that provided details of:

- The names of the landholders on that date
- The locality in which the land was held
- How much land each landholder held
- The nature of the title (freehold or leasehold)
- The date the land was acquired and how acquired
- The date the land was relinquished and how relinquished
- The certificate of title reference

This last piece of information was particularly useful for three reasons. First, it allowed a check to be made on the accuracy of the information. Second, it enabled identification of the particular piece of land to which the information related. Third, it made possible the drawing of farm boundary maps for that date.

Informant Interviewing

Equipped with landholding printouts and reconstructed locality farm maps, it was then a case of establishing whether or not the people who held the land were, in fact, living on that land at the specified date. Informants who had been living in the district at the time and who could provide this information had to be located and interviewed. Mortality obviously placed constraints on how far back this exercise could be carried out but, working in 1981–82, it was found possible to go back to 1905 with a fair degree of confidence in the data.

Once informants had been located, it was a case of working through the locality map with them, farm by farm, and filling in the necessary information: whether or not the listed owners were living on the property at that time; if they were, whether or not they were married; if they were married, who their spouse was (maiden name of wife) and what children they had at the time, if any; what kinship connections they might have had in the locality and the wider district; what kind of farming was being done on the property; what labour, if any, was employed on the farm; details of the families, if any, of these farm workers.

Not all people living in the rural localities were landholders, however. Some were blacksmiths, teachers or assorted farm workers. Tracing these required a different approach. By establishing where each house was in the period in question and by cross-checking with other documentary sources, it was possible to identify who these people were and to fill in details of their families. In other words, using the land records as a guide, the reconstruction exercise involved locating where the houses were in the locality and then carrying out a limited census for each of the households. The location of houses could not be taken for granted between periods, however, since large numbers of them were shifted with farm amalgamations or were destroyed by fire. This procedure was repeated for *all* of the rural localities relative to *each* date, that is, 1905, 1920, 1935, 1950 and 1965.

The equivalent procedure in the two townships was to locate where the houses were at each date and then work through the townships, house by house, filling in household information from informants. Land records and Valuation department information allowed the locating of houses to be done fairly accurately and also indicated whether the occupiers were owners or tenants. As with the rural information, household information for the townships was triangulated with other documentary information to check the accuracy of informants' memories.

In both townships and rural localities, the reconstructed maps – whether of farm boundaries or of house locations – were invaluable in the interview situation, since they acted as *aides de mémoire* and gave a clear sense during the interviews of what had been covered and what still remained to be done. Further triangulation of this information with other documentary materials allowed gaps to be filled and the overall accuracy of the reconstruction to be checked. An important part of the research strategy was therefore to do the reconstruction work *before* embarking on the bulk of interviewing, thus overcoming many of the problems normally associated with oral histories.

Providing equivalent information for the contemporary period was much more straightforward. Local informants were interviewed at the end of 1982 and household information for the district was obtained from them. There was no need to resort to reconstructed farm maps since the informants could easily recollect who was living in what houses at the time.

THE RESULTS

A full discussion of the data that were generated by the historical reconstruction exercise will be left for another context.[10] In the meantime, an overview can be provided of the range of information that was generated on individuals and households and an assessment given of the relative accuracy of that data.

The reconstruction exercise identified 7859 individuals and 2071 households. For each *individual* the following range of information was generated: household belonged to and relative position within it; sex, marital status and whether an adult, a schoolchild or a pre-school child; which school they were attending (if a school child); what generation they were in the district; how long they had lived in the district and how long they remained in the district; how they came to the district and how they left; whether they had kin (up to and including first cousins) in other households in the district; if they owned land in the district then of what type; occupation or, if they were children, occupation of their father.

The range of *household* information that was produced was as follows: locality; number of people living in the household, adults and children; household type (whether family or non-family) and family type (extended, nuclear, conjugal, single parent, and so on); kin in other households in the district; how long the household (as constituted) had been in the district and how long it remained in the district; occupation of the head of household.[11]

TABLE 7.1   *Results of Reconstruction Exercise*

YEAR	NUMBER OF HOUSEHOLDS (Reconstruction)	NUMBER OF INDIVIDUALS (Reconstruction)	NUMBER OF INDIVIDUALS (Census)
1905	187	897	1071 (1906)
1920	253	1074	1193 (1921)
1935	263	1160	1289 (1936)
1950	312	1174	1236 (1951)
1965	332	1229	1305 (1966)
1978	356	1154	1133 (1976)
1982	368	1171	1180 (1981)

An indication of how many individuals and households were identified for each period is provided in Table 7.1.

Table 7.1 also includes some comparative census material against which to judge the accuracy of the reconstruction. Some cautionary comments need to be offered, however, in relation to these census figures. In the first place, the household reconstructions were done as at the end of the designated years, while the censuses were taken in April of the following years. The difference of four months is not substantial, but it needs to be borne in mind.

Second, and more important, the census information is not directly comparable with the reconstruction figures in terms of coverage. The published information from the New Zealand census does not provide direct information on the Kurow district as a unit and the census totals used in the table have therefore been aggregated from locality information. A major complication in this process is the fact that locality designations used in censuses tended to vary from year to year, and this made it difficult to produce a definitive total figure for the district. This meant that official census figures used in the study had to be treated with some caution.

It will be seen from Table 7.1 that the reconstruction figures are sufficiently close to the aggregated census figures to give confidence in the procedures used. The greatest discrepancy occurs in the figures for 1905, when the reconstruction figure is approximately 174 people (16 per cent) short of the 1906 census figure. This requires some comment.

The task of reconstructing 1905 was complicated by the fact that, being the end of the era of large pastoral estates in New Zealand, a sizeable proportion of the population was located on sheep stations and was therefore extremely difficult to trace. These sheep stations existed as occupational enclaves using a predominantly male work-force that was largely single and highly transient. Furthermore, since rabbit infestation was becoming an increasing problem at this time, especially on the large sheep stations, there is every likelihood that large numbers of unidentified rabbiters were working on these stations. There is no accurate way, therefore, of ascertaining who was working on these stations at any given point in time. If the census figures for the sheep stations that were not part of the reconstruction exercise in 1905 are added together, the total arrived at is 180 people – only six more than the perceived discrepancy of 174 (see Table 7.2). This indicates a reasonable accuracy in the reconstruction.[12]

TABLE 7.2   *The Comparison (1905)*

CENSUS (April 1906)	TOTAL	Males	Females
Total District	1071	601	470
Sheep Stations*	180	126	54
Settled Localities	891	475	416

*Excluded from reconstruction exercise

RECONSTRUCTION (December 1905)	TOTAL	Males	Females
Settled Localities	897	469	428

A further confirmation of the accuracy of the reconstruction procedures can be obtained from considering the number of males and females who were in the district. Until 1921 the New Zealand census provided details of the numbers of males and females within each designated locality, and for 1906 the aggregated figure for the Kurow district was 601 males and 470 females (see Table 7.2). This included the sheep stations that were not part of the fieldwork reconstruction. If, however, the 126 males and the 54 females who were on these sheep stations are subtracted from this figure, then the reconstruction for 1905 should have turned up approximately 475 males and 416 females. In fact, the reconstruction accounted for 469 males and 428 females, and again, this gives strong support to the accuracy of the reconstruction methods used.

Finally, mention should be made of the property reconstructions that were carried out in conjunction with the household reconstructions. Working from certificates of title, it was possible to develop for each date a landholding profile for the district including properties in the townships as well as the rural localities. This profile detailed who owned how much land, where, for how long and in what sort of title. By triangulating this landholding data with goovernment valuation data it was possible to put an economic value on individual properties at each date. This gave a breakdown on the unimproved value, the improved value and the total capital value of each property.

In relation to farm properties, informant interviews established what kind of farming was being done on each property at each date. For sheep farms, it was also possible for the years 1890 to 1950 to use government sheep figures to establish how many sheep were being run on each property. Aggregating this information provided an historical profile of pastoral activity for each locality and for the district as a whole.

Overall, then, this approach to historical reconstruction research resulted in a reasonably accurate, comparative framework of understanding within which it was then possible to explore, through oral history interviews, particular aspects of social life, social structure and social change within the district. It is worth re-emphasising that by completing much of the reconstruction research before embarking on the bulk of this interviewing, many of the problems normally associated with the oral history method were avoided. Thernstrom's strictures about the need for 'explicit' historical procedures in locality research were very much taken to heart.

CONCLUSION

In the last ten years or so, the field of community studies has been reconstituted. Part of this was in response to criticisms that had been levelled at the field but a more significant factor was the outcome of incorporating alternative theoretical frameworks and agendas. Where the structural functional framework had been dominant until the mid-1960s now there was increasing recognition that 'community' could be addressed from other theoretical perspectives. As a result, greater attention was paid to locating the local social system in its broader societal context, greater emphasis was placed on issues of process and social change and the historical dimension was confronted more directly and given much greater credence than it had received in the past. With this, however, came the need to develop methodological strategies that would allow sociological concerns and historical analysis to be merged in a manner that would retain the integrity of both disciplines. One such strategy has been discussed – historical reconstruction – and while aspects of the approach, as discussed, rely on features peculiar to the New Zealand situation, the broad principles of triangulating sources and blending oral history and documentary analysis within the context of sociological fieldwork must nevertheless be seen as having more general applicability.

NOTES

1. This re-emergence has seen the focus of study shift from community to locality. In Britain, this has developed from two distinct directions. In the first place, studies by social anthropologists of British rural localities have concentrated on exploring the culture of localism and the identification with place that comes from 'belonging' (see Cohen, 1982, 1983 and 1985). The second development has concentrated on the locality as the spatial focus for the reproduction of labour power within capitalist society (see Cooke, 1982, Massey, 1982, and Urry, 1984). Bradley and Lowe (1984, p. 12) refer to the former as 'the ethnography of localism' and the latter as 'the political economy of capitalist recombination in peripheral regions'. What is being discussed in this article is a third development that is responsive to issues of historical process.
2. Elements of this perspective are to be found in some recent sociological work (for example, Pearson, 1980 and Hall *et al.*, 1983) but a parallel can also be found among historians, particularly with the locality emphasis of the New Urban History (see, for example, Thernstrom, 1964 and 1973, Thernstrom and Sennett, 1969, Katz, 1975 and Griffen and Griffen 1978). Useful overviews of the New Urban History are to be found in Thernstrom (1971) and in Ebner (1973).
3. Sztompka noted that historians have reciprocated with negative stereotypes of their own. Sociologists have been seen as being 'notoriously blind to the past', neglecting 'social dynamics' while focussing entirely on 'social statics', rejecting 'diachronic' approaches in favour of 'synchronic' and so on (1986, p. 322).
4. While the study of community has occupied sociologists for some time, the process of community formation and change has not been extensively

explored. This study sought to address that deficiency. The role of closure and communion were analysed using a framework developed from Weberian theory to highlight the dynamic interplay of contradiction and reinforcement existing between three sets of locality relationships: propinquity (community), property (class) and kinship (family). A key argument in the analysis was that the process of community formation within a locality cannot be adequately understood without considering all three relations together, since they serve collectively to provide the parameters for closure and hence community formation within a locality (see Hall, 1987).

5. University vacations between late 1977 and early 1982 were spent conducting research in the district. The data gathering was then completed during nine months of full time field work in 1982. A range of methods were used in the project including interviewing, participant observation and documentary analysis (for example, land records, parish records, marriage and baptismal registers, school registers, minute books, newspapers, maps and so on). The computer was used to process much of this information.

6. The historical development of the district was considered in relation to four main periods: Initial Settlement (1850 to 1890); Consolidation (1890 to 1920); The Middle Years (1920 to 1950); and The Contemporary Scene (1950 to 1982). These periods correspond roughly to periods in the economic history of New Zealand and are comparable with divisions drawn by other New Zealand researchers (cf Condliffe, 1959, Oliver and Williams, 1981, Hawke, 1985).

7. In line with trends in other rural districts in New Zealand, some erosion of services has taken place in the township. Since 1982 the railway station and the catchment commission have both been closed.

8. Land ownership had theoretical as well as methodological significance for the study. The theoretical significance has been commented on elsewhere (see Hall *et al.*, 1984), so comments can be restricted here to methodology.

9. There are very few pieces of published New Zealand research where extensive use has been made of these certificates of title, but some examples can be found in Waterson (1969), Richtik (1975) and Powell (1971).

10. The main findings of the research have been written up in Hall, 1987.

11. Except in such cases where a household was headed by a widow, a single female parent or a single female, the head of household was taken to be an adult male (that is, in the case of nuclear families, the husband).

12. This checking exercise was possible because station names were used as census locality designations. It was therefore possible to establish how many people were resident at each station.

BIBLIOGRAPHY

K. Arensberg and S. Kimball, *Family and Continuity in Ireland* (Cambridge: Harvard University Press, 1940).
H. M. Bahr and A. Bracken, 'The Middletown of Yore – Population Persistence, Migration and Stratification, 1850–1880', *Rural Sociology*, Vol. 48, No. 1, 1983, pp. 120–32.
C. Bell and H. Newby, *Community Studies* (London: Allen & Unwin, 1971).
C. Bell and H. Newby, *The Sociology of Community – A Selection of Readings* (London: Frank Cass, 1974).
T. Bradley and P. Lowe, 'Locality, Rurality and Social Theory', in T. Bradley and P. Lowe (eds), *Locality and Rurality – Economy and Society in Rural Regions* (Norwich: Geo Books, 1984).
E. H. Carr, *What is History?* (New York: Knopf, 1962).
A. P. Cohen (ed.), *Belonging – Identity and Social Organisation in British Rural Cultures* (Manchester: Manchester University Press, 1982).
A. P. Cohen, *Anthropological Studies of Rural Britain 1968–1983* (London: Social Science Research Council, 1983).
A. P. Cohen, *The Symbolic Construction of Community* (London: Tavistock, 1985).
J. B. Condliffe, *New Zealand in the Making – A Study of Economic and Social Development* (London: Allen & Unwin, 1959).
K. N. Conzen, *Immigrant Milwaukee, 1836–1860 – Accommodation and Community in a Frontier City* (Cambridge, Mass.: Harvard University Press, 1976).
P. Cooke, 'Class Interests, Regional Restructuring and State Formation in Wales', *International Journal of Urban and Regional Research*, Vol. 6, 1982, pp. 187–203.
M. Curti, *The Making of an American Community* (California: Stanford University Press, 1959).
M. H. Ebner, *The New Urban History – Bibliography on Methodology and Historiography* (Monticello, Illinois: Bibliography No. 445, Council of Planning Librarians, 1973).
P. Gibbon, 'Arensberg and Kimball Revisited', *Economy and Society*, Vol. 2, No. 4, 1973, pp. 479–98.
R. Glass, *Conflict in Society* (London: Churchill, 1966).
C. Griffen and S. Griffen, *Natives and Newcomers – The Ordering of Opportunity in mid-19th Century Poughkeepsie* (Cambridge, Mass.: Harvard University Press, 1978).
R. R. Hall, 'Land For The Landless – Settlement of the Otekaike Estate in North Otago (1908)', *The New Zealand Journal of History*, Vol. 19, No. 1, 1985, pp. 38–60.
R. R. Hall, 'Te Kohurau – Continuity and Change in a New Zealand Rural District', PhD Thesis, 1987, Department of Sociology, University of Canterbury, New Zealand.
R. R. Hall, D. C. Thorns and W. E. Willmott, *Community Formation and Change – A Study of Rural and Urban Localities in New Zealand*. Working Paper No. 4 (Christchurch: Department of Sociology, University of Canterbury, 1983).

R. R. Hall, D. C. Thorns and W. E. Willmott, 'Community, Class and Kinship – Bases for Collective Action within Localities', *Environment and Planning D: Society and Space*, Vol. 2, 1984, pp. 201–15.

R. R. Hall, C. Raper, D. C. Thorns and W. E. Willmott, *The Use of Torrens Certificates of Title for Social Science Research, with Special Reference to Locality Studies – A Technical Paper*. Technical Paper No. 1 (Wellington: Social Sciences Research Fund Committee, 1982).

G. R. Hawke, *The Making of New Zealand – An Economic History* (London: Cambridge University Press, 1985).

G. A. Hillery, 'Definition of Community – Areas of Agreement', *Rural Sociology*, Vol. 20, No. 2, 1955, pp. 111–23.

G. A. Hillery, 'A Critique of Selected Community Concepts', *Social Forces*, Vol. 37, No. 3, 1959, pp. 237–42.

M. B. Katz, *The People of Hamilton, Canada West* (Cambridge, Mass.: Harvard University Press, 1975).

R. S. Lynd and H. M. Lynd, *Middletown* (London: Constable, 1929).

R. S. Lynd and H. M. Lynd, *Middletown in Transition* (New York: Harcourt & Brace, 1937).

A. MacFarlane, *Reconstructing Historical Communities* (Cambridge: Cambridge University Press, 1977).

D. Martindale, 'The Formation and Destruction of Communities;, in G. Zollschan and W. Hirsch (eds), *Explorations in Social Change* (London: Routledge & Kegan Paul, 1964).

D. Massey, 'Industrial Restructuring as Class Restructuring – Productive Decentralisation and Local Uniqueness', *Regional Studies*, Vol. 17, 1982, pp. 73–89.

G. Neuwirth, 'A Weberian outline of a Theory of Community', *British Journal of Sociology*, Vol. 20, 1969, No. 2, pp. 148–63.

H. Newby, C. Bell, D. Rose and P. Saunders, *Property, Paternalism and Power* (London: Hutchison, 1978).

W. H. Oliver and B. R. Williams (eds), *The Oxford History of New Zealand* (Wellington: Oxford University Press, 1981).

R. Pahl, *Divisions of Labour* (London: Basil Blackwell, 1984).

T. Parsons, 'The Principal Structures of Community', in C. J. Friedrich (ed.), *Community* (New York: Liberal Arts Press, 1959).

D. G. Pearson, 'Class, Reminiscence–A Research Note', *The New Zealand Journal of History,* Vol. 13, No. 1, 1979, pp. 83–8.

D. G. Pearson, *Johnsonville – Continuity and Change in a New Zealand Township* (Sydney: Allen & Unwin, 1980).

J. M. Powell, 'White Collars and Moleskin Trousers – Politicians, Administrators and Settlers on the Cheviot Estate, 1893–1914', *New Zealand Geographer*, Vol. 27, 1971, No. 2.

A. J. Reiss, 'Some Logical and Methodological Problems in Community Research', *Social Forces*, Vol. 33, No. 1, 1954, pp. 51–7.

J. E. Richtik, 'Changing Patterns of Land Ownership in Eyreton District, 1853–1968', *New Zealand Geographer*, Vol. 31, 1975, No. 1.

R. L. Simpson, 'Sociology of the Community – Current Status and Prospects', *Rural Sociology*, Vol. 30, 1965, No. 2, pp. 127–49.

T. Skocpol, *Vision and Method in Historical Sociology* (Cambridge: Cambridge University Press, 1984).

M. Stacy, 'The Myth of Community Studies', *British Journal of Sociology*, Vol. 20, 1969, No. 2, pp. 134–47.

S. R. Strachan, 'Archives for New Zealand Social History', *The New Zealand Journal of History*, Vol. 13, 1979, No. 1.

W. Sutton and J. Kolaja, 'The Concept of Community', *Rural Sociology*, Vol. 25, 1960, No. 2, pp. 197–203.

P. Sztompka, 'The Renaissance of Historical Orientation in Sociology', *International Sociology*, Vol. 1, No. 3, 1986, pp. 321–37.

S. Thernstrom, *Poverty and Progress – Social Mobility in a Nineteenth Century City* (Cambridge, Mass.: Harvard University Press, 1964).

S. Thernstrom, 'Yankee City Revisited – The Perils of Historical Naivete', *American Sociological Review*, Vol. 30, 1965, pp. 234–42.

S. Thernstrom, 'Reflections on the New Urban History', *Daedalus*, Vol. 100, No. 2, 1971, pp. 359–75.

S. Thernstrom, *The Other Bostonians – Poverty and Progress in the American Metropolis, 1880–1970* (Cambridge, Mass.: Harvard University Press, 1973).

S. Thernstrom and R. Sennett, *Nineteenth Century Cities – Essays in the New Urban History* (New Haven: Yale University Press, 1969).

J. Urry, 'Capitalist Restructuring, Recomposition and the Regions', in T. Bradley and P. Lowe (eds), *Locality and Rurality – Economy and Society in Rural Regions* (Norwich: Geo Books, 1984).

W. L. Warner and P. S. Lunt, *The Social Life of a Modern Community* (New Haven: Yale University Press, 1941).

W. L. Warner and P. S. Lunt, *The Status System of a Modern Community* (New Haven: Yale University Press, 1947).

D. B. Waterson, 'The Matamata Estate, 1904–1959 – Land Transfers and Subdivision in the Waikato', *The New Zealand Journal of History*, Vol. 3, 1969, No. 1.

E. Webb *et al.*, *Unobtrusive Measures – Nonreactive Research in the Social Sciences* (Chicago: Rand McNally, 1971).

R. Wild, *Bradstow – A Study of Status, Class and Power in a Small Australian Town* (Sydney: Angus & Robertson, 1974).

R. Wild, *Heathcote – A Study of Local Government and Resident Action in a Small Australian Town* (Sydney: Allen & Unwin, 1983).

C. Williams, *Open-Cut – The Working Class in an Australian Mining Town* (Sydney: Allen & Unwin, 1981).

8 Urbanisation as Moral Project: Transitions in Twentieth Century Britain

Rosemary Mellor

Sociological explanation is necessarily historical. Historical sociology is thus not some special kind of sociology; rather it is the essence of the discipline. (Abrams, 1982, p. 2)

The changes to British economy and society apparent over the past decade invite appraisal of the terms and conditions of urbanisation. Long-standing divisions have been re-exposed, and long-term relationships, notably those between central and local government, have been redefined. At the same time, conventions as to everyday life – policing, crime, movement, neighbours – are being reassessed. City life and city politics are predominant in the political agenda. With this political realism comes a new interest in the terms and conditions of urbanisation and urban order.

Visibly, cities embody history. Previous generations' investment strategies, bids for wealth and status, attempts to find health, are there, encumbrances to movement or rational use of space, assets or not, depending on their amenity-status. There is a constant accommodation to the artefacts of the past, perhaps less constraining than the conventions of institutions, but requiring ongoing calculation. In another sense, history is ever there – in the streets frequented as daily routine, in memories of past incidents, moments in personal history, in the folklore of home life, in the myths of urban 'village', or front-line confrontation. There is a 'time-geography dealing with the time-space "choreography" of individuals' existence over given time-periods' (Giddens, 1979, p. 205). More than ever, there is consciousness of the precariousness of these rhythms, soon to become history, as the new liberalism which informs the current transition in urbanisation is accepted. Urbanisation, then, is on the agenda. The problem, then, as always, is to select the dimension, or dimensions, by which urbanisation can be assessed.

Urbanisation can be conceptualised as being:

(1) demographic – change in the ratio between urban and rural deriving from the two elements of migration and reproduction;
(2) environmental – change from the 'unbuilt' to the largely 'built' environment;
(3) economic – change in the location of wealth generative capacity, and the stimuli to further wealth creation;
(4) social – changes in social organisation;
(5) political – change in relationship of state and civil society, the basis of reproduction in the state apparatus.

Of these, the first three can be taken as the commonsense understandings of urbanisation. Cities are aggregates of people and buildings; urban regions are complex economic networks; urbanisation means a shift in location of population into a different scale of settlement. In contrast, writers in the sociological tradition emphasise the latter two: sociological theories of urbanisation are presentations in terms of social relationship and politics. Marx and Engels construed urbanisation in terms of alienation and class politics; Simmel and Tonnies in terms of bourgeois individualism; Park and Wirth alternated between pluralist and mass society images of American society; Lefebvre and Castells phrased the discussion in terms of everyday life, state hegemony and urban social movements. Interestingly, each set overestimated the efficacy of urbanisation in achieving the political change they sought by taking their moment of analysis – in each case a transition – as typical and general. The basic assumption is, however, clear – urbanisation is a matter of political redefinition.

The second problem is that of conceptualising and describing change. British urbanisation was, in modern terms, protracted. The movement from a rudimentary pattern of urbanisation before 1500 to the stabilised urban society after 1920 spanned four centuries. This urbanisation took place in a society whose core values were those of deference and respect for tradition, whose national legal system was accepted as universal, where there was a continuity between the medieval and the modern in, for example, the relationships between family members, households, local communities and the state (Mac-Farlane, 1978, 1981). Even when Britain did urbanise (in the first sense) between 1750 and 1920, laws concerning landed property, which had evolved in the sixteenth and seventeenth centuries, preconditioned the form of urban development. These continuities make it difficult to mark out phases or periods for urbanisation. In one of the few essays on the subject, Merrington argues for 'discontinuities' or 'qualitative redefinitions' – one, date/century unspecified, associated with the expansion of a parasitic metropolitan economy focussed on London, the other 'which occurs with factory cities, expanded reproduction of the proletariat, and capitalist agriculture, marks the take-off into an *autonomous* urban growth' (Merrington, 1978). Hall, similarly reacting against evolutionary accounts, in this case of the welfare state, uses the terminology of 'crisis' or alternatively 'rupture, break or breakdown', as well as the less apocalyptic terms 'transition' or 'transitional period' to describe the period 1880–1920 (Hall, 1984).

In this chapter, I wish to argue that there are transitions in the history of urbanisation, periods in which there is a decisive change from one set of conditions to another, and more particularly in which there is an accumulation of social and political pressures for change; in these transitions, the encompassing moral framework to urbanisation is modulated and core institutions are forced to accommodate to the new social forces. One such transition was conceivably that between 1815 and 1848, in which the British state had to concede political rights to the middle classes, reform the institutions of local government, including the police, and abandon principles of *laisser-faire* in the administration of the towns; another was that described by Hall between 1880 and 1920, in which the unbridled power of the rentier capitalist interest was curtailed in terms of principles of state family welfare (Mellor, 1981). The most recent is that of now – a period in which the nation is required to take a stand in relation to competing ideologies of change pointing to new social arrangements.

The attention of this chapter is directed at the latter two of these transitions. Conventionally, there is acceptance of a transition between the 'early modern' and the 'industrial city' (even if there is dispute as to when to locate it). There is not the same recognition of a transition at the end of the nineteenth century from the 'rentier' city of industrialisation to a city (some of) whose resources were allocated in terms of family welfare. This shift in the principles of urban organisation, to those of the 'welfare city' in which the interests of corporate capital were to be restrained, marks the political transition to a mass democracy in which principles of common citizenship were to legitimate resource allocation. Arguably this was *the* urban revolution (Lefebvre, 1970) – the period when social demands broke with established conventions and imposed new duties on state agencies. It is in periods such as this that the novel, the radical, or the unprecedented are established as commonplace, the obvious thing to do. In these periods of social upheaval, demographic imbalance, and economic disequilibrium, social movements and political agitation may coalesce around certain pivotal episodes to remake the ideologies of the political nation. There is consensus as to the political significance of the period; demonstrably there is an equivalent significance for urbanisation.

THE TRANSITION FROM 'RENTIER' TO 'FAMILY WELFARE' URBANISATION

There is a notably turbulent phase in the movement to an urban nation state in the decades 1880–1920 (Dangerfield, 1970). An inchoate surge towards a reconstitution of status for the working class, and for women, culminates in the unrest before, during, and after, the 'Great War': strikes, unionisation of the unskilled, marches of the unemployed, mobilisation of the trade union movement as a political party, women's protest movements, religious protest (at educational reform), socialism, syndicalism, nationalism and counter-nationalistic movements in Ireland. Despite accommodation by the political establishment, only the war brought uneasy domestic order. It is a period in which Britain's hegemony over world markets is under challenge, when foreign capital penetrates domestic markets, defence interests skew investment, and the landed interest crumbles in face of colonial competition. It is also a period of mass unemployment, and quite massive emigration – a net outflow of at least one million per decade is estimated for England and Wales from 1881–1911 (Tranter, 1973, p. 53). At the same time, there was a culmination of the demographic transition which had started in the eighteenth century, in that infant death rates and birth rates fell steadily from the 1870s and more sharply from the 1900s. The practice of state intervention in the towns was consolidated in controls over public health, housing (including rents)[1] and schooling.

None of this change, none of these movements, can be construed as 'urban'. The towns were neither the basis of political association, nor were they the direct target of political protest.[2] Organisation was national rather than local, the target the national state institutions. The different movements were constituents of international movements; they were in the best sense sectarian, in that they mobilised distinct constituencies with emphatic beliefs. They were also short-lived: the great surge of involvement fades as aims – the vote, trade union recognition, national autonomy – are achieved. The popular movements become folk memories as quiescence in a reformed political concensus becomes the norm. The society does, however, restabilise around social principles in which the towns and urban life are directly implicated. The social principles are twofold:

(1) acceptance of a 'rule of law' by which the action of public officals and the maintenance of public order is legitimised;
(2) acceptance of rights to family welfare which provide a pervasive moral code for state policy.

The demand for change rippled through the private as well as the public sphere: family expectations interlinked with welfare reforms, demands for enjoyment for the young (Roberts, 1972), a current as pervasive as that for better material conditions. There is a family history – the realisation of 'affective individualism' (Stone, 1979) seen in the limitation of family size and the individuation of family members, as well as a state history – the political incorporation of the working class through Parliament and the institutional networks of press, church, and local government. Life chances – social mobility, privacy, hedonism – the everyday experience – are one face to the transition; the other is the ritualised, formal, public presentation of local authority, assistance board, or trade union. Private morality is one dimension; public morality – the use of force, the probity of public officials, the use of resources to satisfy an interest group – is another. In that period of transition, the moral universe of the state was widened to encompass some, at least, of these private expectations. Urbanisation was to be very different in the ensuing phase.

STATE FAMILY WELFARE URBANISATION

Change in cities and urban life is seen in:

(1) the transformation in form of the cities from dense urban neighbourhoods to suburban estates and the reinforcement of the norms of privacy;
(2) the enlargement of possibilities for household consumption and display;
(3) change in family size and household composition;
(4) the new style of welfare provision, universalism replacing voluntarism;
(5) working class incorporation in local politics;
(6) acceptance of a rule of law by which state agencies, including local government and the police, were constrained.

The overarching change is that of an institutionalisation of conflict in which a hegemony is achieved for local state agencies which pre-empted further popular mobilisation on local issues. It required an accord between local labour interests and the national state, in which the interests of the 'lumpenbourgeoisie' of small property would be over-ruled, and those of industrial and commercial interests cons-trained.

In this phase of urbanisation, there was a continuity to the moral framework for state action from the 1920s to at least the 1970s. The intricate delegation of powers and cross-referencing of action be-tween central state, local state and voluntary organisations, as well as the balance maintained between the interests of private capital and private consumer, do modify during the period, but always within limits. It has to be assumed that there was a popular democratic consensus that urban living had to be reformed, that it was possible to do so (largely) through the aegis of state agencies, and that indirect levies through personal taxation and local rates, rather than direct levies on capital, should finance this reform. An urban Keynesianism was commonsense even before Keynes. This continuity in the 'moral ethos of the state' (Corrigan, 1980, p. xvii) tends to be overlooked in discussions of specific issues in urban development. Commuting, clearance, labour migration – all point to substantial changes in everyday life which belie the overall continuities from which they stem. The continuities in the political philosophy also articulate poorly with economic development.

Four themes to this can be noted as follows:

(1) unevenness of development: in comparative terms, Britain is unusual in that the peripheral regions had industrialised while the metropolitan core did not.[3] In contrast, the twentieth century is characterised by an intensification of metropolitan dominance, a strong preference on the part of industrial capital for investment in the heartland of the London region, and a strongly held negative status accorded to 'the regions' by state influentials.

(2) volatility of investment. Regional economies are remade, and unmade, in decades. (For instance, Tees-side or the West Midlands.) 'Hypermobile' capital writes off investment with unexpected ease; state interests increasingly do the same. It is unclear whether this volatility is exceptional, relating to the terms on which the British economy is articulated into the world system (or to the intersection of subsidy and private interests), or a common characteristic of old industrial economies.

(3) perpetuation of the 'imperial' status of the City of London as 'clearing house for the world's economic transactions' (Ingham, 1984, p. 7). Britain has, in effect, a world cuckoo lodged in a fragile industrial economy with untold effects on the responses of industrial capital. The distortionate effects on the economy of the London region have only recently been assessed (Thrift, 1987).

(4) extension of markets for private consumption of both goods and services. Demand for housing, consumer durables, including cars, for services, including tourism and leisure, push to recognition of household consumption as stabilising local and regional economies.[4]

Urban and regional literature are strangely silent on two of these themes. There is notable neglect of the effects of the City's integration into world financial markets on regional growth. The concentration of investment there – with some 400 000, many highly paid, workers in the finance sector – and untold spinoffs in construction and rents, professional and personal services, retail and entertainment – is taken for granted; the relationships of the City to industrial investment – and its consequences for long-term growth – is debated, if inconclusively (Coates and Hillard, 1986) but the debate is not represented in academic discussions of recent regional polarisation.[5] The role of the City in association with national government in consolidating the status of the South, is just one of those facts of public life. I can suggest three reasons for this academic neglect: (1) the association of urban growth with industrialisation, which may, for Britain, prove a historic interlude; (2) the practice of assessing economic health by jobs (which reflects the commonsense definitions of urbanisation in terms of people) and not in terms of investment; and (3) the preoccupation with a particular section of the labour force – the unionised, male, manual worker.

There is also indifference to the last of these themes of economic development. The convergence in interest between individuals as consumers in the market and the transnational, national, or local suppliers to local markets is not of concern. As Castells claimed: 'the urban is largely defined . . . in terms of its interaction with the state' (1978, p. 180). There is reluctance to acknowledge that the domination of capital over urbanisation may be exercised through a relationship, that of the 'regulated market' in which 'unfreedom, in the sense of man's subjecton to his productive apparatus' (Marcuse, 1968, p. 41) is encountered in, and through, consumption. As affluence of the core labour force stimulates investment, there must be some recognition of that 'invasive system of ideas and practices we term the market' (Mellor, 1985, p. 43). The emphasis on political economy in urban and regional studies had formalised the role of the state, but overlooked the agency of consumers in establishing markets. The particular alliance of corporate capital with local/national state through the latter part of this period dominated the intellectual agenda.

Under these conditions, urbanisation had certain characteristics. These were:

(1) A stability in population: with the exception of the years of the 'long boom' after 1945, birth rates barely ensured replacement (and the birth surplus of those years was to result in the youth unemployment of the 1980s). International labour migration, in Western European terms restrained, made up the deficit during the boom before being terminated in the face of popular, if politicised, reaction.

(2) Decentralisation: after 1920, suburban investment was encouraged by cheapness of agricultural land and low interest rates as well as government subsidy, and subsequently, despite tight land-use planning controls, decongestion was primed by state provision of rental housing and fiscal incentives to home owners. De-urbanisation accelerated after 1961 with resultant halving of the population of the 'inner cities' in the next 20 years.

(3) State intervention, through local authorities as agencies: this substantially modified the social ecology of the towns. The primary divide between neighbourhoods became one of tenure rather than location, so that insider definitions of status within the tenure groups tended to be overlooked. The black replacement labour force had a restricted location in racialised enclaves.

(4) Dominance of urban policy by ideas of family welfare: 'decent' housing was to strengthen the nuclear unit and stabilise paternal responsibilities, movement from the 'slums' was to be enforced to disperse non-familial, 'disreputable' life styles. Modern towns were to be familial neighbourhoods sustained by a network of state welfare services reinforcing dominant conventions of familial autonomy.[6]

(5) A distinctive and contradictory package of planning ideologies which promoted (i) the protection of the rural heritage from urban development; (ii) decentralisation; (iii) conservation of the old city centres; (iv) modernity in rationalising the dual spheres to the city – 'public' areas of commerce, industry and leisure, 'private' areas of home and neighbourhood; (v) the utility of planning to the family and (vi) the values of community.

(6) Consensus over the delegation of powers from national state to urban influentials which had stabilised as 'municipal socialism'. Delegated powers and local finance meant variability in the provision of welfare services according to local political tradition, yet increasing public apathy opened the way to local corporatism within a 'national-local government system' (Dunleavy, 1981, Byrne, 1982).

It is in this last that stabilisation is most apparent. There is an extraordinary continuity to both the policies and the personnel, despite recession and economic restructuring, war, or the extension of welfare. The lifetime tenure of office/post, the conservatism of the town-hall bureaucracies, the fast-reached traditionalism of local government, all discouraged innovation. A key political figure might dominate local politics from the 1930s to the 1970s (for example, Hull), planning initiatives of the 1920s might be completed in the 1950s (Wythenshawe), the foresight of a chief officer in assembling land might come to fruition a generation later (Swindon [Harloe, 1975]). This continuity was eroding by the 1970s. Whereas the policies of the 1960s were not so different from those of the 1920s, the same assessment could not be made of those of the 1980s. The principles of state housing provision established in the interwar decades were successively abandoned in the 1970s. At the same time, planning policies with inspiration in the first quarter of the century were discredited in the face of inner-city blight and decay of garden estates. Private capital, whose property interests had so long been opposed by town-planning, was to be partnered by the local state (without any apparent ideological strain). Similarly, the discretionary autonomy of local government was to be undermined by financial restrictions and the usurpation of powers by voluntary or statutory bodies without local accountability.

British urbanisation can be said to have entered another 'transition' within a society which, in commonsense terms, is less urban, whose economy is to be effectively transnational, where the state is radically partisan, and in which the retreat from the local provision of welfare will marginalise still further the population of the old cities. Unlike the earlier 'transition', in which influentials in the state establishment and the popular movements were moving towards new norms of state intervention against the immediate interests of the propertied classes, now, the morality of the comfortable body of the nation – those who can behave as free consumers – coincides with that of corporate capital. The rights to welfare of the welfare dependent peripheries are to be curtailed for the benefit of an authoritarian core.

AN AUTHORITARIAN LIBERAL TRANSITION

A transition is evident in specific policies, but these are best seen as indicative of modulation to 'the moral ethos of the state' (Corrigan, 1980, xvii). One moral ethos, that of a social economy in which some definition of collective harmony over-rules individual interest, and in which state action is legitimated by philosophies of social justice, equality of opportunity, humanitarian impulse and/or political rights, is being displaced by another, best termed authoritarian liberalism.[7] In this, private interest, defined as the freedom of choice, to work or to consume, is deemed synonymous with that of public interest. The liberties of the individual are to be guaranteed by the strong state – a state which curtails collective freedom in the name of the rights of the worker, trade-union member, or ratepayer (Gamble, 1985, 1988, Benton, 1986). In any transition, the law in whose terms the previous moral framework was underwritten will become controversial and public order will be breached, and yet as conventions are cast adrift, there is a popular demand for 'paradoxically more state action to guarantee freedom' (Benton, p. 14). So, the moral ethos which urban life had come to assume is being transposed as the policies and institutions which sustained that ethos are discredited. It is tempting to see the onslaught of 'New Right' ideologies as manipulative of popular reactions, or as fronting corporate interests, but if the earlier transition is any guide, the demand for change is as much private as political in its expression.[8] The absence of popular movements for change reflects the institutionalisation of politics and the individuation of need. Not just 'the socially powerful think, see and act differently' (Corrigan and Sayer, 1985, p. 26); we the people, citizen-consumers, do also.

Is it valid to term this last decade or so a transition, using legislative or policy departures as markers to a decisive alteration of social philosophy? Given the choice – the collapse of Ronan Point (1968), the Fair Rent legislation (1972), the prosecution of Poulson or Smith (1974), the White Paper on the Inner Cities (1977) and the public sector cuts of the same year, the right-to-buy provisions of the Housing and Local Government Act (1980) – how can one pinpoint the departure which discredits the old agenda? With the gathering momentum of social change and popular demands for an unencumbered lifestyle throughout the postwar period, is it even helpful to do so? All one can say is that there is a convergence, an accumulation, in shifts in thinking and action that culminates in the unprecedented – the sale of local authority assets, for instance, or the abandonment of the rating system. To judge the extent of this transition it can be compared with that of the earlier period. In what respects can the changes of the past decade or so match those of the earlier transition from rentier to state welfare urbanisation?

THE TRANSFORMATION IN FORM OF THE CITIES

Since 1961, despite restrictive land-use controls, all the indications are of accelerating movement from the core cities. From 1971, the movement is increasingly from the metropolitan regions – an anti-suburban as much as an anti-urban movement. Remoter rural districts and small towns are the recipients of this migration. Britain is seen to have led Europe in this counter-urbanisation which colonises the fringes to the metropolitan economies (Brittan, 1986; Hall, 1987). In everyday life, social-distance is entrenched in ecological separation. There are no predictions that this 'flight to the green' will abate in Britain or in Europe, despite 'gentrification' in the 'command' cities, and the entrapment of low income households in inner-city districts (Champion, 1987).

Household Consumption

De-industrialisation has accentuated the function of the cities as consumption nodes – show-cases and playgrounds for self-indulgence. The surge in consumer spending dominates urban investment strategies. Plans for tourism, shopping malls and atria, leisure centres or marinas, as well as those for 'up-market' housing, all reflect personal spending demands. Personal mobility (and the conference industry) put discrete urban centres in competition, as does the search for heritage or 'theme', so that architecture and town-planning both become exercises in style, in making and holding markets for that estate, neighbourhood, centre or region.[9]

Families and Households

Changes in household composition over the past 25 years are pronounced. A majority of households are one or two person; current predictions for 2001 are for one-third single person. The young leaving home (unemployment and benefit rules permitting), the elderly alone, deferred marriage, low birth rates, abortion, divorce, household fission and reconstitution – all these indicate an extension of the individualism of the earlier transition so that a-familial life styles predominate. These are already conspicuous in London – single, gay, 'yuppy', post-retirement households – and increasingly they gear consumer markets in the regional centres. In different mode, they also characterise the villages and retirement towns of the regional peripheries.

Welfare Provision

The past ten years have seen a reversal in the environmental policies of the welfare state. Housing: fair rents, right to buy, capital expenditure cuts; land-use planning: the reversal of inner-city industrial policies, relaxation of controls on the intensity of commercial development and, more recently, the lifting of restrictions on agricultural land; transport: the deregulation of public transport, with sharp effects on suburban mobility; local authorities: centralisation of control and the delegation of responsibilities to non-accountable agencies, for example, housing associations and urban development corporations; local finance: cuts in the rate-support grant and the substitution of a community charge for the rates. This last will effectively undermine the class gains of the earlier transition in that it will 'narrow the gap which exists between those who use, those who vote for, and those who pay for local government services' (Baker, 1986). And there is no popular resistance to the centralisation, the cuts, or the regressive taxation to be imposed.

Local Politics

The era of corporatism, most marked in the old cities, but in no way confined to these, has been succeeded by a new pluralism and a repoliticisation of local administration. In particular, the coalition between the progressive middle classes, skilled labour and the urban poor – Labourism – which had contained ethnic dissent and absorbed women's interests in family welfare policies, has broken up, leaving a range of interest groups to be harnessed by the 'new urban left' (Gyford, 1983, 1985). But this destabilisation of the norms of local government life is marked outside the big cities as well. The need to respond to central government imperatives, the initiatory role expected of local government in changing economic circumstances, the reincorporation of the middle classes in local politics, and the demands for value for money, all require a more flexible administrative structure, a greater delegation of responsibilities and a participatory style (Stewart, 1985).

The Rule of Law: Local Authorities

In this context, the rule of law refers to (i) the regularisation of local policy through legal enactment and central inspection (including the Audit Commission), and (ii) the bureaucratic organisation of local government in which clientelism and corruption were minimised. Stabilisation implies quiescence – or apathy towards the institutions by which rule is maintained. Changes in the past decade are pronounced:

(1) national state determination of local policies and spending is repeatedly circumvented by local authorities, notably in the urban boroughs, but also, intriguingly, evident in the overspending of the 'shires'. Opposition to changes in local finance spans the parties;

(2) initiatives in local authority service provision mark changes in the universalistic norms of service delivery, for example, decentralisation of social services and housing management, community development, participation in local planning, employment initiatives, equal opportunites policies, leisure/ community centre provision for ethnic groups. The cultivation of consent to local government means close working relationships between agency and client groups;

(3) until relatively recently, public ignorance of the affairs of local authorities was matched by public indifference. If media presentations are any guide, there is a new interest in the affairs of local government.

The Question of Policing

Discussions of urban life have been detached from those of policing. An important aspect of the transition in urban life in the first half of the nineteenth century was the imposition of a professional police force which was to guarantee safe passage in the streets or public places, protect property and regularise activities in poor neighbourhoods. Two basic conditions of modern urban life, (1) what Lefebvre (1968) termed the 'right to the city'[10] – free passage as an individual, regardless of class, ethnicity, gender or age in any public place, and (2) the right to privacy in the neighbourhood (Inglis, 1977), relieved of obligations to neighbours, came to depend on the existence of the police institution as guarantor and mediator of urban order. During the welfare transition, a heavy street presence had been the norm in working-class districts, and in public order situations such as the Dock Strike of 1911, the police role was a military one, but, in subsequent decades, the coercive relationship of the police with urban populations receded from public attention. The 'golden age' of British policing, from about 1920–60 (Reiner, 1985) marked by low recorded crime rates and an insulation of police/crime activity in 'the slums' (Scraton, 1985), may be myth, but like all myth it articulates some perception of social life. Here it is of undisturbed living in an unthreatening environment with ease of access to police and courts. And there is the unquestioned benefit of unrestricted access to all public facilities of the urban area – its shops, colleges, libraries, or workplaces. Policing and cheap regulated public transport were the keys to the opening out of the city from the 1890s onwards (particularly apparent in the recruitment of girls into city-centre shops and offices).

Disputes over policing epitomise the current transition. The irreconcilable expectations of capital/management and workforce have put police back on the front line in an overtly militaristic role; riots have exposed target policing's susceptibility to 'blow back'; the inability of the police to protect against crimes which infringe norms of everyday urban life discredits the routine neighbourhood-caretaker role. Burglary, while often minimal in material effects, violates personal space/identity, assaults/harasssment limit the freedom of movement of the elderly, children, black people and women, and increasingly white men – virtually anyone on the street in a public place (Lea and Young, 1984, Thompson, 1988). This everyday crime is a form of terrorism: the uncertainty of its impact blocks off a once basic right. The response by police to these infringements of the right to the city is to privatise crime.

We are to ward off crime by keeping off the streets, safeguarding property, even detecting the crime – the neighbours are to drop their screen of privacy and watch the neighbourhood. Increasingly, the norms for neighbourhood life become those of suspicion and even hostility towards strangers, fear of transgressing police-defined norms of safe conduct, and a closure of the neighbourhood. The 'amoral familism'[11] of the inner cities may be the prototype for the new urban way of life. Police deploy two styles – the placatory 'good-servant' tone of dealings with the respectable/articulate and the exacerbatory 'precinct-captain' tone of dealings with target areas and populations.

In targeting the outsiders, police amplify the moral outcry and justify authoritarianism, but cannot safeguard a basic freedom.

URBANISATION AS MORAL PROJECT

At the outset, I suggested that sociology has typically considered urbanisation as a matter of politics. In extension, therefore, urbanisation is a matter of political agendas, incorporation of interest groups and recasting of the moral framework which allow truces to be arrived at and negotiations to proceed. The state welfare transition saw, in formal political terms, a recasting of the moral framework by which resource allocation was judged. Basic ideas of fairness – a fair day's work/wage (Hyman and Brough, 1975), and social equity – access to health or housing or education – were substantially recast. The shift in the moral ethos blocked further public discourse in two nation terms. The extension of the franchise had widened the moral universe of the state. At the same time, urbanisation was itself construed as a moral project, one which would satisfy this ethos of fairness and social equity and also regularise the lives of the poor. The moral framework of everyday life was to be redefined through urban reform. Public health measures required new standards of infant care/material responsibility, town-planning detached women from the 'sisterhood of the streets', restrictions on use of housing – overcrowding, lodgers, housekeeping – limited the household and defined work-roles. Even the design of housing – kitchens/parlours/ living rooms – was preceptive.[12] The latent motif in urbanisation as initiated and sponsored by the local state was that of support for the social discipline of a particular family form. Policing, itself a moral project (Storch, 1976), was perhaps of diminishing significance in maintaining neighbourhood and family order.

If there is a transition from this state-family-welfare agenda to one which is authoritarian and liberal, is there an equivalent moral project for urbanisation? There is evident a realignment in the philosophies of state action which do have implications for urban life – the encouragement of entrepreneurship and individual responsibility, the attack on welfare as dependency, the shift of responsibility for care of the elderly and ill to the 'community', or the rephrasing of health care. This version of liberalism promotes charity rather than collectively administered welfare and undermines the professional authority that underpinned the institutions of the welfare state.

Where, then, does social discipline inhere: in the church, the family, the workplace, the pub or the corrective institutions that imposed order on urban populations in the era before the welfare state? In a profound sense, there is disorder in urbanisation as 'procedures, patterns of organisation and institutional mechanisms' (Offe, 1985, p. 6) are discredited. In the ensuing vacuum, other agencies, notably the media and the police, intervene to codify the conventions of public and private behaviour. Increasingly, the police act as moral entrepreneurs setting the boundaries between the respectable and the rough or disreputable, acting as arbiters of neighbourhood life and conduct in the public spaces of the city. In this respect history would seem to have come full circle.

But this is a facile reading of the relationships and mediating influences in the two 'transitions': the interlinkages of the police institution with state and civil society need more detailed empirical exposition than is possible here.[13] One reason for the rather distant attitude of professional historians to their associates, historical sociologists, is the latter's sometimes cavalier attitude to the detail of previous periods – the detail of sequence, connection and acknowledged influence around which the historian's account is built. On many such points of detail this particular attempt to order a discordant pattern of development will be disputed – it assumes too many such accounts. Perhaps embarking on such an enterprise 'is to commit the historical sociologist to a rather agile intellectual life' (Abrams, 1982, p. 333).

NOTES

1. The Glasgow rent strikes of 1915 arguably constitute the pivotal episode in the enforcement of local-authority building and subsidy of working-class housing (Melling, 1983, Damer, 1979).
2. There was widespread support for public health measures and some for town-planning (Pollard, 1959). There is little evidence of campaigns for improvements in local services, even in Glasgow (Fraser, 1985).
3. The failure to industrialise had no bearing on the concentration of wealth there. Lee (1983, p. 22) notes that London accounted for 35.1 per cent of the entire tax assessment for the UK in 1879/80.
4. There is, therefore, 'homogenisation' of local economies (Warde, 1985). But it is not so much women's employment that evens out regional differentials in household income and consumption as the demand for labour in services and retail outlets.

5. There is no reference in, for instance, Massey (1984) or the essays included in Newby (1985). It is also omitted from the Town and Country Planning Association's publication *The North/South Divide* (1987).
6. There is no definitive discussion of the social ideologies of housing policy in the interwar period, but see the essays included in Matrix (1984) and MacKenzie and Rose (1983). More generally, see Wilson (1978).
7. The definition of liberalism adopted is that of Williams, 'a doctrine of certain necessary kinds of freedom, but also, and essentially, a doctrine of possessive individualism' (Williams, 1983, p. 181).
8. The research reported by Taylor-Gooby (1985) is liable to more than one interpretation – see the debate with Marsland (1984).
9. British cities are following the path of American cities in the 1970s in taking 'a historic urban motif and translating it into a saleable package' (Judd, 1979). See, more recently, Hewison (1987).
10. Quoted by Sennett (1977, p. 137), who sees this 'right' as a 'bourgeois prerogative', emphasising the localism of working-class lives.
11. Suttles (1968) described the personalised definitions of responsibility for others, and the significance of demarcations of 'turf'. Marked in contemporary urban life is the virulent hostility to groups marked out as 'moral' outcasts: bikers (even young local boys), gypsies, the mentally ill or ex-prisoners, gays and, of course, black households: each area has its local campaign and tradition of harassment. And, increasingly, there is active defence of domain.
12. The Housing Manual (1927), issued as guidance to local authorities by the Ministry of Health, was much preoccupied with the allocation of floorspace between the women's work quarters and the family living-room, so as to create an environment in which the man would relax at home. Restrictions on lodgers until the 1950s were similarly motivated.
13. Brogden's (1982) exposition of the changing parameters of accountability for local police forces, based on analysis of Liverpool documents, is an excellent example of historical sociology. Much of the recent literature on the police institution emphasises the need for new constitutional safeguards in the absence of the local limits to police authority in which police forces were instituted (Hain, 1979, Lustgarten, 1986, Uglow, 1988).

REFERENCES

P. Abrams, *Historical Sociology* (Shepton Mallet: Open Books, 1982).
K. Baker, 29 January 1986, *The Times*.
S. Benton, 'The Left Embraces Law and Order', *New Statesman* 21 November 1986.
M. Brittan, 'Recent Population Changes', *Population Trends*, 1986, pp. 33–6.
M. Brogden, *The Police: Autonomy and Consent* (London: Academic Press, 1982).
J. Bulpitt, *Territory and Power in the UK* (Manchester: University Press, 1983).

D. Byrne, 'Class and the Local State', *International Journal of Urban and Regional Research*, 1982, Vol. 6.

M. Castells, *City, Class and Power* (London: MacMillan, 1978).

T. Champion, 'Momentous Revival in London's Population', *Town and Country Planning*, March, 1987, pp. 80–4.

D. Coates and J. Hillard (eds), *Economic Decline in Modern Britain* (London: Wheatsheaf, 1986).

P. Corrigan, 'Introduction' to *Capitalism, State Formation and Social Theory* (London: Quartet Books, 1980).

P. Corrigan and D. Sayer, *The Great Arch* (Oxford: Blackwell, 1985).

S. Damer, 'Glasgow 1885–1919', in J. Melling (ed.), *The State, Housing and Social Policy* (London: Croom Helm, 1979).

G. Dangerfield, *The Strange Death of Liberal England* (London: 1935; republished by Granada, 1970).

P. Dunleavy, *The Politics of Mass Housing* (Oxford: Oxford University Press, 1981).

D. Fraser, 'Labour and the Changing City', in G. Gordon (ed.), *Perspectives of the Scottish City* (Aberdeen: Aberdeen University Press, 1985).

A. Gamble, 'Smashing the State', *Marxism Today*, June 1985, pp. 21–6.

A. Gamble, *The Free Economy and the Strong State* (London: Macmillan, 1988).

A. Giddens, *Central Problems in Social Theory* (London: Macmillan, 1979).

J. Gyford, 'The New Urban Left', *New Society*, 21 March 1983.

J. Gyford, *The Politics of Local Socialism* (London: Allen & Unwin, 1985).

P. Hain, *Policing the Police* (London: Calder, 1979).

P. Hall, 'Flight to the Green', *New Society*, 9 January 1987.

S. Hall, 'The Rise of the Representative-Interventionist State', in S. Hall *et al.*, *State and Society in Contemporary Britain* (Oxford: Polity Press, 1984).

M. Harloe, *Swindon: A Town in Transition* (London: Heinemann, 1975).

L. Harris and J. Coakley, *The City of Capital* (London: Blackwell, 1983).

R. Hewison, *The Heritage Industry* (London: Methuen, 1987).

R. Hyman and I. Brough, *Social Values and Industrial Relations* (Oxford: Blackwell, 1975), pp. 30–61.

G. Ingham, *Capitalism Divided? The City and Industry in British Social Development* (London: Macmillan, 1984).

F. Inglis, 'Nation and Community', *Sociological Review*, 1977, pp. 489–513.

D. Judd, 'The Case of Tourism', in G. A. Tobin, *The Changing Structure of the City* (Beverley Hills: Sage, 1979).

J. Lea and J. Young, *What is to be Done about Law and Order?* (London: Penguin, 1984).

C. H. Lee, 'Modern Economic Growth and Structural Change in Scotland', *Scottish Economic and Social History*, 1983, Vol. 3, No. 3.

H. Lefebvre, *Le droit à la ville* (Paris: Anthropos, 1968).

H. Lefebvre, *La révolution urbaine* (Paris: Gallimard, 1970).

L. Lustgarten, *The Governance of Police* (London: Sweet & Maxwell, 1986).

A. MacFarlane, *The Origins of English Individualism* (Oxford: Blackwell, 1978).

A. MacFarlane, *The Justice and the Mare's Ale* (Oxford: Blackwell, 1981).

S. MacKenzie and D. Rose, 'Industrial Change, the Domestic Economy and Home Life', in J. Anderson *et al.* (eds), *Redundant Spaces in Cities and Regions* (London: Academic Press, 1983).

H. Marcuse, *One Dimensional Man* (London: Sphere Books, 1968).

D. Marsland, 'Public Opinion and the Welfare State: Some Problems in the Interpretations of Facts', *Sociology,* 1984, Vol. 18, No. 1.

D. Massey, *Spatial Divisions of Labour* (London: Macmillan, 1984).

Matrix, *Making Space* (London: Pluto Press, 1984).

R. Mellor, 'The Capitalist City 1780–1920', Unit 1, Open University Course, *Urban Change and Conflict* (Milton Keynes: Open University, 1981).

R. Mellor, 'Marxism and the Urban Question', in M. Shaw (ed.), *Marxist Sociology Revisited* (London: Macmillan, 1985).

J. Merrington, 'Town and Country in the Transition to Capitalism'. Reprinted in R. Hilton (ed.), *The Transition of Feudalism to Capitalism* (London: Verso, 1978).

Ministry of Health, *Housing Manual* (London: HMSO, 1927).

H. Newby (ed.), *Restructuring Capital* (London: Macmillan, 1985).

C. Offe, *Disorganised Capitalism* (Oxford: Polity Press, 1985).

S. Pollard, *A History of Labour in Sheffield* (Liverpool: Liverpool University Press, 1959).

R. Reiner, *The Politics of Policing* (London: Wheatsheaf, 1985).

R. Roberts, *The Classic Slum* (London: Penguin, 1972).

P. Scraton, *The State of Policing* (London: Pluto Press, 1985).

R. Sennett, *The Fall of Public Man* (New York: Knopf, 1977).

J. Stewart, *The New Management of Local Government* (London: Allen & Unwin, 1985).

L. Stone, *The Family, Sex and Marriage in England 1500–1800* (London: Penguin, 1979).

R. D. Storch, 'The Policeman as Domestic Missionary', *Journal of Social History*, 1976, Vol. 9.

G. D. Suttles, *The Social Order of the Slum* (Chicago: University Press, 1968).

P. Taylor-Goodby, 'Attitudes to Welfare, *Journal of Social Policy*, 1985, pp. 73–82.

K. Thompson, *Under Siege: Racial Violence in Britain* (London: Penguin, 1988).

N. Thrift, 'The Fixers: The Urban Geography of International Commercial Capital', in J. Henderson and M. Castells, *Global Restructuring and Territorial Development* (London and New York: Sage, 1987), pp. 203–33.

Town and Country Planning Association, *The North/South Divide* (London: TCPA, 1987).

N. Tranter, *Population Since the Industrial Revolution* (London: Croom Helm, 1973).

S. Uglow, *Policing Liberal Society* (Oxford: Oxford University Press, 1988).

A. Warde, 'The Homogenisation of Space', in H. Newby (ed.), *Restructuring Capital* (London: Macmillan, 1985).

R. Williams, *Keywords* (London: Fontana, 1983).

E. Wilson, *Women and the Welfare State* (London: Tavistock, 1978).

9 Aye Tae the Fore: The Fife Miners in the 1984–85 Strike

Suzanne Najam

INTRODUCTION

This chapter engages with the failure of traditional accounts of working-class consciousness to explain the mechanisms promoting or inhibiting radical beliefs. These, too often, have been overly-concerned with assessing the ability of the working class to fulfil its historic role as characterised by Marxist definitions, or have concentrated on the descriptive analysis of areas and times during which radical activity took place. The first type of approach adopts a simplistic perspective that fails to grasp the complex nature of belief, and the ambiguities and contradictions that it may contain. The second disengages particular episodes from the flow of time and thus fails to account for the relationship of radical stances to their historical background.[1]

Explanations have tended to give unsophisticated accounts of the relationship between objective and subjective conditions for action and, consequently, have failed to indicate the ways in which a broad social imagery may, or may not, be related to an overtly political world view. Further, accounts have largely been static, with little attention to the reproduction of radical consciousness among workers over time, or of the role of historical awareness in the creation of radical identities and beliefs. What is necessary is to approach the subject area less with a predetermined idea of what is to count as a 'valid' description of radical discourse and simplistic notions of the relationship between objective and subjective conditions for action but, rather, to examine what mechanisms are crucial to the creation and perpetuation of perceptual orientations in general in order to avoid the laden assumptions of 'class consciousness'.

This said, the topic under review is concerned with radical subject-ive understandings. The key mechanisms within social life which are seen as central to the production and reproduction of radical con-sciousness are the areas of work, community, industrial organisation and relations, and political institutions. It is in these spheres that actors learn, through experience and informal socialisation, both the past and the present of the social group. The research upon which this chapter is based attempts to examine the formation of consciousness over time, how the history of the group is understood and becomes incorporated within identity and beliefs, yet how the meaning of this history is changed by action in the objective world. As it is beyond the scope of this chapter adequately to tackle all of these areas, it will concentrate, albeit briefly, on some of the key ways in which a sense of the past is mobilised by radical actors, and how this may interact with contemporary actuality.[2]

THE ROLE OF SIGNIFICANT HISTORY

Central to an understanding of the production and reproduction of radicalism is the concept of an historical legacy transmitted through intergenerational interaction. This legacy serves to locate individuals within their familial and communal past by its transmission through personalised stories relating to relatives or group members, thereby providing the material which explains who 'I' am, 'we' and 'they' are. In addition to providing a means of identification, it also offers communal values of expected behaviour and understandings of the world through its stories. Yet this historical understanding is not to be seen as the totality of an 'objective' past, but as an history of what is regarded as significant to the lives of social groups.

The historical legacy is different to a 'sense of the past' in that this latter may be an unfocussed understanding, without implications for the receivers, whereas a legacy contains an implicit means of understanding the world. In this sense, an historical legacy is that which is given to future generations; a gift which carries both a sense of duty and obligation. What is drawn from the legacy depends upon what is required or needed from it, and how the sense of obligation is understood. It is, as such, an encapsulated sense of the past which offers a particular interpretation of the world.[3]

This historical interpretation is seen as a 'significant history'. It is a history existing outwith time but which contains key understandings which, mobilised in differing spatio-temporal circumstances, have vital consequences for the playing out of 'situated history'; that is, what Heller would call the 'historical present'.[4] It provides the frame of meaning within which actors attempt to make sense of their lives and, at the same time, thus acts as a 'cultural repertoire' for action.[5] By its mobilisation in time and space, the historical legacy is perpetuated within the group; that is, its utilisation helps reproduce significant history whilst, at the same time, both enlarging it and reinforcing it through continuing relevance.

Yet this reproduction is dependent upon two factors; namely, that the substance of significant history has a continuing relevance for actors through its applicability to, and ability to make sense of, the actuality of people's lives, and, further, that it is possible to perpetuate this legacy through the presence of enabling objective conditions; that is, that perpetuation is dependent upon whether contemporary events either confirm or contradict the legacy. It is with the purpose of analysing the relationship between the past and present, and the ways in which a sense of the past interacts with situated history to reproduce or transform belief, that an examination will be made of key factors involved in the attitudes of the Fife miners during the 1984–85 strike.

THE FIFE COALFIELD DURING 1984–85

By 1984 the miners of the Fife coalfield, as was the case with the British coalfield as a whole, would appear superficially to have been ill-equipped to embark on what many soon realised would be a long industrial dispute. The mining industry no longer dominated the county in the way it had done in former years. Compared with the last prolonged strike in the 1920s, when the county contained some 65 pits (in 1926), and employment figures stood in the 20 000s (28 140 in 1921), by 1984 there were just three pits – Comrie, Seafield and the Frances – which employed just 3818 men. Correspondingly, there had been a dramatic decline in the size of the mining communities which had eroded many of the traditional support systems upon which the miners had historically depended. The withdrawal of the pit from the centre of community life had profound consequences for the ability of the miners to sustain a strike. The industry was no longer the major source of employment for local inhabitants or, therefore, vital to their interests. The remaining collieries were large, modernised and cosmopolitan productive units, drawing men in from all over Fife, thereby making coordination of activity potentially difficult to attain. Lastly, and perhaps crucially, the divorce of the pits from the communities meant that the miners' Union was no longer central to everyday life, dominating the concerns and activities of the miners' families as it had done in earlier periods.

Yet, despite these vast changes in the strength of the industry, at the beginning of the strike the Fife miners were one hundred per cent solid, and between 90 to 92 per cent would return *en masse* in March 1985, the majority of the remainder only returning to work in the last few weeks.[6] Like other areas, organisational bases were soon established around the coalfield, arranging and sending out pickets, collecting and distributing funds and provisions, organising political meetings and social events, and even getting babies born to miners' wives 'adopted' by workers in Dundee. Paralleling the activities of the local Councils of Action of the interwar period, ten Strike Centres were set up around the county co-ordinated from a Central Headquarters in Dysart. It was in these that activities centred, plans were made and executed, analysis given and morale sustained.

As elsewhere, the stresses of the strike were intense. Marriages became embittered, and in some cases collapsed, as tempers flared, morale fluctuated and families sunk deeper into debt. For activists, the Strike Centres became second homes as they worked around the clock, and they suffered physical exhaustion, mental fatigue and despondency. It was a demanding year, and for the Seafield men 13 months, having been out in a local dispute since Febuary 1984.

Yet despite the hard work, material hardship and periods of despair the miners agree it was also a great year. Once again the communities drew together for mutual aid and all sections rallied around the strike. The Union became integrated once more into the communities due to the exigencies of the dispute. Further, it was a period in which personal inner resources were discovered, developed or tested – whether individuals found themselves confronting new ideas, suddenly addressing large meetings around Britain for the first time, or improving their golf handicaps during periods of relaxation in what turned out to be a fine summer.

Thus despite the debilitated state of the industry the Fife miners found the resources and conviction to sustain themselves through a year of unprecedented struggle and in the face of the growing awareness of the inevitability of defeat. What requires explanation, therefore, is the strength of the mechanisms existing within the area which enabled this response despite unpropitious objective circumstances. Yet, further, an analysis must be given of the ways in which objective conditions during the strike served to undermine established perceptual mechanisms already under assault from industrial decline and by the end had engendered both an enhanced radicalism and a growing demoralisation. It is through the analysis of the strike that one can reach a fuller understanding of the inherent fragility and complexity underlying the adherence to a radical stance, and how this may be affected over time by changing spatio-temporal circumstances. What shall be argued is that a crucial source of strength for the Fife miners is the presence of an historical legacy of political radicalism, systematised locally by the Communist Party (CP), but that the 1984–85 strike served to highlight that this legacy is now under severe strain as circumstances have acted to disengage the radical discourse from actuality.

THE HISTORICAL LEGACY

The Fife coalfield, therefore, is a suitable target area for a study dealing with the nature of the mechanisms which promote the production and reproduction of political radicalism due to its solidarity during the 1984–85 strike. Yet this is increased by the proven ability of the Fife miners to perpetuate a radical consciousness over time, thus allowing one to analyse this ability over prolonged periods and in the face of changing historical circumstances.

Fife has had a reputation for industrial militancy since 1870 when the Fife miners reputedly became the first in Europe to win the eight-hour day, and one of political extremism since the 1920s.[7] It was at this time that Fife won notoriety due to the activities of the Communist Party of Great Britain and mining communities during the interwar depression. Internal squabbles between the old Lib-Lab union leadership and the young communist militants led firstly to the establishment of the breakaway Fife Miners' Reform Union in 1923, and then to the setting up of the communist-led United Mineworkers of Scotland in 1929, which found its strongest base in the county. Militant activities spread beyond the concerns of the mining industry into community support for the young Soviet Union and the Spanish Civil War, and to mass action against such problems as evictions and the Means Test.[8] Despite a decline in support for communism in the late 1930s and a right-wing backlash in the Union against communist miners in the 1950s, Party members have continued to be prominent locally. In 1942 Abe Moffat, a communist miner from Lumphinnans became the first President of the Scottish miners' union, to be replaced by his brother Alec in 1961. The county and townships regularly returned communist councillors until 1974 (and more irregularly since that time), and by 1984 communists were still in local Union leadership – three of the four officials for Seafield at the commencement of the strike being Party members, one of whom was a Regional Councillor.

Radical politics, therefore, play an integral part in the objective historical legacy of the Fife miners, and, through the importance of the industry locally, of the southern part of the county itself; this being that part within which the coalfield lies. Given the nature of the history of the industry in the area, and of the struggles of the past generations against the oppressive conditions of the old coal owners, the transmission of the regional legacy is a particularistic one, which has been rendered coherent by the availability of a systematised world view articulated by the CP. The significant history of Fife is thus essentially a conflictual and oppositional one.

This legacy is integrated into personal experience in relation to familial history which ties, through biographical stories, into the wider spatio-temporal legacy to instill identity. That this interrelationship between regional and personal histories provides a major source of individual understanding and motivation can be seen from the following statement from a miner in his 30s:

[A sense o' history] makes me proud, and ah am proud tae be a miner. Proud tae be brought-up in a mining communi'y. Proud o' being the son o' a miner. Ah think ah'm proud because ma feyther had tae struggle. It makes ye proud, that he fought fur onything he got, and ah'm the same. Onything ah've got ah warked fur. Naebody's gave onything tae me. Ah get alot o' sa'isfaction ootae that. Nothing's been honded tae me on a plate.

Further, as many local residents have some past connection to the industry, the community also continues to feel an identification with the miners despite the decline of the industry locally. The legacy has a county appeal. It is this factor which is held to account for the rallying of the local inhabitants to the strike call. One 33-year-old argues:

In this area the decline o' the pits *changes* the communi'y. Ah
mean, it daesnae *end* the communi'y. The communi'y continues,
but the communi'y's changed. The militancy's still there, when the
need arises. What pleased me aboot Cowdenbeath was the fact that
when the strike call went oot it wasnae just the miners in the toon,
ye know, that rallied tae the call but the toon itsel. Because the
toon realised that although we've got nae pits alot o'men are still
employed in the pits, and the tradition o' militancy come tae the
surface. And the toon stood firm wi' the miners, which pleased me
nae end at all, ken. Ah mean, we've only lost oor pits in living
memory. Ah mean, ah can mind the pits gaeing and ah'm only 33.
The tradition's still there. Alot o' the alder men are fra' mining. Ah
mean, ye'll no' gae intae a hoose in this area and no' find somebody
who's no' got, at present or in the recent past, somebody in their
family has something tae dae wi' mining.

If this tradition operates within the working-class community through
past ties, it has much stronger effects on the actions of the miners
themselves. It is again the presence of the legacy which can be held to
underlie the miners beliefs as to why they were solid during the
strike. The following quotation indicates how the historical legacy
provides a cultural repertoire of precedent:

Ah think the militancy o' the Fife miners in that strike is, in fact, a
na'ural process fra' previous strikes and previous struggles o' their
feythers and grandfeythers. Ah mean, the lad Brian Easton we
talked aboot, who was the Secretary o' the Strike Commi'ee in this
strike, his grandfeyther was imprisoned in 1921 fur his role in the
strike that took place at that time. There's a cer'ain historical
tradition.

The particularistic nature of militancy in Fife has been given a distinct
orientation by the activities of the CP in the area. The dominance of
the Party historically, and the role still played by local activists has
coloured the direction of campaigns. Both Party and non-Party
members see the CP as having historically provided local leadership.
A statement from a leading communist from Cowdenbeath shows
how this political legacy has affected the potentiality for action:

Well, ah keep coming back tae this communist thing, but the
people who've led the Fife miners have been the communists over

the years. They have ayeways provided the main core o' leaders. In
the biggest pit in Fife, Wullie Clarke, Johnnie Neilson, leading
communists. The Workshops, the delegates were communists. Ah
mean, oor local Strike Commi'ee, o' the ten on the Strike
Commi'ee there were seven members o' the Communist Party who
directed the way in which the local struggle was conducted. And
that has been the element in Fife that wasnae elsewhere. There has
been this *influence* historically through the Moffats, McArthurs,
the Jimmy Millers, the Wullie Clarkes and Johnnie Neilsons. The
young lads who've come up as communist leadership. And if ye
read aboot the strike and hoo the propaganda was conducted, ah
mean, it was conducted in a different way here. Well, ah don't
know whether ye've no'iced those great, big adverts that the Coal
Board took oot, pu'ing their case tae the people. Well, Fife was the
only area in which the *miners* put oot the same full page, took oot
another full page answering the case in the same public way. That
was done in Fife and wasnae done elsewhere. Big pages in the
newspapers *answering* the same kindae things.

This quotation clearly relates what is seen as the politically progressive stance of the Fife miners to the historical role played by the CP. In
this way we can see how the past activities of the communists are an
implicit element within the reservoir of historical knowledge drawn
upon in the strike to make sense of, and deal with, the confrontation;
that is, it is a part of the particularistic sense of history and identity
relating to the county which is reproduced in younger men. This
tradition of radicalism establishes a precedent for political and
experiential possibilities. Both young and old miners hold common
perceptions of Fife's history as one of great militancy, yet this is not a
static description of the past but a force which has continuing
ramifications for contemporary miners. The legacy is a dynamic
phenomenon informing attitudes and actions. This knowledge of the
past serves to harden young men. There is a close inter-relationship
between political and industrial commitment and knowledge of past
conditions and actions. It is amongst the most radical of the younger
miners that one can find the greatest awareness of the historical
legacy as an active force of continuing relevance. As the following
quotation indicates, this is an interactive process wherein experience
in the present and knowledge of the collective past act as political
education:

Oh, yes. Oh, yes, [knowledge o' the past] affects [their actions]. Ye are *yoo*. Ye are conscious. Most o' them consciously try and learn fra' the past. And they have some bitterness fra' the past, as well as some great *examples* fra' the past. And these remain wi' ye all yur life, these examples. The examples o' treachery as well as the examples o' extreme solidarity stay wi' ye all yur life. There's a determination tae live-up tae the past. That they will no' be lesser men.

The mobilisation of the legacy was thus an integral part of the ability to understand and sustain motivation in 1984–85 for contemporary miners by providing guidelines, standards and examples. Yet perceptions of past struggle also manifest themselves as a sense of obligation to those whose previous conflicts have produced the benefits currently enjoyed. Combined with this is a feeling that there is a duty to carry on for future generations. This places miners in a past/present/future configuration whereby decisions and actions currently undertaken are made in reference to both past and future expectations. It is this which provides the dynamic for thought and action. One miner in his 20s states:

[Coming fra' a mining family and what ma feyther told me] affects *me*. It affects me in as much tae say that ah thought ah had a du'y tae cairry it on. Tae cairry on trying tae win mair benefits and be'er conditions and that fur the miners. Because ma feyther and ma forefeythers fought fur the conditions that ah'm able tae enjoy just noo. And ah think these conditions, which are far be'er than what *they* had, ah think they could still be extended. So ah would say it's ma du'y tae try and be'er the conditions even further fur ma sons and fu'ure generations.

This sense of the past, understood in terms of hardship and conflict was, therefore, an enabling factor during 1984–85, providing a frame of meaning and establishing precedents for attitudes and actions. Yet if the radical legacy was mobilised during the strike and was given a renewed legitimacy through the year-long dispute, it was also a time of testing for that history as the miners sought to equate their past to the present. The growing realisation during the course of the strike that their reputation greatly outweighed the reality placed the radical identity under severe strain. What requires explanation is how subjective understandings, both historical and contemporary, interacted with the objective circumstances of the strike and laid the basis for both enhanced radicalisation and increasing demoralisation. Yet within this, one needs to examine how certain sections of the miners were better able to sustain commitment. It is only thus that one can come to appreciate both the positive and negative aspects of the historical legacy.

TAKING ON THE WORLD

At the beginning of the strike morale and faith in the ability to secure a victory ran high. Looking back to the years of Union strength and to the national strikes of 1972 and 1974, initial optimism was grounded on beliefs about the power of the NUM within the British trade-union movement. One retired miner succinctly sums up this belief:

> The miners have *ayeways*, historically speaking, miners have ayeways led, they have been the advance guard o' the British warking class in *all* their struggles. And the people *look* tae the miners tae fight. And, in fact, many warkers will say tae ye, 'Christ, if they can beat the miners, what chance ha' we got?' Because we *are* the best organised, because we're the *easiest* tae organise, because o' the na'ure o' the industry.

For younger miners, brought up surrounded by stories about the invincibility of their Union, and to believe that they, by industrial muscle power, could topple governments, there was a strong belief that they could win. These ideas gained credence due to the youthful nature of the participants for, as many older men had left the industry on redundancy, there were increasingly fewer miners with experience to counsel wisdom. One 24-year-old argues:

> [We thought we were] a law unto oorsel. We *thought* we were when we went on strike, because in '72 and '74, ye see, wi' sheer muscle-power we crushed the government. And alot o' people thought, when we walked oot in '84, that we were gaeing tae crush them again. If we stuck 5000 pickets in a huddle we were gaeing tae shut the whole country doon. And we would dae it, ken. It was a sortae romantic thing. Still talking like 1974. 'Away tae the power stations and shut everything doon.'

The Fife miners, therefore, entered the dispute in good spirits, and were quick to erect an organisational framework to deal with the responsibilities the dispute would entail. As the younger men were without experience of long-term struggle it was a period of personal and educational development. As the strike intensified, the demands of the situation drew out personal resources and qualities that few were aware they possessed. One 30-year-old expresses this:

> . . . ah realised alot o' things masel that ah could dae that perhaps before the strike ah just didnae think ah was capable o' daeing. Well, ah went tae speak at public mee'ings, which ah had verra li'le experience o' before the strike. And ah could organise other people, which ah think is a tremendous abili'y fur onybody, tae be able tae sit doon and organise other people intae action. It's easy enough tae get aff yur ain backside and gae and dae something, but tae organise other people and tae cairry them forrad is something else.

If the strike developed personal qualities, it was also an education for participants who gained a fuller political insight into the nature of the British state and the operation of its power structures. One young miner, inactive before the strike, shows how his experiences gave him a greater insight into such forces:

> Ah *seen* the state machine in action. Ah *seen* what they were daeing tae us, ken. Ah would gae tae mee'ings and listen tae Scargill saying something and it would say something to'ally different on the telly at night. Ken, they would be telling ye that there were 50 people warking in the paper and that, and ah'd stond there every day and see naebody gae up tae their wark, or twa folk and that.

For many the strike led to changes in previously held beliefs and outlooks. The necessities of the strike demanded a reorientation both in social values and normative expectations. The same young man, who had previously denied contemporary legitimacy to the legacy, explains how it changed his outlooks:

> Ye see, ah used tae have alot o' ambition before the strike. Ah wasnae intae the Union or that. Ah went tae college and got a Higher National in engineering, and all ah thought aboot then was that ah wanted taeget away fra' [the industry]. Ah wasnae wanting

tae wark wi' ma honds. Ah wasnae wanting tae wark in an industry such as that. Ah didnae want tae be associa'ed wi' it. But noo it's changed, see. The strike changed me alot. Ah seen such things, ken. Values that ah had, ken, fur material things and that. Ah was wanting cars and bikes and valueing things raither than people. And ah was reading the tory press who were telling me that everything was a' richt. And all these sneers aboot Scargill and that. And ah couldnae see what they were daeing tae people, ken. And when ah came oot on strike it was *me* that was there. Ye know, it wasnae British Leyland or the dockers or that, it was *me* that was in that position. Ah mean, ye get back tae yursel. And it makes ye realise [what ah thought before's] *no'* what it's aboot. And ah says, 'Well, maybe there's something worth fighting fur here.'

This quotation clearly demonstrates the ways in which younger men who had denied contemporary relevancy to significant history came to accredit it with a continuing importance through the circumstances of the strike. Thus, the strike provided an awareness which could encourage a greater radicalisation among the miners through their personal experiences and those gained through contact with the state, judiciary and media. One 71-year-old ex-miner aptly sums up the effects on the younger generation:

Ah think in many respects they are *mair* politicised noo. Fur example, if ye take before the strike, if ah had been talking tae warkers in a pub or onywhere else, and trying tae explain tae them that the state was no' neutral, that the state was an instrument o' whatever current socie'y that exists, that they create a state tae perpetuate their ain image, their ain interests, ah wouldae had a great deal o' difficulty in explaining that. And ah *had* a great deal o' difficulty explaining that. Ge'ing people tae accept that. Ye have nae trouble convincing a miner aboot that *noo*. Because they've seen the way the judiciary and the polis were used against them in that strike. They understond *much* mair clearly than their fore-feythers did that the state is no' neutral. They understond that crystal clear because they've got the bluid tae show it. They've got the marks tae show it.

As this quotation indicates, the younger generation, through the conflict, have gained a legitimation within the context of the legacy.

They have become part of the conflictual history of the miners, and in so doing have enriched the legacy; that is, that through their actions a new chapter has been added. A miner in his 30s argues:

> There's a cer'ain pride and digni'y in the folk that took pairt in '84–85. Ye'll get alot o' them, ye know, at the pits, ye know, 'We should forget aboot it. We got beat,' ye ken. And miners are a funny breed, they tend tae be, hoo can ah put it, ah'll no' say chauv. . ., aye, they're chauvinistic in a cer'ain way. And if ye talk tae them aboot pride and digni'y they tend tae shy off, ye know. They're 'cissy' wards and that, ye know. But at the same time, when ye sit and talk tae them, even the ones that say, 'Och, we should forget aboot the strike,' ye know. Ye get them talking and, 'Och, ah remember the picket-lines at Bilston Glen.' And, 'Och, ah remember this,' and 'Ah remember that.' And ye can see it in their eyes, ken. They were *proud*, proud o' what they done. Alot o' them dinnae understond the historical implications o' the strike. Ah mean, it was the same in 1926. It wasnae till many years aifter when ye can look at it in the context o' what was happening at that time, ye know, tae fully understond the effect o' the strike. And it's when ye can look at it in hindsight, maybe five, ten, 15 years time fra' noo, when ye can look at the '84–85 strike, and the impact it had on socie'y in Britain. And alot o' them dinnae realise that, ye ken. But ah reckon, when alot o' them grow-up, they'll be si'ing there wi' their wee grandbairns on their knees, and they'll be, 'Ah remember in '84–85. . .,' ye ken what ah mean. And there'll be pride, and there'll be digni'y there, and ye can feel it. They might no' *talk* aboot it, but ye can *feel* it, ye ken.

By fulfilling a role in the perpetuation of this history due to the activities of the strike, therefore, younger men have been enabled to take their place alongside their forebears. Thus the strike has served to instill in contemporary miners feelings of worth whereby their hardships have raised their sense of self-esteem in relation to older generations. One 33-year-old expresses this clearly:

> The '84–85 strike changed ma life dramatically. Changed ma ootlook tae ma life dramatically. Tae me, ah suppose, the '84–85 strike, in a nutshell means this. Ah've ayeways been interested in history, in the history o' this area and the history o' the mines, and ah like nothing be'er than tae sit in the company o' yur ald miners

and listen tae their tales o' the pit and the '26 strike. And ah used tae sit in awe at some o' these alder men. Their tales o' their hairdships and what they'd done in 1926. Ah can noo look at they men right in the eye, as an equal, because o' the '84–85 strike. Ah mean, ah'm no' saying oor time is any easier or hairder than they'n, but ah'm equal, and that means alot tae me, ye know, as an individual. Ah dinnae look up tae them noo, ah dinnae look doon on them, ah'm equal. That means alot. [The strike] was a bit ah didnae want tae dae. Ah mean, let's face it, who the hell wants tae gae on strike fur a year? In fact, who maybe wants tae gae on strike at all? But ah'm proud, and ah gained three things fra' that strike that'll last me fur the rest o' ma life, and that's pride, digni'y and self-respect. And, ah mean, they're things that cannae be bought. Ah'm proud in the sense that ah stood-up fur ma job, ma communi'y and ma femily. Ah've got digni'y in the fact ah stood firm, and ah've got self-respect in that ah can look onybody in the eye. Ah can look [the ald boys] in the eye as equals, and that means a lot. Ah'm proud in the fact ah stood firm. Ah was oot on strike fur so lang. Ah suffered so much. It was haird at the *time*.

The period 1984–85, therefore, provided a dual legitimation; of the history of the miners as essentially one of conflict and hardship, and of the rightful place of the younger generation within that legacy. The past and present combined within understandings of the strike, and act out into the future through their incorporation within contemporary belief. Yet if these experiences were a positive source of strength to the miners, there was a negative side. Whilst optimistic at the start of the strike, there soon grew the awareness that the miners did not have the strength to defeat the NCB, and that the world within which they currently existed had radically changed. Objective conditions, both in the sense of their own importance and numerical force and in relation to the tactics which they adopted, had changed, as had the political climate of the country as a whole. As such, the year was one in which the miners had to reorientate their perceptions of themselves, their industry, and their places within British society.

BACKS AGAINST THE WALL

The optimism of the early months was soon seen to having been built on ignorance and self-delusion. There was a lack of preparation on the part of the miners nationally, a failure to perceive the diminished power which they could bring to the strike, and little awareness of the scale of opposition that would come from the state. Under these circumstances the miners were often lacking a clear direction and strategy. But it was the mobilisation of the myth of the miners which was largely responsible for the failure adequately to confront the situation.

Wielding the victorious image of 1974, the miners had dwelt on, rather than learnt from, that strike. Beguiled by the legacy, they accepted the glory and had failed to see how circumstances had changed. In this way 1974, the miners' greatest victory, laid the ground for their greatest defeat, for it led them into 1984–85 with outmoded tactics and attitudes. The Tory government, on the other hand, was quickly perceived to have learnt from the past even if the miners had not. Indeed, soon, though perhaps not soon enough, the miners began to see that the harshness and determination of the government was due precisely to 1974. Seeing 1974 as the retribution for 1926, their willingness to live in the past did not extend to seeing 1974 as perhaps requiring retribution also. As one man in his 50s argues:

Well, obviously it's a government that represents, this is raither cliche-ridden, a cer'ain class in socie'y, and they ha' done their job! If there's one thing aboot them, they had warked oot their strategy fur dealing wi' the miners *verra* carefully, verra well, and they had organised their troops. That's one thing, ye've got tae hond it tae them, they had learnt lessons fra' the past. They werenae like Arthur fighting the strike in 1984 wi' the tools they'd fought the strike in 1974. They had *learnt* lessons. They knew what they had tae dae and they did it. We're dealing wi' a verra clever enemy. Who *dae* learn lessons. Who *dae* organise their troops. Who *knew* what they were aboot. *Knew* where they were gaeing. Alot o' times during the strike the miners *didnae know* where they were gaeing. *Didnae* know what they were targe'ing fur. In fact, when we were having discussions here aboot where we were gaeing there was this *unclarity* aboot what we should be daeing at cer'ain times. '*Why* should we be picke'ing there?' 'Should we be attempting tae dae *this*?' There was a lack o' an overall strategy aboot what we were attempting tae dae.

The concentration of overall decision-making at NUM Headquarters in Sheffield thereby acted to enhance feelings of powerlessness, for the ability to effect strategic action was beyond the Fife miners' control. Thus, despite the thoroughness of local organisation in Fife, the miners saw the government as possessing a strategy which the national Union, often directionless and outmanoeuvred, did not. This tactical failure became highlighted from 18 June 1984 when some 10 000 pickets assembled at the Orgreave coking plant. It is this date which is most commonly identified as being the occasion when doubts became clarified into certainty. Despite local solidarities, outside Scotland the strike would be lost. One man describes the significance of Orgreave:

> The lads came back fra' Orgreave [knowing] that they werenae gaeing tae win, because they had put *all* o' their resources, all o' their forces intae one place at one time. They had gone tae various pickets like Ravenscraig and Hunterston, and whenever they turned-up there was ayeways mair police than them. And they were *ayeways* looking fur a victory, and they were *ayeways* being defeated. And they went tae Orgreave, and Arthur summoned his 'army', his 'Spartacus army o' peasants'! Fra' all over Britain. And the police had set it up. Orgreave was created *specifically* tae defeat them. Whereas on previous occasions they had been turning the buses *away*, closing the roads, they were saying, 'Come in, lads. Park yur bus there.' They were *welcoming* them in. And they set them up. An ambush. *Created*. They picked the time and the place tae inflict the defeat . . . [So] the lads came back fra' Orgreave *knowing*. They had gone there in high spirits, wi' buses fra' all over Britain. The Sco'ish miners, the Welsh miners and all the rest o' it. And it was Scargill's 'Saltley Gates'.

From this point the miners became more fully on the defensive. Whilst the strike was, by its nature, defensive in the sense of being to protect jobs and communities, while there was a hope of winning there had also been an assertive side to the strike. From Autumn onwards, however, the growing awareness of governmental opposition, public hostility and tactical failure led to the realisation of the inevitability of defeat. The legacy was falling apart. Yet all of the sample stayed out for the whole year despite this knowledge. One man describes how, in the last analysis it was blind hope and loyalty to each other and the Union that kept them motivated:

They lived in hope. One day the news would be guid and ye'd be up. The next day the news would be bad and ye'd be doon. And ye were like that through-oot the strike. Ye know, when NACODS come oot it looked as though [there'd be a break-through]. So ye lived in *hope* while yur be'er senses were telling ye, 'Ach, it's away. We've lost.' But ye lived in hope. Ye were *clinging* tae *hope*. Ye were clinging tae *loyalty*. Loyalty tae the Union. Loyalty tae yur fellows. But within ye, [ye knew].

By the end of the strike exhaustion and despondency had become widespread even among activists. For many, the last few months were simply going through the motions, waiting for the end. When it did come in many senses it was a relief. One communist recalls the last day:

Ah was si'ing in the Strike Centre and fur aboot the last twa months o' the strike it was impossible tae get onybody tae *talk* aboot the strike in the Strike Centre. Naebody wanted tae talk aboot it. *Didnae* want tae analyse what was happening. They were just gaeing through the motions. They didnae want tae *think* aboot what was inevitable. They *knew* the strike was lost. They had known that since before Christmas. Nae langer wanted tae *talk* aboot, tae *analyse* what was gaeing tae happen. Just waiting. We were si'ing in the Strike Centre when the announcement came over, and it was the twa things, the sense o' relief, *most* people were relieved it was over. Ah mean, they heaved a sigh o' relief. And ah dinnae think onybody said *onything* aifter that. They just wondered when and hoo they'd gae back.

On a national level the miners' strike was defeated. Faced with a divided membership responding differentially to a divisive issue, adopting outmoded tactics in a climate of industrial uncertainty, and confronted by a hostile Board and government it is improbable perhaps that it could have been otherwise. In such circumstances, the militancy of one small area is no longer of importance; it is the national level which counts on all major issues. Yet the local legacy was crucial in sustaining morale, and this may be seen most particularly in the aftermath when, whilst some have sunk into apathy and despair, others are still prepared to man the barricades. It is amongst those most fully integrated into the political and industrial significant history of the Fife miners that these latter may be found.

LIVING WITH DEFEAT

Although Fife as a whole was a solid area there is a great deal of difference to be found among the men since the strike. For many, the loss of faith most obviously relates to the defeat and resulting split in the Union. This is compounded by what is seen as a 'no-win' situation. British Coal is now seen as being in a position where it can, and is, imposing its own terms on the vanquished. It is felt that further industrial action would merely advance the opportunity to effect more closures. Losing the Frances due to fire on 4 February 1985, one month before the end of the strike, in August 1986 the announcement was made to close West Fife's remaining pit. The miners' fears for the future are enhanced by the local unemployment situation in the county. One 30-year-old communist Union official comments on the prevailing attitude among the rank and file:

> People are *scared* tae gae on strike noo. They're scared because they could be dismissed quite easily . . . . they're scared tae lose their jobs basically. Ah mean, the fact there's miners still dismissed aifter the strike, who've been dismissed fur the last twa yeas, is no' a threat tae they individual miners, it's a threat tae the rest o' us. If yoo step ootae line, yoo'll get that tae. . . . Plus, another thing tae, is that [the Tories] have decimated industry. We've lost so much o' oor manufacturing base that there's verra few places left.

The air of uncertainty and the perceived authoritarianism of management has served to disenchant many of the rank and file, who now wish to leave the industry. One official from Comrie, which was, in fact, closed shortly after the interview, states:

> . . . prior tae the strike, ah enjoyed ma wark. Ah liked the pit, ah just liked ma wark. But aifter it, the men are doon, like. There's just, ah cannae explain it, there's just the uncer'ainty o' what's happening tae us fur a stairt, ah think. Especially at Comrie. Everybody's wanting oot. They're wanting oot. They dinnae *want* tae stay in the industry. And it's just that naebody gives a shit, like. [The strike's] took the guts ootae us.

For some miners the atmosphere in the pits after the strike was such that they chose to leave the industry on the generous redundancy terms being offered to decrease the workforce, as they felt they could no longer remain. The bitterness and resentment had tarnished the pit. One 50-year-old explains why he left:

> Ah only warked twa days in the pit and it was twa days tae much. Och, ah couldnae wark wi' what was left. Just scab miners, ye know, them that broke the strike. And we no'iced right away that the management, it was a different a'itude wi' them, ken. There was nae negotiating, they were gaeing tae kick the ball. And ah just *couldnae* wark there because, tae be quite honest wi' ye, ah warked that monday night shift and there was a scab miner taunting me in the lamp cabin, on the surface before we went doon the pit that night. This one who was the leading scab in this area, he says, 'There's an awfy smell in here.' But he was *deliberately* taunting me because he kent he had the protection o' management and he was trying tae get me secked. And ah was gaeing tae smash his lamp back intae his face, ye ken. Ah was! But then ah kent what was happening. And there was another scab miner threatened me doon the pit. And ah came hame, and ah went tae ma bed and ah just told ma wife ah wasnae gaeing back, ken. And that was it.

Yet such demoralisation can be most readily perceived among those of the sample without clearly systematised political beliefs. It is among the politically unaligned that one can find sentiments such as that to be found in the following statement from a man in his 40s:

> We went back defeated, ye ken, and we got it intae oor heid that we lost the ba'le but no' the war. But me, as far as ah'm concerned, ah think the war is lost.

Among CP members, however, can be found a lesser disillusionment, for their world view more readily enabled them to transcend the post-strike depression. If anything, their experiences during the strike merely crystallised already formulated beliefs. It is among such men that we can see how the strike legitimised the legacy. One communist in his 50s sums this up:

> It didnae change ma views . . . . It *reinforced* what ah'd ayeways felt politically. Reinforced all the things ah'd been *fed* on since ah was a boy. The role o' the state, the role o' the police, the role o' the media, hoo people responded. What it was all aboot. It

reinforced everything that ah had ayeways believed in. That's what it did tae me.

Further it is among the communists and more left-wing of the Labour Party members that one can perceive both a greater awareness of the failings of the strike, and a preparedness to engage in such debates in order to re-establish a strong Union and, through this, morale. A statement from one young communist shows this continuing optimism:

> Well, the role o' the miners in the labour movement *noo* is the same as what it's ayeways been. The miners, tae me, had a number o' important principles that were close tae their hairts. No' just the fraterni'y o' the industry but everything that went *wi'* that. Obviously striving fur socialism, a ward that's sometimes looked doon on noo, and Thatcher's said she wants tae get rid o' it. So there's that principle o' socialism, that concept. There's also alot o' other things aboot *internationalism* wi' other people through-oot the warld. And all these sortae concepts that the labour movement had fur *years* were there because, no' just the miners, but mainly the miners, could *inject* they sortae things intae the labour movement. And the miners' Union could *still* dae that because although we took a hammering over one year, that daesnae mean tae say that the principles ye ayeways stood fur is *wrang*. And it's *injecting* that back intae the labour movement. We could still *dae* that.

For some, however, radicalism has been enhanced by the bitterness from the strike, and there is both a perception that conflict will return to the industry and a preparedness to engage in further conflict. Thus, whilst all the men interviewed said they would strike again, for some this was qualified, for others there was a greater willingness. One militant Labour Party member expresses this attitude well:

> Ah think the Coal Board, or British Coal as they call theirsel noo, are ge'ing rid o' alot o' men, but what they're gaeing tae be left wi', and ah don't think they've realised, is a haird-core o'militant miners. Because it's no' every miner that wants oot. And ah think they're gaeing tae make a stick tae break their ain back. We'll be kicked, ah mean, we're kicked the noo, but ye'll only take so

much, and we'll be back. We'll come back again. . . . Ah would dae it again. Ah would dae it again. Ah would dae it again. Tomorrow. Ah've got tae fight fur this industry fur ma son.

CONCLUSION

It has been argued that the historical legacy of the Fife miners played a crucial role in the 1984–85 strike. Located within a region which has displayed a strong commitment to radical activity over time, contemporary miners were able to draw upon this both subjectively, in the instilling of identify and framing of meaning in which to comprehend events, and practically, to order their response to the year-long dispute. Yet whilst this was a source of strength it also had a negative side in that, beguiled by past visions of strength, they had failed to see a disjuncture between the fixed nature of the radical discourse and the changing nature of reality.

When faced with current actuality it proved hard to sustain radicalism in the face of contemporary objective conditions. The declining strength of the miners, and the inability of traditional support systems to withstand the opposing forces highlighted contradictions within the legacy. When historically-proven tactics failed to ensure victory many miners were left both directionless and bewildered. Such continuing commitment as can be found is among those whose systematised political world views meant they were better able to withstand the assaults upon them, and who were able to emerge from the struggle with the will to continue battered but in tact. It is among such men that we can see how the legacy still acted to provide a crucial basis for morale and understanding; by enabling them to maintain a sense of order and identity in the chaos.

However, this is not an unqualified statement for they too have been subject to the doubts and ambiguities induced by the current situation within their industry. These conclusions, therefore, may help enlighten broader understandings as to the nature, and means, of subjective understandings, for, if radical workers have found it difficult to sustain motivation and take action, this poses questions for more general explanations on working-class consciousness.

The Fife miners are not typical of miners as a whole, the strength of their opposition clearly displays that, as, indeed, the miners are not typical of the British workforce as a whole. What is, therefore, of interest is that, if it is hard to sustain political radicalism in an area traditionally militant, there are consequent implications for the wider working class. More manifestly, it shows that in a society in which major change occurs at a higher structural level, the radicalism of one group or area is little able to affect wider social, political or industrial change. In such circumstances it becomes easier to comprehend the underlying fragility of a militant stance.

This does not mean, however, that industrial change must necessarily spell the end of such a tradition. In relation to the Fife miners, as more men leave the pits, political activists are beginning to move out into the communities and are attempting to establish a wider communal base in their new undertakings. Thus, although the effectiveness of the legacy in providing the means to attempt to direct and control their lives has been weakened, the embedded nature of the radical tradition within the locality, and its activities at the local level, are continuing to enable the legacy to perpetuate, albeit on a different material base, as the industry continues to decline.

NOTES

1. Both of these orientations can be found within J. Foster, *Class Struggle and the Industrial Revolution* (London: Methuen, 1974) which not only offers a simplistic account of the orientations of the Oldham working class in the nineteenth century due to his determination to locate events within a Marxist-Leninist approach, but which also, despite an analysis over time, fails to account adequately for the changing nature of subjective understandings.
2. The sample was constructed in order to indicate key factors of difference between radical and non-radical orientations. To this end, 40 miners were placed along a radical/non-radical continuum. The non-radical section comprised nine politically-unaligned men who were used as a 'bench-mark' against which to assess the particularity of the radical section, which included both CP and Labour Party members. However, it must be remembered that the term 'non-radical' is a relative one. Such men were non-radical by comparison with the radical section but, in other areas or industries (Nottingham, for example), such men may well be regarded as militants.
3. See, for example, P. Abrams, *Historical Sociology* (Shepton Mallet: Open Books, 1982); R. Williams, *Marxism and Literature* (Oxford: Oxford University Press, 1977); Z. Bauman, *Memories of Class: The Pre-History and After-Life of Class* (London: Routledge & Kegan Paul, 1982).

4. A. Heller, *A Theory of History* (London: Routledge, 1982).
5. C. Tilly, '19th Century Origins of our 20th Century Collective Action Repertoire', *CRSO Working Paper*, no. 244, Michigan, September, 1981.
6. Whilst it is clearly difficult to establish exact figures on the return to work, these percentages are based on estimates given by a range of local and national NUM, SCEBTA, COSA and BACM officials.
7. S. Najam, 'The "Winning" of the Eight-Hour Day: An Historical Analysis of the Origins of Militancy among the Fife Miners', Edinburgh: unpublished paper, 1986, argues that the Fife miners were not, indeed, the first to win the eight-hour day. Historical documentation from the period is in clear disagreement with the arguments put forward by R. Page Arnot, *The History of the Scottish Miners* (London: Unwin Brothers, 1955) to this effect. It would appear that Page Arnot's argument may be based on a misrepresentation of a letter written by Fife Union leader, Davie Proudfoot, to Allen Hutt in London and to which Page Arnot would have had access. This letter is reprinted in I. MacDougall (ed.), *Militant Miners* (Edinburgh: Polygon, 1981). However, this belief is widely held by the Fife miners and referred to frequently to assert their historical militancy. In this sense, objective truth is of less importance than what the miners believe, and its consequences for identity.
8. S. F. MacIntyre, *Little Moscows: Communism and Working-Class Militancy in Inter-War Britian* (London: Croom Helm, 1980).

10 History and Sociology in the New Economic Sociology: A Discourse in Search of a Method

Roger Penn

This chapter involves a critical examination of the articulation of historical and sociological modes of analysis within what has come to be called the 'new economic sociology'. It will demonstrate that the use of historical data within many of the best-known and best-respected texts in this field is both casual and tendentious. Such conclusions raise serious questions about the capacity of contemporary sociologists to utilise historical material in a satisfactory way.

THE CONTEXT: THE HISTORICISATION OF SOCIO-LOGICAL DISCOURSE

There can be little doubt that sociological discourse underwent a profound shift between the mid-1960s and the latter 1970s both in Britain and elsewhere in advanced societies. The earlier period was dominated by the trans-historical theoretical approaches associated with structural-functionalism and specifically with the works of Talcott Parsons. In this mode of analysis an attempt was made to discover the essential structures of any social system in the same way as economics, in its neo-classical form, had uncovered the basic parameters of all market-based economic systems. Structural-functionalism was felt to be impressive both in terms of its abstraction and of its universal applicability. Although conflict theorists in Britain like Lockwood (1956) and Dahrendorf (1959) raised serious objections to the assumptions of Parsonian universalism in the late 1950s, it was the dominant theoretical stance in Western sociology by the early 1960s.

However, over the next 15 years or so, sociology in Britain became more and more historical in its orientation, although in a rather peculiar and partial way. At the theoretical level, the works of Marx and Weber and, to a lesser extent, Durkheim, were used increasingly to demonstrate the historical specificity of contemporary society. The political events of the 1960s – the failure of the Wilson Labour governments, student radicalism and increasing worker militancy – helped to reinforce this theoretical shift. Sociologists increasingly became aware of at least some historical analyses and incorporated them into their own discourse. However, these readings were generally selective and highly partial. For example, most sociologists had grasped Thompson's *Making of the English Working Class* (1963), and Hobsbawm's writings on the aristocracy of labour (1964), but few seemed to be aware of the criticisms of either position. Here we witness a tendency that has become pronounced in the 1980s of accepting certain historical arguments as 'given' and as bench-marks against which sociologists can examine contemporary social change.

In the cases of Thompson and Hobsbawm, a recognition of the partial nature of their arguments and the debates surrounding their historical interpretations of the British working class can be dramatic. For instance, if Thompson failed to demonstrate the existence of a working class by the 1830s, when did it come into being? Indeed, under what conditions can we talk about a working class at all in social science? Put baldly, if there has never been a working class in Britain over the last two hundred years, then why, as is currently fashionable in left-wing political discourse, should one discuss its current demise? Now, I am not saying that there is or there is not a working class at the moment, but what I *am* suggesting is that there is no reason to assume that there was one in the 1830s because one historian has suggested there might have been. Indeed, as I argued in my book, *Skilled Workers in the Class Structure* (1985), one of the paradoxes of the articulation of the notions of the 'traditional' working class and the 'labour aristocracy' in sociological images of the British working class is that they mutually contradict one another. For instance, Hoggart (1959), Lockwood (1960) and Anderson (1965) all discussed the homogeneous working class of the interwar years. Foster (1976) and Roberts (1971), on the other hand, emphasised the sectionalism of the British working class during exactly the same period. Similarly, Dahrendorf (1964 and 1980) suggested that the postwar period was witnessing an increasing differentiation of the class structures of advanced societies, whereas Hobsbawm (1981) can find a homogeneous working class in the 1950s and 1960s and laments the increasing sectionalism of the 1970s. Such confusions indicate considerable conceptual and empirical muddle, but more critically they reveal a profound naivety about the nature of historical science and a major failure to incorporate one of its essential characteristics – the contested nature of historical interpretation. Indeed, the use of selective historical referents involves a profound misunderstanding of the nature of historical science. Historical science does not consist of the establishment of a set of facts that sociologists can trawl at will for data that supports a preconceived, so-called 'theoretical' scheme. Such a mistaken view is not even positivistic, since no positivist ever claimed such a position for historical accounts. Historical science involves a series of debates, classic examples of which are the debates about the causes of the French Revolution, the standard of living of the British working class prior to 1850 or the class nature of the seventeenth-century English Civil War. These debates are essentially matrices in which a wide range of theoretical positions are present and in which the evidence presented is never unproblematic. Sociologists who enter this terrain without such an orientation will select the evidence that they want to fit their preconceived 'theoretical' abstractions and their accounts will be still-born.

THE NEW ECONOMIC SOCIOLOGY OR HOW NOT TO PROCEED

The 'New Economic Sociology' was a term coined to encompass the works of radical economic sociologists like Braverman, Edwards, Gordon and Reich. These authors, in a series of texts, have recast the shape of industrial sociology over the last 15 years or so. These writers' texts represent critical moments in the genealogy of contemporary economic sociology. Writers as diverse as Thompson (1983) and Rose (1988) regard these texts as central to modern accounts of work and stratification. In this part of the chapter I will examine their historical 'method' and seek to show that their approaches are cavalier and selective. In a strange admixture of theoreticism and crypto-positivism, they select historical data to fit their preconceived, *a priori* schemes. By so doing, they present clear examples of how not to integrate sociology and history.

Braverman's 'Labor and Monopoly Capital'

Here, I shall not attempt to summarise Braverman's theoretical stance or his argument in its entirety. I shall focus rather on how he marshalls his empirical evidence to support his thesis that skilled work is being eliminated in modern capitalist societies. The bulk of the empirical support for his claims is to be found in Chapter 9 of *Labor and Monopoly Capital* – the chapter entitled 'Machinery'. The argument can be summarised as follows.

Braverman suggests that developments in automated machinery provide the opportunity for management to achieve control through mechanical means. The main example provided involves the utilisation of numerical control-units on machine tools. Prior to the development of electronically-based control systems, which are both cheap and reliable, most metalworking had remained the sphere of skilled machinists. According to Braverman, numerical control leads to the progressive deskilling of machinists as their skills are increasingly embodied in computerised control repertoires that have been produced elsewhere by technical specialists. The skilled machinist is rendered obsolete by the processes of subdivision of work outlined above. Braverman then proceeds to suggest that the same processes have been at work in a range of other occupational milieux which have been the traditional preserve of skilled craftsmen – boilermaking, heavy plate construction, sheetmetal shops, construction work, baking, furniture production, meatpacking, clothing and typesetting. Furthermore, computerisation also leads to the progressive elimination of maintenance skills with the increasing emergence of self-diagnostic maintenance routines. The net result of all these trends is that there is a decreasing need for either production or maintenance skills amongst manual workers in the USA.

However, this use of a supposed typical occupation plus a series of *etcetera* clauses is highly dubious as an explanatory procedure. It is as if one used the handloom weaver as the exemplar occupation for characterising the industrial revolution. As I demonstrated in my 1986 article entitled 'Where have all the craftsmen gone?', only two of the major skilled manual occupations in the USA witnessed falling numbers in the period between 1950 and 1970 – machinists and compositors. Of the others, many, such as electricians and pipefitters, increased much faster than the overall growth of the labour force (see Tables 10.1 and 10.2 and Figure 10.1). Of even greater

TABLE 10.1   *Occupational Change in the USA, 1940–80 (percentages)*

	1940	1950	1960	1970	1980
Professional	7.3	8.5	10.7	11.6	11.8
Managerial	8.2	8.6	7.9	8.1	10.0
Clerical	16.6	12.1	14.1	17.8	29.6
Craftsmen	11.1	13.8	13.5	13.9	13.0
Operatives	18.2	19.9	18.8	17.9	19.2
Labourers	6.9	6.5	5.1	4.8	
Farmers	11.3	7.3	3.7	1.8	2.9
Farm labourers	6.9	4.2	2.4	1.3	
Service workers	6.0	7.6	8.5	11.3	13.1
Domestic servants	4.7	2.5	2.6	1.5	

N	45.1 million	57.6 million	64.3 million	79.7 million	104 million

SOURCES   Decennial Censuses of US Population.

TABLE 10.2   *Trends in Craft Work in the USA, 1940–80 (absolute numbers)*

Occupation	1940	1950	1960	1970	1980
Carpenters	558 313	985 443	923 837	921 848	1 305 868
Painters: construction and maintenance	322 159	431 109	416 040	359 462	422 470
Machinists	609 773	533 726	515 532	390 184	510 699
Millwrights		60 193	67 876	81 025	134 076
Toolmakers		156 992	186 602	206 775	193 890
Electricians	197 222	324 046	355 522	482 763	625 813
Plumbers and pipefitters	173 915	295 990	331 012	398 159	502 004
Welders	124 741	275 545	386 622	565 505	791 028
Compositors and typesetters	158 072	178 696	182 937	162 504	70 515
Mechanics and repairmen	863 731	1 767 618	2 300 690	2 502 995	3 982 515

SOURCES   Same as table 10.1

embarrassment to the Braverman thesis, as is clear from Figure 10.1, machinists increased quite dramatically between 1970 and 1980.

I am not suggesting that these data are unproblematic – far from it! However, such data are widely available and suggest a complex pattern to the evolution of skilled manual work in modern America. What comes as perhaps no surprise is that sociologists have focussed

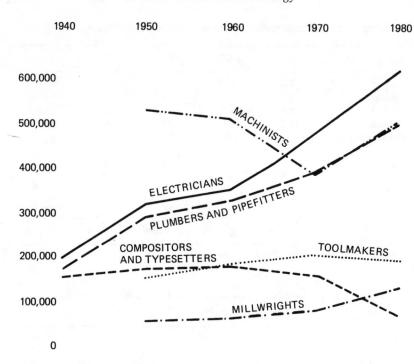

SOURCE *Table 10.2.*

FIGURE 10.1 *A Graph of Occupational Trends in the USA, 1940–80, for Selected Craft Jobs*

considerable attention on the two least typical skilled manual occupations – machinists (see Burawoy, 1979, Noble, 1977 and 1984, Jones, 1982, Hartmann et al., 1983, and Duhm and Muckenberger, 1983) and compositors (see Zimbalist, 1981, Rogers and Friedman, 1980, Martin, 1981, Wallace and Kalleberg, 1982, and Cockburn, 1983). On the other hand, groups like electricians, pipefitters or plumbers have received significantly less occupational analysis. Such selectivity is highly damaging to rigorous empirical inquiry.

Braverman demonstrates clearly how *not* to conduct research into skilled work in modern conditions. His method involves the construction of a complex conceptual architecture that is supported by recourse to examples that fit the argument. He makes *no* attempt to look for counter-examples, which, as has been demonstrated, abound. His style is *ex cathedra*, his claims immense, but his evidence is weak in the extreme. The question that must be raised is why so many sociologists have been impressed by these arguments and why many still fail to admit that their emperor really had no clothes. It is my belief that it is the general lack of either historical training, historical skills or even much in the way of common sense that is endemic within the institutional nexus of contemporary sociology that accounts for this state of affairs.

Edwards' 'Contested Terrain'

Edwards' *Contested Terrain: The Transformation of the Workplace in the Twentieth Century* (1979) manages to make Braverman's use of data look masterful! The argument purports to demonstrate how traditional patterns of personalised managerial control in the nineteenth century were superseded by new forms of 'structural' control in the twentieth century. The first form of 'structural' control, according to Edwards, is termed 'technical' and involves the situation where the worker is controlled by the physical arrangement of technology. Edwards clearly has the automobile industry in mind here. However, this type of domination, according to Edwards, produces new contradictions – industrial unionism in particular – and a new form of control emerges. This is labelled 'bureaucratic' control and describes the situation where control is embedded in 'work rules, promotion procedures, discipline, wage scales, definition of responsibilities, and the like'.

Edwards' analysis proceeds to fit evidence into this procrustean bed. A series of large firms – GM, Ford, IBM, GE, International Harvester and Polaroid – are used to illustrate the abstract scheme. The reasons why these firms are selected is never revealed in the text nor any indication given as to their representativeness. Furthermore, Edwards does not seem to have much of a grasp of the empirical developments of the American workforce in the twentieth century. For example, he claims that both technical and bureaucratic control strategies were a response to workers' struggles. Indeed, as a neo-Marxist account 'class struggles' *must* be given such a position of prominence. However, Edwards does not demonstrate this specific link which is so critical to his argument. For instance, meatpacking and electrical products manufacture, which were both industries in the forefront of mechanised forms of control (see Brody, 1964,

Schatz, 1985), were not in the vanguard of labour struggles prior to the introduction of mechanisation and an intense division of labour. Indeed, the most militant industries, such as coal mining (see Bernstein, 1960) or metalworking (see Haydu, 1984 and 1988) did not experience technical control strategies in the period before 1940. Likewise, the embryonic computer industry or the film industry were not great fields of labour conflict during World War II. Indeed, it would appear more plausible to suggest that innovations in control strategies have occurred more often in quiescent rather than militant industries throughout the twentieth century in America.

However, Edwards' approach is not based upon an evaluation of competing theories, still less upon a cautious approach to his sources of information. Again and again he presents evidence as self-evident and as capable thereby of clinching his *a priori* schemes. Such a non-interpretative sociology has no place in modern academic discourse.

Gordon, Edwards and Reich's *Segmented Work, Divided Workers*

If Edwards' *Contested Terrain* offers a peculiar method of analysis, Gordon, Edwards and Reich's *Segmented Work, Divided Workers* can only be described as bizarre. Abstractionism is allowed full play in this text, almost completely untrammelled by such recalcitrant features as adequate supporting data. The argument has, of course, the virtue of being clear. We are presented with a 'unified theory' of the development of the American working class. The authors suggest that there have been three cycles to this development. The first, from the early nineteenth century to the 1890s, is labelled 'initial proletarianization'. In this epoch workers enter into waged labour but this work remains 'untransformed'. In other words, there is a 'formal' but not a 'real' subordination of labour. In the second phase from the late nineteenth century to the 1930s, employers are held by the authors to have secured this real subordination and thereby reduced jobs to a common deskilled condition and produced an homogeneous working class. This period of 'homogenisation' is succeeded in the post-World War II era by a period of 'segmentation', wherein the workforce is divided into a primary segment of autonomous, well-paid, self-directed workers and a secondary segment of repetitive, poorly paid, heavily-controlled workers.

Each of these cycles further involves three internal phases – exploration, consolidation and decay. In majestic dialectical fashion each period of working-class life is linked to 'long swings' in the economic system which determine the processes of transformation outlined. Many may admire such a wonderful theory but, sad to relate, it does not seem to correspond to empirical data. As Brody (1984) has shown in his magisterial review of their claims, 'the authors have not established a full mastery of the events that they are describing. Beyond that, suspicion begins to mount that they have been swept up in a game of brainstorming, so that, in the end, if the facts do not square with the theory, so much the worse for the facts' (p. 703).

Two examples should suffice to reveal the poverty of their method. Firstly, Gordon, Edwards and Reich pronounce that the period from 1873 to 1899 was one of 'stagnation'. This is a dictate of their theory and allegedly based on empirical data. However, total commodity output in the United States increased by 54 per cent per decade between 1869 and 1899 which is 5 per cent higher than the overall average for all decades between 1839 and 1899 (data cited by Brody, 1984, and taken from Gallman, 1960). Brody's review produces a series of similar pieces of data that reveal the *a priori* selectivity of the authors' use of data. They also argue that immigrants to the United States in the nineteenth century 'tended mainly to expand the ranks of those doing unskilled work' (Gordon, Edwards and Reich, p. 74). However, as various US Censuses have revealed, immigrants from Europe were critical for the development of the new skills generated throughout the nineteenth century (see A. Edwards, *Population: Comparative Occupation Statistics for the United States, 1870 to 1940* (US Government Printing Office, Washington, 1943, and Penn, 1989). This is a critical area since it suggests a pervasive division within the American working class around the axis of skill which is associated with ethnic divisions (see Mackenzie, 1973, and Form, 1976 and 1985). However, if such a divide is a persistent feature of the pattern of social stratification within the American working class throughout the *longue durée* of industrial capitalism, the heuristic advantages of Gordon, Edwards and Reich's complex conceptual architectonics become nugatory.

CONCLUSIONS

This chapter has been highly critical of some of the central texts within the new economic sociology. These books represent a style of sociological analysis that has to be challenged. In particular, this combination of so-called 'theory' and evidence is a disastrous example of how to integrate historical analysis within sociology. The great strength of historical science is its experience in the use of evidence. These skills appear to be in short supply within the contemporary sociological profession. Recently, the discipline has been challenged for its failure in Britain to develop satisfactory advanced quantitative research methods. This is, for the most part, a fair criticism. However, my own view is that this problem merely reflects a more general crisis within contemporary sociology wherein there is an endemic failure to develop theoretical arguments within rigorous empirical analysis.

There are, of course, many examples of successful analyses which link sociology and history within contemporary economic sociology. The papers by Bradley and Fevre reprinted in this collection offer a far more rigorous integration of evidence and theoretical development than the texts which have been criticised in this chapter. However, the evidence is that the latter texts hold the higher ground within contemporary economic sociology. Until they are dislodged and there is a general recognition of the need for extensive historical research on the part of sociologists, we cannot be sanguine about the link between historical and sociological reasoning in the contemporary analysis of society.

REFERENCES

P. Anderson, 'Origins of the Present Crisis' in P. Anderson and R. Blackburn (eds), *Towards Socialism* (London: Collins, 1965).
I. Bernstein, *The Lean Years: A History of the American Worker 1920–1933* (New York: Houghton Mifflin, 1960).
H. Braverman, *Labor and Monopoly Capital: The Degradation of Work in the Twentieth Century* (New York: Monthly Review Press, 1974).
D. Brody, *The Butcher Workmen: A Study of Unionization* (Cambridge, Mass.: Harvard University Press, 1964).
D. Brody, 'Review of *Segmented Work, Divided Workers*' in *Journal of Interdisciplinary History*, XIV, 3, Winter, 1984.
M. Burawoy, *Manufacturing Consent: Changes in the Labor Process under Monopoly Capitalism* (Chicago: University of Chicago Press, 1979).
C. Cockburn, *Brothers: Male Dominance and Technological Change* (London: Pluto Press, 1983).

R. Dahrendorf, *Class and Class Conflict in Industrial Society* (Stanford: Stanford University Press, 1959).

R. Dahrendorf, 'Recent Changes in the Class Structure of European Societies', *Daedalus*, Winter 1964.

R. Dahrendorf, 'Twenty-Five Years of Socio-Political Analysis: Notes and Reflections', *Government and Opposition*, 15, 3/4, 1980.

R. Duhm and U. Muckenburger, 'Computerization and Control Strategies at Plant Level', *Policy Studies*, 3, 4, 1983.

R. Edwards, *Contested Terrain: The Transformation of the Workplace in the Twentieth Century* (New York: Basic Books, 1979).

W. Form, *Blue-Collar Stratification: Auto Workers in Four Countries* (Princeton: Princeton University Press, 1976).

W. Form, *Divided We Stand: Working Class Stratification in America* (Urbana: University of Illinois Press, 1985).

J. Foster, 'British Imperialism and the Labour Aristocracy' in J. Skelley (ed.), *The General Strike* (London: Lawrence & Wishart, 1976).

R. Gallman,'Commodity Output, 1839–1899' in National Bureau of Economic Research, *Trends in the American Economy in the Nineteenth Century* (Princeton: Harvard University Press, 1960).

D. Gordon, R. Edwards and M. Reich, *Segmented Work, Divided Workers* (Cambridge: Cambridge University Press, 1982).

G. Hartmann, I. Nicholas and M. Warner, 'Computerized Machine Tools, Manpower Consequences and Skill Utilization', *British Journal of Industrial Relations*, XXI, 2, July, 1983.

J. Haydu, 'British and American Solutions for the "Labor Problem": Employer Strategies in the Metal Trades, 1898–1901', Paper presented to the Annual Meeting of the Pacific Sociological Association, Seattle, 1984.

J. Haydu, *Between Craft and Class* (Berkeley: University of California Press, 1988).

E. Hobsbawm, *Labouring Men* (London: Weidenfeld, 1964).

E. Hobsbawm, 'The Forward March of Labour Halted?' in E. Hobsbawm and M. Jacques (eds) *The Forward March of Labour Halted?* (London: Verso, 1981).

R. Hoggart, *The Uses of Literacy* (Harmondsworth: Penguin, 1959).

B. Jones, 'Destruction or Redistribution of Engineering Skills? The Case of Numerical Control' in S. Wood (ed.), *The Degradation of Work* (London: Hutchinson, 1982).

D. Lockwood, 'Some Remarks on the "Social System" ', *British Journal of Sociology*, 7, 1956.

D. Lockwood, 'The "New Working Class" ', *European Journal of Sociology*, 1, 2, 1960.

G. Mackenzie, *The Aristocracy of Labor: The Position of Skilled Craftsmen in the American Class Structure* (Cambridge: Cambridge University Press, 1973).

R. Martin, *New Technology and Industrial Relations in Fleet Street* (Oxford: Clarendon Press, 1981).

D. Noble, *America By Design: Science, Technology and the Rise of Corporate Capitalism* (Oxford: Oxford University Press, 1977).

D. Noble, *Forces of Production: A Social History of Industrial Automation*

(New York: Alfred Knopf, 1984).

R. D. Penn, *Skilled Workers in the Class Structure* (Cambridge: Cambridge University Press, 1985).

R. D. Penn, 'Where Have All the Craftsmen Gone? Trends in Skilled Labor in the United States of America since 1940', *British Journal of Sociology* XXXVII, 4, December 1986.

R. D. Penn, *Class, Power and Technology: Skilled Workers in Britain and America* (Oxford: Polity Press, 1989).

R. Roberts, *The Classic Slum* (Manchester: Manchester University Press, 1971).

T. Rogers and N. Friedman, *Printers Face Automation* (Lexington, Mass.: D. C. Heath, 1980).

M. Rose, *Industrial Behaviour* (2nd edn) (Harmondsworth: Penguin, 1988).

R. W. Schatz, *The Electrical Workers: A History of Labor at General Electric and Westinghouse 1923–60* (Urbana: University of Illinois Press, 1985).

E. P. Thompson, *The Making of the English Working Class* (London: Gollancz, 1963).

P. Thompson, *The Nature of Work* (London: Macmillan, 1983).

M. Wallace and A. Kalleberg, 'Industrial Transformation and the Decline of Craft: The Decomposition of Skill in the Printing Industry, 1931–1978', *American Sociological Review*, 47, 3, 1982.

A. Zimbalist, 'Technology and the Labor Process in the Printing Industry', in A. Zimbalist (ed), *Case Studies on the Labor Process* (New York: Monthly Review Press, 1981).

11 Change and Continuity in History and Sociology: The Case of Industrial Paternalism
Harriet Bradley

'The past is a foreign country; they do things differently there.'

INTRODUCTION

To some extent this chapter is a challenge to L. P. Hartley's dictum, cited above. It is, of course, quite true that people behaved differently in the past and that they acted under different meanings and motivations. This is, in part, what makes the study of history so exciting; at times the historian feels much the same way as a social anthropologist confronted with a new civilisation and its (as yet quite incomprehensible) culture. However, it is also the case that people do things the same in the past. This is not to make claims for the existence of any underlying structure of human motivation or universal meanings-system; it is simply to imply that forms of behaving and thinking are passed on from generation to generation, embedded in the culture and built into the structures of institutions. It is for this reason that the sociologist can enter the terrain of history; and it is for this reason, too, that she *must* do so if she is to comprehend fully the persistence of these culturally embedded and structurally inbuilt forms of behaviour and thought.

In the following pages I have tried to elaborate an example of the benefits of an historical approach within sociology, following the example of Philip Abrams (1982). My basic argument is that historical and sociological methods are complementary; and by using the example of a certain type of industrial practice I have tried to show

177

how historical and sociological methods, each taken alone, may lead to an imperfect understanding of the phenomenon under study, in this case to an underestimation of its extent and persistence. The industrial practice is that of paternalism, which I studied as part of my research into the East Midlands hosiery industry (Bradley, 1987).

Industrial paternalism, rather in the same way as the extended family, is always being diagnosed by historians and sociologists as doomed and dying. Where cases of it are discovered it tends to be seen as an anachronistic relic, soon to be swept away by the inevitable course of industrial development, bureaucracy and rationalisation. This is in part due to the way it is often linked to dichotomous models of social development of the kind so usefully and critically surveyed by Kumar in 'Prophecy and Progress' (1978). Paternalism (again like the extended family) is seen as part of the 'old order' of society, 'traditional', 'feudal' or whatever label is employed; the tendencies associated with the modernisation of society, in particular that broad spectrum of changes referred to as 'rationalisation' by Weber, will be structurally incompatible with it, leading assuredly to its redundancy and demise. Yet paternalism (like the extended family) has obstinately refused to die. Indeed, it is my claim that it is a healthy and vital part of contemporary industrial life, although its existence has been largely disregarded by industrial relations experts and its social significance is therefore little recognised.

My own study of industrial relations in hosiery over the past two centuries revealed a long-standing and continuing tradition of paternalism in the locality, although the nature of practices and strategies used by 'paternalist' employers had changed over the period under study. This led me to develop a typology of different forms of paternalism, which are likely to be found in differing social and historical contexts. In the remainder of this chapter, I start by outlining what historians and sociologists have said about paternalism and the problems of method which characteristically arise. I then go on to present my typology to illustrate how a combined historical/ sociological approach may surmount these problems and deficiencies. Next I make some general points about the survival of paternalism and its sociological significance, concluding with a brief comment on the prospects for a historical sociology.

STUDYING PATERNALISM: THE HISTORICAL APPROACH

As is to be expected, historians have tended to see paternalism as a phenomenon specific to particular times and places. For example, E. P. Thompson has written extensively about paternalism in the eighteenth century, seeing it as an intrinsic part of the old 'moral economy' which was about to be superseded by the 'rationality' of market-based capitalism, backed up by utilitarian political economy and the ethic of individualism. In the eighteenth century and the early decades of the nineteenth, paternalism was espoused by both working people and the landed classes (aristocracy and gentry) in a (basically vain) attempt to counter the rising social power of the class of capitalist entrepreneurs, the poor appealing to the old order for justice and protection, the rich evoking its connotations of social responsibility and community (Thompson, 1971, 1978). A similar perspective is employed in David Roberts' fine study 'Paternalism in Early Victorian England' (1978). For Roberts, paternalism is essentially an ideology,[1] involving an organicist vision of an orderly and hierarchical society, in which the nexus of relations between the ranks or classes is founded on the basis of certain reciprocal rights and duties. Thus, the duty of the rich is to rule, guide and help the poor, the duty of the poor to obey, be grateful and offer deference. Like Thompson, Roberts regards this as the vision of the old aristocratic order, now in decline, but he argues that it was to some extent regenerated in an attempt to deal with the social dislocation brought about by industrialisation. This regeneration, however, could only be carried out by industrial employers in certain circumstances. Its classic location was the isolated rural 'factory village' (in Lancashire and Derbyshire, for example) where employing families were able to involve themselves in all aspects of the employees' lives, dealing thus with the 'whole man' (and woman); the lavish care and provision of such employers was expensive and beyond the reach of the mass of smaller competitors; thus, as industrial capitalism established itself as a mass and typically urban phenomenon (from about 1850), Roberts argues that paternalism began to die out.

This view is challenged, however, in Patrick Joyce's book *Work, Society and Politics*; far from paternalism dying out in the 1850s, Joyce argues that, in Lancashire at least, it achieved its classic flowering after the collapse of Chartism, as factory owners used it to reconcile their employees to the harsh industrial environment and to rekindle a sense of community. This was accomplished by incorporating family and community into factory life, often by utilising family employment and recruitment systems; the appeal to family loyalties was a major part of its success. For example, elaborate celebrations and rituals marked major biographical events in the employer's family (a son coming of age, a marriage). Joyce concludes that, rather than being antipathetic to paternalism as Roberts had maintained, the urban environment became its 'chief seat' in the late Victorian period; 'industrial paternalism was both pervasive and succesful' (Joyce, 1980, pp. 136, 154).

From these three examples, we can see that the historian's method of concentrating on a particular time and period holds the danger of seeing a phenomenon as the privileged product of that time and place *alone* (which must then demonstrate all the necessary preconditions for the phenomenon's existence). Thus, apparent contradictions between the accounts of Roberts and Joyce (paternalism as rural or as urban phenomenon, as an organicist or familial ideology and so on) could be resolved by tracing the way in which the forms, practices and ideologies of paternalism vary in response to change in the social, economic and intellectual environment, To do this would, of course, involve employing a broader time perspective than is generally favoured by historians and emphasising continuities rather than the discontinuities emphasised by Thompson, Roberts and Joyce. Sociology might seem admirably well placed to do this.

TYPOLOGISING PATERNALISM: SOCIOLOGICAL APPROACHES

Obviously, the way in which sociologists approach the analysis of a phenomenon such as paternalism is different from that of historians. Rather than developing a narrative account of particular instances, their concern is to specify the conditions under which such a phenomenon can (or cannot) emerge. This objective may be achieved by adopting a markedly historical approach focussing on particular periods. Howard Newby's writings on paternalism, for example, are carefully grounded in historical investigation. His conclusions bear some similarities to those of Roberts; for Newby, too, paternalistic relationships are more compatible with the rural environment, and in the twentieth century paternalism and its other half (the deferential response) are most likely to linger on in agricultural communities, where farmers are in close personal contact with their 'deferential workers' (Newby, 1979). In the urban context, too, Newby tends to equate paternalism with face to face relationships; his argument is that the development of large-scale industrial enterprises and impersonal, bureaucratic systems is inimical to the particularistic paternalism characteristic of the employee/employer relationship in early capitalist enterprises, which took their model from the Puritan household. This again bears resemblances to Roberts' account, except that for Newby *small* firms rather than *large* ones are the typical users of paternalism. This is because Newby's core emphasis is on personal links rather on expenditure on care and welfare provision. The conclusion is that the modern industrial environment is not conducive to paternalism (Newby, 1977).

A similar conclusion is reached by Abercrombie and Hill, who, however, employ a more classically 'sociological' strategy in their study of paternalism, attempting to construct ideal types of patronage and paternalism. In the resultant model, the idea of concern for the 'whole man' (or woman) is central; for them, paternalism is a form of social organisation which hinges on the ideology of personal care and which transcends the naked economism of the cash nexus. The paternalist employer continues to feel concern for employees after they have left the factory gates. Thus, the course of industrial development, with its inexorable push to increased enterprise size and bureaucratic impersonality (vide Marx and Weber), threatens paternalism. Unlike Roberts and Newby, however, they conceive that its continuation is possible even in a large and bureaucratised firm, if impersonality is overlaid by an ideology of personal care and a collective provision for employee welfare. This, Abercrombie and Hill maintain, has been the case in postwar Japan, where the paternalistic relations of early capitalist development have been strengthened rather than weakened by the policies of the great corporations. Thus, as well as extensive welfare provision (including the provision of company housing for married and dormitory quarters for single workers), Japanese firms like Hitachi and Nissan may involve themselves considerably in the family life of their employees.[2] However, Abercrombie and Hill argue that in most other countries (notably Britain and America) the ideology of personal care is no more than lip service and therefore many firms which have been rather sloppily labelled 'paternalist' by industrial sociologists are in fact nothing of the kind; their involvement with their employees is strictly limited to the cash nexus (Abercrombie and Hill, 1976).

It is certainly the case that the term is often rather casually used in case studies of modern firms without due attention to explaining exactly what is implied by its use; paternalism is often assumed rather than defined. In the East Midlands context, two interesting and very different studies of hosiery firms (Edwards and Scullion, 1982, Westwood, 1984) use the word to describe the management practice and control strategies observed by the researchers. But no specific definition is provided in either case. Alan Fox is one industrial sociologist who *has* provided us with a typology of management styles and practices which includes paternalism. For Fox, as for Roberts, the key to the understanding of paternalism is ideology, in this case what he calls a 'unitary' ideology, that is, the belief in the identity of interests of employers and employees. Fox distinguishes between two forms of paternalism – 'traditional', in which management and workers both hold the unitary view, and 'modern' or 'sophisticated' paternalism, in which management espouse a pluralist perspective (competing but reconcilable interests) while workers cling to unitarism (Fox, 1964). Such an account does not, I think, stand up to empirical investigation. However, the important step taken by Fox is to distinguish *two* forms of paternalism, which in some sense are historically successive; this offers us a way to explore the survival of paternalism, albeit in changed form, within a late capitalist industrial environment.

Sociologists' accounts, then, hold up the *possibility* of looking at continuities of paternalism and its persistence beyond a single time and place. However, the characteristic sociological method of developing abstract ahistorical or transhistorical categories, in the form of ideal types or generalised descriptive typologies, tends to mitigate against this study of continuities. Such typologies, in abstracting what are seen as the essential delineating features of a phenomenon, often based on the form it takes at one particular time and place, may well lose sensitivity to change, and to the way such forms may mutate over time. Concrete examples are then matched up against the typologies and found wanting, as in the Abercrombie and Hill case outlined above. Thus, in this particular case, sociologists just as much as historians have tended to underestimate the extent to which paternalism (albeit in changed form) may persist over time; this in turn has led to neglect of the important role still played by paternalist strategy in producing harmonistic industrial relations in the contemporary context.

THE CHANGING FORMS OF PATERNALISM

Historians, by concentrating on change, tend to overlook continuities. Sociologists, while attempting to trace out continuities, often obliterate the effects of change. By taking a historical/sociological approach, combining elements of narrative reconstruction with typological construction, we might be able to produce an account sensitive to both continuities and change.

Fox's account of the two types of paternalism provides a starting point for such an endeavour; but his concentration on ideology gives too restricted a view of paternalism, which is better envisaged as a type of social nexus involving a variety of relationships, practices, ideas and symbols. In the hosiery study, therefore, I looked at the changing forms which these might take (a firm, for example, might give up providing housing for workers, but establish a pension scheme, or lavish parties at the employer's home might be replaced by annual works' outings). While many such changes were evident, it also became clear that they were occurring within a set of social relationships which placed the employer or the firm in the role of *father* to his workforce. This seemed to me to be a defining feature of paternalism. Within this framework I was able to distinguish four forms of paternalism which evolved within the East Midlands industrial environment; these I label *classic paternalism*, *factory paternalism*, *neo-paternalism* and *pseudo-paternalism*.[3] Taken together these constituted a clear tradition of paternalism in the locality, with a core of leading firms providing a model for new entrants.

Classic paternalism, the earliest form, is closely linked to the old 'moral economy' described by Roberts and Thompson. Accordingly, it was upheld in the East Midlands communities, especially in the rural areas, by prominent aristocrats and landlords, such as the Dukes of Rutland and Newcastle, Lady Byron and Earl Howe. These notables provided moral support and aid of various kinds (including gifts of food, grants of land for allotments, temporary employment, funds for emigration schemes, friendly societies and trade unions, charitable support during strikes) for the local working people (mainly framework knitters) throughout the turbulent decades of the late eighteenth and early nineteenth centuries. A tribute by framework-knitter poet, William Jones, to the Duke of Rutland praises him for his moral leadership and 'love parental'. This was more easily provided, clearly, by the very rich, but the style was copied by less elevated people, gentry, clergy and some of the hosiery masters; Jones paid similar tributes to his own employer, a Mr Preston.

This long-standing tradition of aristocratic patronage and paternalism was to provide a model for hosiers and other industrial employers who wished to build up their own social power, influence and status in the local communities. If, in the long run, they wished to supplant the landowners in the political sphere, they had to prove themselves capable of shouldering similar social responsibilities. An even stronger model was also available in the locality; in Derbyshire there were a few notable instances of the factory villages described by Roberts. Here spinning mills had been set up such as those of Sir Richard Arkwright at Cromford, the Strutt family at Belper and the Hollins (of Viyella fame) at Pleasley and Via Gellia. All these provided in a spectacular manner for their employees, as they sought to attract reluctant working people into their mills: cottages, schools, shops, sporting facilities, libraries (even in the case of the canny Arkwright a pub), were all laid on for employees and whole families recruited to live and work in the villages. The working routine was enlivened by a lavish series of festivals, feasts and entertainments, some to celebrate special events, some part of the factory annual calendar. At one such party to celebrate the Reform Bill, the Strutts entertained their workforce at their home with 4800 lbs of beef, 3184 lbs of plum pudding and 2550 quarts of ale.[4]

Although hosiery production was at this stage still organised on a putting out basis, some large employers like the Morleys of Nottingham, the Biggs brothers and Robert Walker of Leicester were building up similar reputations for concern for their workers' well-being, helping them in times of sickness and keeping them on as workers in their inefficient old age. These employers (apart from the Biggs who went bankrupt) were to carry their paternalism with them into the factory environment.

Classic paternalism, then, lasted through the eighteenth century and the first half of the nineteenth; it displayed all the characteristics described by Roberts: concern with the personal well-being of employees and their families, transcending the economic to enter the moral sphere, close personal links with work people, generous expenditure on welfare provision and social entertainments, the latter serving to reinforce the solidary link between employer and employees, and organicist or unitarist images of employer and employee linked tightly by mutual respect and common interest.

Many of these characteristics were also displayed in factory paternalism, although in a muted form; as Roberts has argued, few could afford to keep up the spectacular largesse of families like the Strutts. In addition, the place of the new paternalists in the urban environment (men like Biggs, Morley and Walker were all heavily involved in local, sometimes even national politics) led to their charitable efforts being spread more diffusely through the community (a point also noted by Roberts). However, this most emphatically did not imply the decline of paternalism. If anything, it took a stronger hold in its new muted form, as the more moderate provision involved was within the reach of some of the middle-sized firms which established themselves in this period.

Hosiery production moved into the factories in the 1850s. Some of the first factory owners, like Morleys, Walkers, A. J. Mundella of Nottingham, Corahs of Leicester and Atkins of Hinckley set the pattern which was copied by employers in other industries when the industrial structure of Nottingham and Leicester diversified in the last quarter of the century (Boots was an outstanding example among the latter). The early factory owners took pride in maintaining the best possible factory conditions for their workers and laying on a range of services, from pensions to sports clubs, from 'gypsy excursions' to factory parties. On the whole, these provisions now tended to be confined to within the work environment, but some village hosiers provided housing for work people and one or two factories showed their concern for the 'whole man' by employing clergymen to lead services in the factory.

Such measures were described by Nottingham employer, William Felkin, as tending to 'identify more clearly and plainly the true interests of the employers and employed' (Felkin, 1867, p. 555), and unitarist ideology was employed by other paternalists such as Samuel Morley and Corahs. However, perhaps more striking was the persistent use of family imagery and the playing up of family links (including the employment of whole families in the factory and the use of the family as the major means of recruitment). Documents produced by these companies emphasise the importance of family service in the factory (the Shipman family employed by Atkins notched up a total of 377 years combined service)! Significantly, factory relations themselves are described in analogies to the family: for example, Arthur Atkins advised his work people as 'a father would a son', Corahs took 'an almost paternal interest' in their employees, one family member considering 'all the workpeople as brothers and sisters' (Atkins, 1972, Webb, 1948).[5]

In much contemporary writing there is a tendency to equate paternalism with attacks on unionism, perhaps because of the use of the ideology of common interests; however, the East Midlands study reveals interesting ambiguities on this point (perhaps mirroring Fox's distinction between 'traditional' and 'sophisticated' paternalism). Some paternalists were certainly bitterly anti-union, going to enormous lengths to demonstrate their opposition. Others, such as Morley and Mundella, were extremely progressive in their attitudes to unions, accepting them as legitimate voices of their workers' feelings and believing that the way to stabilise industrial relations was to develop proper institutions of collective bargaining and arbitration. Perhaps more important to paternalism than simple hostility to unions is the idea of reciprocal rights and duties. Trade unions, thus, can be accepted as long as they espouse 'responsible' and 'co-operative' attitudes to industry. Where the sense of reciprocity is outraged, paternalist employers can become obstinately authoritarian (just like real fathers)! John Biggs, for example, identified even by the Chartist leader Thomas Cooper as a truly compassionate and concerned employer, stood out fiercely against his workers when they went on strike.[6]

There are, then, clear continuities between classic and factory paternalism, in terms of similar practices and attitudes. Paternalism in this area had become an industrial tradition upheld by a core group of employers, who also tended to be among the most successful, thus setting an example to non-paternalist competitors. Similar continuities can be observed between factory paternalism and neo-paternalism.[7] This latter began to evolve in the interwar period and established itself after World War II. The major change is that the progress of bureaucratic development, the growing size of firms (some of which now established branch factories or were involved in mergers and takeovers) and in some cases the shift from private to public ownership, began to break down the strong tradition of personal communication between members of the owning family and the work people.[8] Many of the nineteenth-century paternalists took pride in knowing all their employees by name (and this was still the case in many of the smaller paternalist firms which I visited in the

1980s). In these new circumstances it became necessary to substitute (as did Corahs, for example) the notion of the 'good firm' for that of the 'good employer'.

The other major area of change was in the nature of provisions which the firms continued to make. While increased material prosperity and government welfare policies made provisions like housing, holiday facilities or libraries redundant, new facilities like canteens and pensioners' clubs took their place. Firms, too, reacted to changes in the industrial relations climate, instituting advisory committees and house journals to maintain communication, suggestion schemes with prizes, and so forth. The same old firms, however, are found adopting the neo-paternalist mode (Corahs, Hollins, Atkins). Characteristic of this new form is the incorporation of trade unions into the structure of the firm (as described by Nichols and Beynon, 1977) so that it, too, is seen as part of the 'big factory family'. A major continuity, however, is that family themes and imagery continued to be deployed, despite the growing reality of bureaucratic impersonality. Family recruitment is still a common feature in the hosiery industry today, and firms continue to employ family metaphors in their publicity material.

Finally, another common variant is what I have called pseudo-paternalism. This is characteristic of small firms, which are very numerous in the hosiery industry. These, as Roberts pointed out, are simply unable to afford the cost of welfare provision or spending in the community; the personal care tactics of these firms are thus limited to the maintenance of strong personal links and close communication, combined with the use of family symbolism and family recruitment. This may represent a very genuine concern for workers' well-being. In such firms unions *are* characteristically unwelcome, management considering them to be redundant because of the closeness of day-to-day shopfloor interactions. As in the larger contemporary paternalist firms, the importance of family commitments is also emphasised by the flexibility of individual working arrangements, which allow female employees to fit their working hours to family and child care needs.

THE PERSISTENCE OF PATERNALISM

I have traced the development of industrial paternalism in the East Midlands area, showing the evolution of four distinct variants. It

might be objected that these consitute four quite separate phenomena. For example, the type of industrial practices I have called
factory paternalism have elsewhere been described as welfarism.[9]
Two arguments can be made here. First, as I have tried to demonstrate, these variants were linked in a clear tradition of paternalism,
which was part of the general industrial climate in the area, but which
was also upheld by a core group of key firms which were committed
to paternalism in its various forms. Thus one can trace out the
continuities of this form of industrial practice within these firms.
Secondly, as should have become evident, a unifying strand in all
variants is the persistent use of a family framework for making sense
of industrial life. This use of family symbolism, the appeal to family
links and loyalties, I take to be the defining feature of paternalism in
industry, rather than the common accompaniments of unitarist
ideology, welfare provision or the ethic of personal care and social
responsibility; my perception of paternalism, thus, is closest to that of
Joyce.[10] The centrality of family symbolism is revealed by the
comparative historical sociological method, since it appears as a
feature of all separate instances of paternalism, although other
factors may have been regarded by the chroniclers as more important.

To demonstrate the continuing use of paternalist strategies is not,
of course, to demonstrate that paternalism works. However, while
evidence on this is not so readily available in the hosiery case, what
there is suggests that it does. Direct evidence of this comes in the
form of a series of tributes from workers to the paternalists – verbal
tributes, poems, deputations, gifts, presentations – ranging from the
flowery and formal to the simple and informal; a considerable body
of these exist covering the period from the early nineteenth century
through to the 1980s.[11] Although these expressions of gratitude and
affection may be instituted by a few 'trusties' rather than the body of
the workforce, it is likely that these long-serving employees set the
tone for the factory. One would not want to suggest that all hosiery
workers at all times felt commitment and regard towards paternalistic
employers; but, at the level of common sense it is hardly surprising if
people prefer a concerned boss to an uncaring one! Where the
concern is not genuine, but is more cynically adopted, as is sometimes
the case with neo-paternalist firms, paternalism is at its most vulnerable and in such cases may fail.

Indirect evidence of its working in hosiery also comes from the
generally successful record of the paternalist firms (Corahs, Atkins,

Mundellas) who achieved economic prosperity in a notoriously cut-throat and unstable industry, imputing their own success at least in part to their good industrial relations climate, which enabled them to pursue market policies founded on reliability and quality of output. Moreover, in the industry as a whole, the consolidation of factory paternalism was concomitant with improved industrial relations and the decline of strikes and violent confrontation. Other factors were involved here, but paternalism seems to me to have been one crucial component in the promotion of industrial harmony and class pacification.

The use of family metaphor was crucial to its effectiveness, an effectiveness insufficiently recognised by historians of class and labour relations. In the East Midlands, as in Joyce's Lancashire, paternalism had a broader role in promoting social harmony within a community which had been riven by conflict during the early phases of industrialisation. This it achieved partly by emphasising family identities and family loyalties in opposition to class identities and loyalties; thus, employers committed to preserving the family firm and workers committed to ensuring family survival can indeed be seen to share common interests, in this respect over-riding class differentials and antagonisms.

Studying a phenomenon over a long period also highlights the factors which are most favourable to its origination and persistence. East Midlands employers turned to paternalism originally to overcome problems of labour shortage in a period hostile to the factory environment. But such a climate of industrial relations also helped to allay the fears about the moral and physical welfare of employees, especially young children and women, which characterised the public response to the establishment of mills and factories in the area. This suggests that a paternalist approach is often adopted where the workforce is seen as vulnerable, in need of care and protection. In the contemporary context, this is most likely to be the case where the workforce is largely female. In addition, the family metaphors of paternalism seem to work particularly well with women, who, as prime bearers of responsibility for family welfare, respond strongly to notions of family priority. Paternalism is also clearly promoted by the continuation of family ownership (which is still common in the hosiery industry). Ownership is a more significant factor than size of firm and the shift from private to public ownership represents a crisis point for paternalism which it cannot always survive. A final important factor is the position which a firm or industry holds within a community; where that community becomes identified with an industry and sees industrial relations within it as a crucial matter of public concern, a spirit of paternalism is likely to be fostered. This is most likely to happen in a single-industry town or where a particular firm employs a large proportion of the populace (see Martin and Fryer, 1973, Lane and Roberts, 1971).

Once a tradition of paternalism has become firmly established, continuities of personnel and the climate of expectations will encourage its continuation, unless some major crisis or upheaval threatens the whole system. In the East Midlands, change of ownership was the most likely cause of its breakdown; the Pilkington and Casterton studies provide examples of other forms of crisis.

I have suggested that the significance of paternalism has been underrated. There are three aspects of this I want to raise. First, paternalism continues to be an important type of management strategy, especially where an industry (hosiery, confectionery) has an established tradition of it. Recent research into women's work suggests that it may be widespread among firms, both large and small, which employ mainly women. Pseudo-paternalism, in particular, may well be common in the new small firms springing up as a result of current economic restructuring. At the other end of the scale neo-paternalism is likely to be encouraged as the entry of Japanese firms and the influence of Japanese competitors lead to a 'Japanisation' of British industry. The spirit of breathless admiration for this 'new' type of industrial practice seems partly misplaced; we are merely seeing a recrudescence of many practices well-rooted in British industrial tradition. But emulation of Japan is bringing paternalism to industries with no previous tradition of it (the car industry, engineering).

This has social implications beyond the firm. Paternalism, with its stress on the family priorities, its emphasis on the equivalences of family and work, fits all too nicely into the political climate in which Margaret Thatcher has declared that there is no such thing as society, only families. As in the nineteenth century, industrial paternalism has an insidious role in the restructuring of class relations as capitalism evolves into a new phase, and gender too is implicated here. Where work relations are seen as harmonising with family relations, the assignment of women to inferior work roles, particularly in the expanding personal services sector, can continue to be justified as 'natural'.

Finally, the survival of paternalism, invalidating the view that it is incompatible with 'progress' and 'modernity', raises basic doubts about prevailing sociological models of modernity and development; in particular it challenges two widely held assumptions. The first is the view, derived especially from Weber but common to Marxism and many other macro-sociological models, that industrial development inexorably leads to the replacement of all other forms of social action by economically 'rational' behaviour. Freer's admirable account of nineteenth-century Leicester industrialists (1975) is one study which explicitly challenges that view, revealing the persistence of other forms of motivation ('affective' and 'traditional', to use the Weberian terms); economically rational choices were rejected in favour of family priorities: employment of family members, for example, or checking a company's growth to ensure the feasibility of continued private family control. In my interviews with hosiery owners in the 1980s I found exactly the same choices being made. I would argue that such findings throw into doubt the whole notion of rationality in social action as currently espoused by sociologists of all persuasions, but particularly by industrial sociologists. The over-rationalised view of human behaviour needs modification; and a serious acceptance that forms of behaviour we might designate traditional and emotional are not just hangovers of a bygone socio-logical epoch. Related to this, another central assumption within industrial sociology, held by the mainstream and Marxists alike, is that industrial relations are necessarily of an adversarial nature. The image of the manager and the union leader (both male of course!) locked in combat, be it class war, pecuniary competition or skilful negotiation, is pervasive throughout the discipline. Yet whole tracts of industrial relations (especially those involving women) do not conform to this pattern. This is not to deny that class conflicts and competitive interests are present in the workplace, but simply to point out that other forces and forms of experience and motivation are also at play. It is paternalism's strong card that it recognises these and plays up to them. If sociologists recognise them, too, moving beyond the purely economistic model, they will be able to give a better account of industrial life and the social world in general.

THE PROSPECTS FOR HISTORICAL SOCIOLOGY

I hope I have provided a small example of the advantages of an historical/sociological approach, emphasising both continuity and change, in developing a clearer and more coherent understanding of a particular phenomenon. Neglecting either element, I have argued, may lead to an imperfect comprehension of a phenomenon, in which one element may assume a disproportionate significance *vis-à-vis* other elements.

There is no space here to deal adequately with the problems of this approach, which are dealt with in other chapters in this volume. However, I should raise briefly the issue of the comparability of data which are different in kind. Historical data are characteristically random, limited, incomplete and preselected (in a variety of ways); contemporary data can be systematically collected, can be limitlessly generated, can be if not complete at least fairly representative, but, by contrast, are selected by the researcher and thus more subject to a certain type of manipulation and bias. Moreover, it may seem illegitimate to extract data, for purposes of comparison, from their specific context. A nineteenth-century firm, even when it bears the same name as a current one, operates embedded in different strata of meanings, not all of which are amenable to excavation. I have argued here that we can to some extent get round this by means of the uncovering of tradition, which can be achieved by careful narrative reconstruction. But even so, these methodological disjunctions mean that the claims we make must remain relatively modest. The historical sociologist cannot aspire to finality or to the predictive certainties of the statistician. Findings must be seen as suggestive, not conclusive.

In the current intellectual climate, however, a little more modesty in the claims of sociologists might be both becoming and prudent. The discipline is currently facing a challenge from postmodernist philosophy, with its embargo on meta-narratives and its characteristic portrayal of social reality as made up of fragmented and incommensurable language games (Lyotard, 1984). This may call for reappraisal of many of our approaches to the analysis of social structure, while apparently legitimating the presentation of particular micronarratives (the historian's traditional method). While not suggesting that we should capitulate to the postmodernist critiques, it seems to me that one of the ways forward for sociology (though by no means the only one) is an affirmation of the links with history that already characterises the work of some individual sociological researchers.

Lawrence Stone in a recent rewriting of his 1970's article about history and the social sciences argues that social scientists (especially sociologists) have tended to see history as a resource, a databank from which to draw support for their models and theories, while maintaining an uninterested or even contemptuous attitude towards historical methods and concerns, for example, the method of descriptive narrative. While acknowledging the important contributions of social science to the 'new history', Stone seems to feel that currently the social sciences (especially sociology) are in such a state of disintegration and internal disarray that historians should draw away from them. This implies a return to the old state of the disciplines, whereby the study of societies was dislocated and fragmented between the past and the present. Such a refragmentation, I believe, would be to the loss of all the disciplines and a turning away from the vision of a 'scholarly comparative social science and a comparative history . . . the beginning of a true "science humaine"' (Shils, quoted Stone, 1987 p. 16): but if it is not to occur, sociologists may need to reconsider their views on history and develop a greater respect for the narrative method.

NOTES

1. I use 'ideology' here and throughout the chapter not in the sense of opposition to any 'true' or 'scientific' analysis of society, but simply to connote a set of ideas by which people make sense of or interpret their environment. In this usage any society can and does yield a number of differing ideologies.
2. See, for example, the research of Dore (1973) and of Woronoff (1983).
3. This typology is described more fully in Chapter 6 of my PhD thesis, where a detailed narrative account of each type is provided (Bradley, 1987).
4. This example is taken from the study of the Strutts and the Arkwrights by Fitton and Wadsworth (1958). My knowledge of classic paternalism draws heavily on this text and also studies by Chapman (1967), Wells (1968) and an older company history by Piggott (1949).
5. Material on factory paternalism was drawn from a variety of sources, of which histories produced by the companies were perhaps the most interesting; other sources included biographies, employees' poetry, local histories and pamphlets.
6. This may perhaps throw some light on the way paternalism sometimes seems to vanish when conflict breaks out; see Lane and Roberts' famous study of the Pilkington strike (1971). The sense of betrayed rights/duties may be felt by either party, as Martin and Fryer's study of Casterton reveals (1973).
7. I have adopted this term as it is used by Nichols and Beynon in their 'Chemco' study (1977) in reference to a very similar pattern of industrial relations. However, in many ways 'bureaucratic' or 'institutionalised paternalism' might be a more apt label for what I describe.

8. In one recorded case the owner of the firm sometimes brought his wife with him on his weekly tour round the factory, to the great gratification of the female employees.
9. For example, see Nelson (1975).
10. Martin and Fryer, although their (implicit) definition of paternalism seems to revolve around attitudes generated by the relationship of benevolence and deference, also emphasise in their study of Casterton Mills the importance of family links and family recruitment.
11. This evidence is fully described in Bradley, 1987.

BIBLIOGRAPHY

N. Abercrombie and S. Hill, 'Paternalism and Patronage', *British Journal of Sociology*, 1976, pp. 413–29.

P. Abrams, *Historical Sociology* (Shepton Mallet: Open Books, 1982).

Atkins, *Atkins of Hinckley 1722–1972*, 1972.

H. Bradley, 'Degradation and Resegmentation: Social and Technological Change in the East Midlands Hosiery Industry 1800–1960', unpublished PhD, University of Durham, 1987.

S. Chapman, *The Early Factory Masters* (Newton Abbott: David & Charles, 1967).

R. Dore, *British Factory, Japanese Factory* (London: Allen & Unwin, 1973).

P. Edwards and H. Scullion, *The Social Origin of Industrial Conflict* (Oxford: Basil Blackwell, 1982).

W. Felkin, *A History of the Machine Wrought Hosiery and Lace Manufacture* (New York: Augustus Kelley, 1967).

R. Fitton and A. Wadsworth, *The Strutts and the Arkwrights* (Manchester: Manchester University Press, 1978).

A. Fox, *Beyond Contract* (London: Faber & Faber, 1964).

D. Freer, 'Business Families in Victorian Leicester: a Study in Historical Sociology', unpublished M.Phil, University of Leicester, 1975.

P. Joyce, *Work, Society and Politics* (Brighton: Harvester, 1980).

K. Kumar, *Prophecy and Progress* (Harmondsworth: Penguin, 1978).

T. Lane and K. Roberts, *Strike at Pilkingtons* (London: Fontana, 1971).

J. P. Lyotard, *The Postmodern Condition* (Manchester: Manchester University Press, 1984).

R. Martin and R. Fryer, *Redundancy and Paternalist Capitalism* (London: Allen & Unwin, 1973).

D. Nelson, *Managers and Workers* (Wisconsin: Wisconsin University Press, 1975).

H. Newby, 'Paternalism and Capitalism' in R. Scase, (ed.) *Industrial Society: Class, Cleavage and Control* (London: Allen & Unwin, 1977).

H. Newby, *The Deferential Worker* (Harmondsworth: Penguin, 1979).

T. Nichols and H. Beynon, *Living With Capitalism* (London: Routledge & Kegan Paul, 1977).

S. Piggott, *Hollins: a Study in Industry* (Nottingham: Hollins, 1949).

D. Roberts, *Paternalism in Early Victorian England* (London: Croom Helm, 1978).

L. Stone, *The Past and the Present Revisited* (London: Routledge & Kegan Paul, 1987).

E. P. Thompson, 'The Moral Economy of the English Crowd in the Eighteenth Century', *Past and Present*, Vol. 50, 1971, pp. 76–136.

E. P. Thompson, 'Eighteenth-century English Society: Class Struggle Without Class', *Social History*, Vol. 3, 1, 1978, pp. 133–65.

C. W. Webb, *A Historical Record of N Corah and Sons Ltd*, 1948.

F. A. Wells, *Hollins and Viyella* (Newton Abbott: David & Charles, 1968).

S. Westwood, *All Day, Every Day* (London: Pluto, 1984).

J. Woronoff, *Japan's Wasted Workers* (New Jersey: Allanheld & Osmun, 1983).

12 Sub/contracting and Industrial Development
Ralph Fevre

It is some time since the Department of Employment confirmed that the use of contractors and subcontractors in British industry was increasing (*Employment Gazette*, October 1985), and recent studies (see, for example, *Guardian*, 24 September 1986) would appear to suggest that this trend is not confined to the nationalised industries and services where contracting out has been a method of privatisation. Although we now know a great deal about the effect of this trend on the workforce (for recent examples see *Guardian*, 21 January 1987, *Listener*, 12 November 1987 and Hurstfield, 1987a, 1987b), the theory of contracting and subcontracting remains underdeveloped. Researchers who have tried to look beyond the social effects of contracting-out enter a realm of some confusion. For example, Ascher (1987) concludes that it is doubtful whether contracting out public services has been more efficient or cheaper (also see Fevre, 1986). This chapter begins with the assumption that some knowledge of the place of contractors and subcontractors in the history of industrial change will help to clear away some of the confusion inherent in contemporary explanations of this form of industrial organisation. But before we consider the historical data, we must first *define* the form of industrial organisation which interests us.

WHAT IS SUB/CONTRACTING?

In general I will use the term 'sub/contracting' to refer to both contracting – a simple relationship between the client (the principal) and a contractor – and sub/contracting (where the client is also under contract) since in practice it is frequently unclear whether the client is a principal or also a contractor. For example, contemporary wool textile firms are frequently contracted by garment manufacturers and even (although this is more common in other branches of the textile industry) retailers. The companies that such wool textile firms themselves contract to undertake work on their behalf are therefore strictly termed subcontractors rather than contractors.

The term is meant to include contracts with an organisation, firm, gang, or individual (if self-employed), to undertake work on things – materials, machinery, land, buildings and so on – which are not their own property.[1] A historical example of sub-contracting is the 'outwork' system in textiles where a weaver, for example, owned a loom but not the yarn which she/he wove into cloth in his/her workshop. Contemporary examples include labour-only sub-contracting in construction (often described as the 'lump') within which a gang provides labour for a specified task to a main contractor who is responsible for building some construction on behalf of the principal.

THE LESSONS OF HISTORY

Littler warns of the 'ahistorical . . . nature of most organization theory and analysis' (1979, p. 1, see also Goffee, 1981), but, as far as sub/contracting is concerned, the shortcomings of contemporary analysis result as much from bad history as from no history. This bad history (for related comment see the chapter by Penn, this volume) purports to show that the (historical) evidence for a single path of industrial development is overwhelming *and* that this path takes economies through successive and *different* types of industrial organisation. Thus the conventional view of economic history (including marxist accounts) assumes that the rise of the capitalist mode of production and the Factory System showed sub/contracting to be an inferior and primitive form of organisation, and that where this form survived it did so as a relic of the earlier primitive type (often as a substitute for technical change). But if sub/contracting is a backward form of organisation why should it appear to be regarded as a useful innovation by employers (and governments) in advanced industrial countries? In the remainder of this chapter I will use a historical case study to suggest that the assumptions which produce this anomaly are wrong and, incidentally, to shed some light on the reasons for increases (and decreases) in sub/contracting.

If our assumptions about the nature of industrial development are wrong then the economic historians must take some of the blame.[2]

Berg (1985, pp. 16–17) has recently summarised the new directions taken by economic historians who have been stimulated (by current industrial change) to take a fresh look at the history of industrial development. In fact, the challenge to conventional assumptions about *sub/contracting* was issued over 20 years ago, by Sidney Pollard:

> Subcontract . . . does not itself form a 'stage', but may be compatible with different stages of development of industrial capitalism, according to technical and commercial needs and managerial competence. It survives, in many forms, into the factory age; in some industries it survives until today, and is not necessarily inefficient or anachronistic. It is in fact, only the dogmatism of classical political economy as developed in the nineteenth century which looked upon the capitalist-owner-entrepreneur facing an individual, propertyless worker, as the 'normal', highest finite form of organisation, which has led us to ignore or minimize the importance of surviving systems of subcontract, group-contract or co-operation. (Pollard, 1965, p. 39)

This challenge was repeated by Littler (1979) in respect of internal sub/contracting (with which I will deal only briefly) and by Andrew Friedman, both writing in the late 1970s. Although the current increase in sub/contracting had not yet been observed, Friedman argued that this form of organisation could be both a 'resource base' for development and a central feature of advanced capitalist enterprise (Friedman, 1978, p. 35).

In the following pages I will test these heretical views against the evidence from the history of one British industry, textiles, and especially the two branches of the *wool* textile industry, woollen and worsted. Using the (wool) textile industry as a case study at least has the virtue of familiarity to sociologists[3] and I will, in the main use familiar texts to construct this history.[4]

A Short History of Sub/contracting in Wool Textiles

In wool textiles (and some related industries) sub/contracting has been an important (even dominant) form of organisation. Before the late eighteenth century, when the industrial revolution in this industry began,[5] commodity production occurred under both capitalist and non-capitalist modes of production. Under the former, most work was done in the producers' own homes as a form of sub/contracting known as outwork, 'capitalist outwork' according to Clapham (quoted by Thompson, 1974, p. 287). Outworkers were paid by 'capitalist organisers' to perform one or other of the tasks of production. They worked on materials which belonged to the organisers but owned the tools with which they worked. Supervision was not exercised directly but at the warehouse door where the outworker might be fined for slow or poor quality work.

It is likely that by 1700 the majority of producers were capitalist outworkers, and that their numbers increased still further in the late eighteenth and early nineteenth centuries. In the worsted section of the wool textile industry a complex hierarchy of contractors and sub/contractors was reduced to a relatively simple relationship between principals, intermediaries (the 'putters-out') and sub/contractors (who were in time relegated to the same degraded level as the handloom weaver). In the same period some *woollen* producers were only now being converted to *capitalist* outwork from petty commodity production and in time most of the 'small clothiers' became handloom weavers. As in worsted, outworkers were not direct employees. Payment occurred on the completion of the specific piece of work they had agreed to undertake. 'Wage' advances were not yet common and even in the worsted section were viewed as debt rather than as continuous payments to an employee by the organiser.

Marx shows that at this time outwork was also extended as 'an outside department of the factory' (1974, p. 437). A proportion of the expansion in textile outwork in the nineteenth century was due to the existence of outwork processes which complemented those undertaken in the factories. Indeed where outworkers (or prisoners or the occupants of work houses) were sub/contracted to undertake complementary processes to those undertaken in the factories, the number of outworkers would often greatly outnumber the number of employees. The best-documented example is the extension of outwork weaving on handlooms which accompanied the growth of mechanised spinning in factories. All textile branches had factory spinners who put out weaving and auxiliary tasks but there were also other mixes of factory and outwork processes. In a worsted factory spinners put out wool to be combed by individual outworkers and commission shops up to the 1850s and there are even examples of the owners of power looms putting out work to hand combers and spinners in worsted and to spinners in the woollen section; indeed it was in woollen production, of all the textile branches, that the 'mixed' system survived the longest.

It is clear that the existence of a 'technological gap' (Heywood, 1976, p. 108) created by the mechanisation of spinning does not completely account for this extension of outwork. For one thing, outwork was often extended simply to cater for mass markets in areas of production unaffected by mechanisation. For another, outworkers were sometimes put to work by mill owners who had machinery at work on similar or identical processes. There were several examples of mill owners contracting outworkers to perform the same tasks as, or close substitutes to, those undertaken by machines. Most numerous amongst these were the cases where capitalists used both hand and powerloom weavers. Again the phenomenon was general to all textiles and there were even isolated examples of mill-owners dispensing with power looms to return to all-outwork production. The woollen section also included examples of 'masters' who used both outworking weavers and power looms but of most interest here was the 'semi-domestic' system in which the usual sub/contracting relationship between outwork and the Factory System was reversed.

While there are many examples of the owners of woollen mills using outworkers, the Yorkshire woollen section also included sub/contracted factories. Fulling, finishing, carding, scribbling and spinning were all sub/contracted in this way. The carding and scribbling mills, for example, acted (although not exclusively) as 'service stations' to the small clothiers (Heaton, 1972, p. 80). This practice began in the latter half of the eighteenth century and was continued at least until 1830. Most mills in the semi-domestic systems were 'public' and could be sub/contracted by any client to undertake carding and so on.

Before we turn to sub/contracting within and between factories, we must first conclude the story of the outworkers, a story which did not end with the nineteenth century. In 1850 perhaps one half of the wool textile workers in Britain were hand-technology outworkers and much of the outwork-factory system in this and other textile industries was not dismantled until the extension of legislative protection to workers in small workshops in the latter half of the century. Even when enacted, however, the legislation proved difficult to enforce and its effects are ambiguous (Samuel, 1977, p. 15).

In related industries outwork remained *dominant* into the next century, in clothing and Nottingham lace manufacture, for example.

This was also the case in the wool textile industries of other countries. Outwork was still predominant, for example, in French worsted weaving and combing at the turn of the century. Even in Britain there was still ample evidence of a continued role for outworkers in the twentieth century. In 1903, for example, there were complaints of the problems that sub/contracting by 'bagwomen' could create for textile outworkers (Anderson, 1922, p. 90) and many wool textile sub/ contractors were working in non-mechanised workshops in 1907 (Clapham, 1907, pp. 129–30). The sub/contractors who undertook preparation for weaving in the 1970s were hardly more likely to have machinery; furthermore, much of a process (burling and mending) which followed weaving was still undertaken by outworkers in their own homes. In fact outmending was believed to be on the increase (see also Allen and Wolkowitz, 1987); and advertisements for menders frequently appeared in the West Yorkshire newspapers.

Many of the characteristic features of outwork were transferred intact to the early factories. A whole array of 'transitional forms' (Marx, 1974, pp. 44–6) had been developed before 1850. These ranged from the cottage factories of Coventry to the charging of textile operatives for rent of machinery, use of power, and for faulty work. This last practice replicated the outwork sub/contract in that costs were transferred to the worker and penalties were enforced *after* a piece of work was completed. In the larger Yorkshire wool textile mills there were many looms owned wholly or partly by the weavers themselves. Yorkshire wool textiles also had the 'room and power' tradition where hopeful masters could rent space in a mill, possibly even machinery, and buy power and perhaps borrow wage advances and operating capital from the landlord.

Sub/contracting *within* (manu)factories began before the Industrial Revolution and continued within factories proper well into the twentieth century. In the internal sub/contract system of the cotton spinners the mule spinners were paid by the piece and passed on a proportion of this payment in time wages to assistants (piecers and scavengers). These assistants were *not* generally family members but were recruited and supervised by the spinners, and assistants had no guarantee, no matter how long they worked, of taking over machines of their own. The cotton spinners' internal sub/contract system was retained until the 1960s and woollen spinners also acted as contractors in the twentieth century (a circumstance reflected, in the woollen spinners' favour, in the comparison with the wages of worsted spinners where this type of sub/contracting was rare).

Elements of sub/contracting remained in the employment of other workers, too. Ordinary textile operatives were still liable to face deductions for power and cleaning after 1900, there were still masters who rented 'room and power', and an internal sub/contracting system remained in dyeing before 1920. Nevertheless, sub/contracting within wool textile firms had ceased to grow, but sub/contracting *between* firms was increasing in one section (worsted) at least.

The history of the wool textile industry supports Pollard's claim that sub/contracting is the most important 'survival' from capitalist outwork to influence industrial capitalism (1965, p. 8) to the extent that the modern organisational pattern appears to follow lines laid down in the sub/contracting relationships established in earlier periods.[6] After the Industrial Revolution worsted spinners put out work to hand combers and sometimes to handloom weavers. A similar pattern emerged after general mechanisation. Now worsted spinners used the services of (mechanised) commission combing firms and increasingly sold yarn to 'manufacturers' without looms who, like the old handloom organisers, had their (mechanised) weaving done on commission. Furthermore, this pattern was accentuated as the nineteenth, and the twentieth, century progressed. The disintegration of worsted (and cotton) spinning and weaving firms became common and more and more of worsted production became the concern of 'topmakers' who sub/contracted combers, 'manufacturers' who sub/contracted weavers, and commission dyers and even spinners.

In the first half of the twentieth century integration was often purely nominal and the integrated worsted firm still relied on middlemen and sub/contractors. This was never simply a matter of small firms working on sub/contract to establish themselves while larger firms acted as principals. Both wool textile sections always consisted of a small number of large firms and a large number of small firms, but some of the *largest* firms were sub/contractors. Both large and small worsted firms worked on commission but the few large firms (until after World War II most large units were in fact cartels) usually worked on commission for small or medium sized companies. Indeed, until later in the twentieth century, large firms only survived as sub/contractors.

The commission system continued to account for much of wool textile production after World War II. For example, Rainnie described the work of commission spinners in the 1960s:

Some of the tops or wool supplied to these firms to be spun into yarn is the property of firms described as merchant converters who have specialized in the buying of wool or tops and the selling (sometimes reinforced by a brand name) of yarns. They own no drawing sets, spinning or doubling spindles and are quite divorced from the production process. This specialization of function can be found in most sections of the industry. In the weaving section there are firms which own looms and process material supplied by other firms some of whom are known as merchant converters or manufacturers without looms. The latter type of firm usually buys yarn, designs the cloth, has it woven on commission, sends it to be dyed and finished on a commission basis and then merchants it. Specialized commission weavers, like specialized commission spinners tend to be small firms, but commission combers are among the largest firms in their section of the industry. (Rainnie, 1965, p. 56)

Rainnie also found extensive use of sub/contracting in rag grinding, and in the preparation of yarn for weaving (1965, pp. 18, 24). In 1969 the Atkins Report noted that

. . . a significant amount of commission combing, spinning and weaving is still carried out, and the majority of the non-integrated dyers and finishers operate on a commission basis. (Atkins, 1969, p. 18)

Figures were not available for all sections of the industry but 45 per cent of raw wool preparation, 30 per cent of worsted cloth finishing, and 20 per cent of worsted burling and mending were done on commission (in the latter case by outworkers).[7]

The most important contemporary form of sub/contracting in wool textiles may not, however, lie in the commission system but in 'outward processing', This is the practice whereby firms in advanced industrialised countries like West Germany contract out certain processes to their nominal competitors in less developed countries. UK manufacturers have had close links with continental firms for over a century and although, in the late 1970s, they claimed to be opposed to it, they had made use of outward processing. Of particular interest were the links established between UK wool textile producers and those in Comecon countries, especially Poland.

Sub/contracting is perhaps even more widespread in textile production outside Britain, not only in West Germany and Italy (see below p. 210) but also further afield: in the Middle East and North Africa, for example, where large multi-national firms use hand-technology sub/contractors.

History and Theory

According to the conventional view adopted by economic historians and by many marxist writers,[8] the development of the capitalist mode of production in advance of the Factory System did *not* come about through capitalist outwork. Sub/contracting is one of the reasons advanced to explain the 'backward' aspect of capitalist outwork. It is singled out as an obstacle to capitalist development. Braverman, for example, writes that capitalist organisers disregarded 'the difference between labour power and the labour that can be gotten out of it' (1974, pp. 60–1), and the work of Braverman – together with that of another labour process theorist, Marglin – is a useful example of the influence of (mistaken) conventional assumptions about history on contemporary theory (cf Goffee, 1981, Littler, 1979, 1982).

The conventional view seeks the roots of capitalist development where there is assumed to be no sub/contracting and finds them outside the outwork sector altogether, in the hand-powered *manu*factories. It is assumed that sub/contracting was absent where workers were gathered in a workshop owned by a capitalist, and it is also assumed that capitalists turned to manufactories precisely because they substituted direct supervision for contracting (Marglin, 1974, p. 94). The obstacles to the development of the capitalist mode of production were removed by manufactories (Braverman, 1974, pp. 59, 73).

Where the conventional view argues that manufactories dispensed with the obstacle (to industrial change) of sub/contracting, so much more forcefully is this argument developed in respect of the Factory System itself. This view begins with the assumption that the Industrial Revolution began a *sectional* struggle between hand- and mechanised technology where the former is identified with outwork, but the unmechanised sector is also thought to have an additional handicap in an already unequal struggle in its adherence to sub/contracting as a method of organisation. The factory has dispensed with sub/contracting and therefore ensured its own success. The further development of the Factory System is retarded where any internal vestiges of sub/contracting remain (Marglin, 1974, p. 102). Sub/ contracting is therefore seen as at best transitional and at worst non-capitalist and an obstacle to industrial capitalism. It is always a relic and has no modern forms (Braverman, 1974, pp. 61–4). It survives in the latter half of the nineteenth century only in special circumstances (Braverman, 1974, pp. 61–4, Marglin, 1974, p. 97). Later sub/contracting is a throwback to pre-industrial times or at least the early nineteenth century when capitalists had not realised (in either sense) the advantages of direct employment.

The conventional view, when applied to wool textiles either before or after the Industrial Revolution, is wrong. This is clear from the work of some conventional economic historians as well as from other histories. There are, for example, four errors in the conventional view of the superiority of manufactories. Firstly, sub/contracting had not been largely superseded in large workshops in the period of manufacture. Secondly, large workshops (with more than ten workers) of any kind were rare and usually unsuccessful. They were not the source of later capitalist development. Thirdly, the scarcity of large workshops can be explained by their *inability* to compete with enterprises which relied wholly on sub/contracting. Sub/contracting was simply more profitable (Deane quoted by Schremmer, 1976, p. 88). Finally, the successful workshops were not owned by capitalists at all but were rather the small shops of the petty commodity producers or sub/contracted outworkers. Indeed small workshops were characteristic of capitalist outwork. Far from being an obstacle to development, sub/contracting relations were one of the strengths of capitalist outwork and helped it to increase wool textile output and extend the capitalist mode of production.

Sub/contracting also helped mill owners to develop the Factory System: it reduced their costs and gave them flexibility and capital. Help of this kind was needed – even in the early stages of industrial capitalism when starting costs were low. Early factory failures were legion, in Yorkshire woollen and elsewhere, indeed failure was more likely than success. While the low level of starting costs itself suggests that these costs were spread to burden the sub/contractors as well as the capitalist, sub/contracting proved essential to an enterprise which did not wish to join the list of early factory casualties. In woollen service mills were given a head start in the race to an integrated Factory System by their sub/contracting relations. Although they never made up the bulk of the nucleus of mills which grew into the later vertically-integrated factories, service mills included some firms which would later become giants. In worsted access to the resources of the outwork sector meant that capital accumulation was 'never a serious problem' (Sigsworth, 1958, p.177) and many capitalist organisers went on to own mills.

From 1770 the development of industrial capitalism in wool textiles was accomplished through changes in sub/contracting. These changes did *not* involve the decline of sub/contracting which is assumed in the conventional view. For decades sub/contracted outwork was as much an essential component of industrial capitalism as the Factory System and the latter developed through sub/contracting work either internally or to outworkers. Finally, when direct employment did become general, it did so in factories but these factories were dependent on internal sub/contracting and inter-firm sub/contracting.

Recent economic histories have found more to criticise in the conventional view than its mistaken view of sub/contracting. One alternative, the theory of 'protoindustrialisation' – which suggests that the development of industrial capitalism required a transitional ('protoindustrial') phase when typically, agriculture and industry were combined in the person of the 'peasant outworker' – appears to be a blind alley since it retains too many of the conventional assumptions. A summary of general criticism of this approach is supplied by Berg (1985) while Hudson (1981) makes specific criticisms of its application to wool textiles. Berg's alternative is the one proposed a decade ago by a sociologist: to oppose the whole idea of 'the invariant nature of the single path to modernity' (Corrigan, 1977, p. 487). Berg opts for a 'multi-linear' perspective which allows that industrial change need not mean the elimination of older forms, and that their persistence can sometimes be essential. In the case of sub/contracting, therefore, this form of organisation should be viewed as one possible path of development and not as an obstacle to change. If this seems a reasonable (provisional) conclusion the next question we would wish to ask is why – why does sub/contracting become a way of developing in some cases and not others?

The Advantages and Disadvantages of Sub/contracting

If we seek an answer to this question in terms of varying comparative advantages between sub/contract and direct employment we will be disappointed since, on closer inspection, we find that in any period equally persuasive arguments can be made in favour of each option.

According to the conventional view the difficult (if not impossible) part is to make a coherent argument in favour of sub/contracting. An attempt to do this follows.

The conventional view emphasises the weaknesses of a system which relies on sub/contracting (the risks of embezzlement of materials, high levels of investment in stocks and so on) but neglects its strengths. For example, the high level of investment in variable capital in capitalist outwork was complemented by negligible investment in constant capital. While capitalist organisers were obliged to invest in raw materials for all their sub/contractors, the number of workers at their disposal was not limited by the extent of their investment in buildings or tools.

Under capitalist outwork, sub/contracting allowed each capitalist to put many more hands to work than if production had been concentrated in the capitalist's premises. Even if the speed of turnover of capital was limited, the volume of turnover could be expanded quite rapidly. Furthermore, sub/contracting limited the proportions of an organiser's time and resources which were involved in production and so made possible the expansion of purchasing and selling activities. This, together with ready access to new sources of labour through sub/contracting, permitted faster rates of growth on a small capital base.

Moreover, sub/contracting enabled the capitalist organiser to respond quickly to improved trade, and, more importantly, to a recession. The enterprise which relied on outworkers was not burdened by having to pay workers who might not be fully employed. Sub/contracting not only gave the capitalist organiser the opportunity to extend the business but minimised the costs of such expansion.

A similar argument in favour of sub/contracting could be made in relation to outwork and the Factory System. As in earlier periods, sub/contracting relations ensured that the work was undertaken by those with an 'interest in production' (Mann, 1971, p. 116) and Bythell also points out that principals got the 'managerial services' of the putters-out/intermediaries for free (1978, p. 86). Secondly, sub/contracting relations between outwork and the factory helped the client capitalist to cope, where the factory enterprise proved too inflexible to do so, with fluctuations in trade over both the long and the short term and at the minimum cost. For example, the principal was able to lay off gradually when required. Costs of a more fixed character than those induced by trade fluctuations were also reduced as were risks and uncertainties in general.

What of the advantages of internal sub/contracting systems *within* the Factory System? It is clear that the sub/contracting element of the organisation of mule spinning offered advantages to the employers. Those mill owners who used the system escaped responsibiity for violations of factory legislation and benefited from reduced costs (recruitment and supervision), and the usual advantages of having employees with 'an interest in production': whereas outwork sub/ contractors had engaged in 'ruinous undercutting', mule spinners drove their piecers harder and also increased the amount of unpaid labour time they contributed.

This analysis of the advantages of sub/contracting before the factory, between the factory and outwork, and within the factory suggests some common advantages of sub/contracting systems (to principals). The *flexibility* allowed by sub/contracting permits the principal to pass on the effects of fluctuations in the product and labour markets. The *minimisation of costs* is the second advantage to those who use sub/contractors. Savings on the costs of overheads and of fixed capital are the most obvious but there are also savings to be made on labour costs. For example, the sub/contractor recruits, trains and selects workers. Of course, labour costs form an element of the sub/contractor's payment but the principal is usually in a position to ensure that not all of these are passed on; in outwork for example:

> The workmen of the first class being scattered over a wide tract of the country, and being mutual competitors for work and wages, can seldom conspire with one another, and never with any effect, against their employers. But supposing them to do so in some degree, they would lock up as much of their own capital as their masters; that is, they would lose as much interest of money in their unemployed looms and loom shops, as he would lose in the capital advanced to them in yarn for weaving. (Ure, 1967, p. 281)

Furthermore, it is possible that labour costs are at a low level even if the sub/contractor is able to pass them on. Sub/contracting may allow the creation of a differentiated labour market in which employees of a sub/contractor are non-unionised and badly-paid. Sub/contracting may also permit 'co-exploitation'. This is Hobsbawm's term (but see Marx, 1974, p. 519) for the result of the process which 'made many members of the labour aristocracy into the co-employers of their mates, and their unskilled workers' (1964, pp. 297–8). The former operated under the pressure of incentives but this pressure was passed on to subordinates without generalising the incentives: 'these set the pace and the rest had no option but to follow it!' (Hobsbawn, 1964, p. 353).

Hobsbawn is thinking particularly of *internal* sub/contracting but co-exploitation of a kind can also exist in its other forms. It is not necessary in this respect to have intermediaries who undertake super-exploitation (contrary to Dobb's opinion, 1975, p. 266). As Marx noted (1974, p. 535), intermediaries may prove expensive even if their activities (like those of merchant capital) are more visible and more readily criticised as immoral. Capital may benefit from lower costs of exploitation because 'direct exploitation of labour costs labour' (Marx, 1974, p. 557) and these costs are minimised where labour has an 'interest in production'. The classic example of this interest is the outworking family which increased production when trade slumped and so increased the gap between supply and demand.

But while flexibility, lower costs and co-exploitation give obvious benefits to principals, they do not make sub/contracting a superior system to direct employment. The outworking family which increased production in a slump also tended to reduce production when demand rose, and for every advantage that accrues from dispensing with direct control of labour and capital a disadvantage can be found. For example, Bythell (1978, p. 182) agrees that manufactories were crippled by costs which did not affect the capitalist organiser (the cost of the workshop, its tools and its maintenance, the cost of heat and light, and possibly the expense of supervision) but goes on to argue that manufactories offered *advantages* over outwork:

. . . wages could be paid on a time- rather than a piece-basis, patterns could be kept secret, materials kept clean, and delivery dates met with greater certainty. (Bythell, 1978, p. 184)

It is possible that economic historians once assumed that direct employment was superior to sub/contracting because this fitted their (mono)linear view of industrial development. We must not make a similar mistake by assuming an absolute advantage for sub/contracting in certain of the paths of change which comprise the revised multi-linear view of development (cf Friedman, 1977). It would be more sensible at this stage to talk instead of (semi-permanent) *traditions* and (possibly less permanent) *fashions* in types of organisation. From this perspective the conventional histories are simply reflecting the prejudices of the fashion- advisers of the early

Industrial Revolution, Pollard's 'dogmatism of classical political economy' (see p. 198 above, also see Berg, 1985, pp. 42, 46).

CONCLUSIONS

Provided we are not too concerned that the case study has been, in the main, limited to a single industry,[9] we can now list a new set of assumptions from which we can begin analysis of contemporary events. Firstly, sub/contracting is no longer assumed to be a primitive form but, as Pollard writes, 'may be compatible with different stages of the development of industrial capitalism' (1965, p. 39). Secondly, sub/contracting is not a naturally worse (or better) form of organisation. Finally, sub/contracting trends may be explained by changes in fashion.

Contemporary arguments about sub/contracting are strangely familiar. They recall, for example, the discussion of flexibility (on pp. 208–9 above). In 1980 the Wool Textile Economic Development Council told the industry that it would like to see sub/contracting extended:

> . . . the Italian woollen industry centered on Prato consists, unlike much of the UK industry, of very small producers who manufacture fabrics on a commission basis. The fabrics are commissioned by the imprannotori, in some way similar to convertors but with greater power and influence . . . The effect of this system has been to give the Italian industry great flexibility . . . This has had a profound effect upon the UK industry's ability to compete in both home and overseas markets, on non-price as well as price factors.
>
> The EDC hopes that the UK industry will learn from the Italian experience outlined above. (Wool Textile EDC, 1980, pp. 20–1)

This wish is curiously similar to one expressed in comparable circumstances (West Country wool textile producers were experiencing intense competition from Yorkshire) two centuries earlier (Mann, 1971, p. 116).

Similar echoes (of arguments about growth and capital availability as well as flexibility) are to be found in the writings of a contemporary exponent of 'a new (sic) flexible approach to organization' in the United States:

It is hard to imagine a better way for a company to grow than by having people work for it as if they were part of the company without having expensive capital investments committed to the work they do. More managers should consider contracting out many tasks performed in house right now. (Harrigan, 1985, p. 4)

and in the work of Atkinson (1984 and see *Guardian*, 18 April 1984), arguably the best of current writers on the 'flexible firm' (his term). Indeed the recent work of Anna Pollert (1988) suggests that Atkinson and other participants in the 'flexibility' debate have considerably over-stated the significance of current trends towards increased flexibility (especially as far as temporary workers are concerned). Furthermore, the historical echoes are not limited to those who are concerned with the advantages of contracting. Trade unionists arguing against contracting out in the British Steel Corporation (BSC) in the 1980s (Fevre, 1986) repeated some of the arguments used by textile trade unionists in the 1930s who blamed 'manufacturers' and 'middlemen' for increasing 'the cost of production without performing any useful function' (Hilton, 1935, p. 308).

Almost all of the arguments in favour of sub/contracting rehearsed on pp. 207–9 above apply equally as well in the late twentieth century (see Fevre, 1989) as they did in the eighteenth or nineteenth centuries, yet this chapter has suggested that, so far as the historical case study is concerned, these arguments are no more persuasive than arguments which emphasise the *disadvantages* of sub/contracting. Might this not also be true today? If it were, then the current trend towards contracting out would be just that, a trend or fashion.

To say that the current trend towards contracting out is dictated by fashions in types of organisation is not to suggest that all enterprises have the same freedom to follow this fashion. Many sorts of limitations exist: the technical and managerial limitations mentioned by Pollard, the strength of organised labour and so on, but these are only the factors which limit the *opportunities* for sub/contracting (Atkinson, 1984). They do not determine whether an enterprise which has such opportunities will decide to contract out. Similarly, industry as a whole can be limited by general factors which make sub/contracting more or less attractive. Chief amongst such factors are legislative restrictions on the sub/contractors (for contemporary effects of removing such restrictions, see Hurstfield, 1987a and *Listener*, 12 November 1987), but, as with individual employers, these factors affect opportunities and do not determine choices.

Two contemporary examples support the suggestion that sub/ contracting has been extended because it has become *fashionable* once more. This is certainly what seems to have happened in BSC where, without any sort of reliable costing exercise, management's extreme caution about contracting out was replaced overnight by the desire to replace large numbers of direct employees with outside contractors (Fevre, 1989). It costs this argument little to concede that this overnight change in policy was stimulated by the Conservative government's favourable opinion of contracting out as a method of privatisation and this government's desire that BSC should reduce direct employment even if this did not reduce costs. In this case the fashion-followers were the government rather than the policy-makers inside BSC (who soon found this enthusiasm infectious, however).

Ascher (1987) describes contracting out in public services in similar terms. She thinks that this movement may have more to do with reducing direct employment than costs and establishes that weakening the trade unions is an important, covert aim of the policy. Although she does not describe contracting out as a fashion, her accounts of 'new right' arguments and political lobbying in its favour, of the way hospitals have implemented it, and of likely future swings of opinion away from the policy, all support the suggestion made in this chapter: that sub/contracting is a fad.

If this view is even close to the truth then two consequences should follow. Firstly, the term 'fashion' should immediately suggest to *sociologists* that a question has been asked rather than answered; and they may observe that – no matter whether they wish to use the term fashion' or not – there is no obvious reason why a similar question should not be asked of other aspects of industrial organisation than sub/contracting. Useful research into the organisation of production therefore implies investigation of the origins of 'new fashions', of the mechanisms by which they are disseminated, and of the circumstances under which they are adopted or ignored. An example of just such an approach is provided by Pollert's critical commentary (1987, 1988) on the work of Atkinson and colleagues at the Institute of Manpower Studies. Of particular interest to the present author, however, are the logical (rather than merely circumstantial) proofs which are required if we are to explain why employers do not follow the more 'rational' decision-making processes with which sociologists usually credit the business world.

Secondly, if fashion and tradition[10] are what determine trends in sub/contracting, those who wish to argue against contracting out can do so on economic as well as social grounds. Until now such arguments have had little force since they encounter a dilemma. The social argument is that contracting out makes things worse for the workers, but it is assumed that this is probably good news for management: reduced and more insecure employment, lower wages, worse conditions and so on will mean greater productivity and lower costs (this was, of course, the Conservative government's argument in favour of contracting out nationalised industries and services). But if there are equally good economic arguments against contracting out, if the choice of which argument to believe simply depends on fashion, then the dilemma no longer exists: making a social case against contracting out no longer disqualifies one from presenting economic arguments as well.[11]

NOTES

1. Because the materials on which work is undertaken are often commodities, sub/contracting may exist where – as in some examples of outwork – (a) the sub/contractor has no option but to sell to this one buyer, and (b) bought the materials from him/her. 'Property' is used here in the sense that Weber (1964) uses it: to refer to things which one is free to buy and sell and to pass on to one's heirs.
2. Rather less blame attaches to (under)development theorists because they have long since abandoned the assumptions about industrial change which are in question here. Unfortunately both economic historians and writers on contemporary matters appear to have ignored their work (for notable exceptions see Hudson, 1981, pp. 52–3 and Gerry, 1983).
3. For example, through the work of Bendix (1956) and Smelser (1959); and latterly Anderson (1971), Braverman (1974), Joyce (1980), Marglin (1974), and Melossi and Pavarini (1981).
4. Where at all possible I have tried to save space by *not* providing detailed references to these texts and readers are referred instead to the bibliography at the end of the chapter (which also includes material on subcontracting in other industries). This bibliography is not complete, however; for example, it does not include several very useful articles published in the journal *Textile History*, and a full bibliography is available on request.
5. The writer with the closest knowledge of the early Yorkshire mills concludes that there was an 'almost 100 year transition' to the factory in wool textiles (Jenkins, 1975, p. 1).

6. At the most remote level, this continuity can also be seen in the continued importance of piece wages. Less remotely, outmending is a direct descendant of capitalist outwork: handloom weaving families did most of their own mending. Readers should also note that differences between the organisation of woollen and worsted before the Factory System help to explain differences in the pattern of sub/contracting between the two sections in the twentieth century.

7. Interestingly, the Atkins Report found no *independent* commission combers in the industry in 1969, but at least one firm of this type (Yorkshire Combers Ltd) was set up with help from prospective clients, in the 1970s.

8. And others: one doubts that Weber would find in sub/contracting the forms of 'appropriation' necessary to ensure the 'maximum formal rationality of capitalist accounting' (see Weber, 1964).

9. There are, in any event, other suitable case studies: the automobile and defence industries, for example.

10. In both textiles and steel (Fevre, 1989) sub/contracting can be viewed as the 'historically available solution'.

11. There is a curious irony here since some economic historians blamed sub/contracting for the worst social consequences of the Industrial Revolution while at the same time seeing it as a backward system of organisation. Readers should note that, while economic arguments against sub/contracting have not been entirely absent from the contemporary literature, they have usually been limited to particular cases where comparative costings are available or to accusations of poorer quality work by sub/contractors (cf Fevre, 1986, Hurstfield, 1987a; note that Ascher, 1987 is much more wary of these claims than Fevre or Hurstfield).

BIBLIOGRAPHY

S. Allen and C. Wolkowitz, *Homeworking – Myths and Realities* (Basingstoke: MacMillan Education, 1987).

A. M. Anderson, *Women in the Factory* (London: John Murray, 1922).

M. Anderson, *Family Structure in Nineteenth Century Lancashire* (Cambridge: Cambridge University Press, 1971).

K. Ascher, *The Politics of Privatisation: Contracting Out the Public Services* (London: Macmillan, 1987).

W. S. Atkins, *The Strategic Future of the Wool Textile Industry* (London: NEDO/HMSO, 1969).

J. Atkinson, *Emerging UK Work Patterns* (Brighton: Institute for Manpower Studies, 1984).

R. Bendix, *Work and Authority in Industry* (London: John Wiley, 1956).

M. Berg (ed.), *Technology and Toil in Nineteenth Century Britain* (London: CSE Books, 1979).

M. Berg, *The Age of Manufactures* (Oxford: Basil Blackwell, 1985).

M. Bienefeld, *Working Hours in British Industry: An Economic History* (London: Weidenfeld & Nicholson, 1972).

H. Braverman, *Labor and Monopoly Capital* (New York: Monthly Review Press, 1974).

D. Bythell, *The Handloom Weavers* (Cambridge: Cambridge University Press, 1969).

D. Bythell, *The Sweated Trades: Outwork in Nineteenth Century Britain* (London: Batsford, 1978).

J. H. Clapham, *The Woollen and Worsted Industries* (London: Methuen, 1907).

P. R. D. C. Corrigan, 'Feudal relics or capitalist monuments?' *Sociology*, Vol. 11, 1977, pp. 435–63.

F. Crouzet, *Capital Formation in the Industrial Revolution* (London: Methuen, 1972).

M. Dobb, *Studies in the Development of Capitalism* (London: Routledge, 1975).

M. Dunford and D. Perrons, *The Arena of Capital* (London: Macmillan, 1983).

R. Fevre, 'Contract work in the recession' in K. Purcell *et al.* (eds), *The Changing Experience of Employment* (London: Macmillan, 1986).

R. Fevre, *Wales is Closed* (Nottingham: Spokesman, 1989).

A. Friedman, *Industry and Labor* (London: Macmillan, 1977).

C. Gerry, *Recession, Restructuring and the Rediscovery of the 'Black Economy'*. Paper to Annual Conference of British Sociological Association, Cardiff, 1983.

R. E. Goffee, 'The butty system and the Kent coalfield', *Bulletin of the Society for the Study of Labour History*, No. 34, 1977, pp. 41–55.

R. E. Goffee, 'Incorporation and conflict: a case study of subcontracting in the coal industry', *Sociological Review*, Vol. 29, No. 3, 1981, pp. 475–97.

D. Gregory, *Regional Transformation and the Industrial Revolution: A Geography of the Yorkshire Woollen Industry* (London: Macmillan, 1982).

B. Hammond and J. L. Hammond, *The Skilled Labourer 1760–1832* (London: Longmans, 1919).

K. Harrigan, *Strategic Flexibility: A Management Guide to Changing Times* (Lexington, Mass.: D. C. Heath, 1985).

N. Harte and K. Ponting (eds), *Textile History and Economic History* (Manchester: Manchester University Press, 1973).

H. Heaton, *The Yorkshire Woollen and Worsted Industries* (Oxford: Oxford University Press, 1965).

H. Heaton, 'Financing the Industrial Revolution' in Crouzet 1972.

C. Heywood, 'The rural hosiery industry of the lower Champagne region 1750–1850', *Textile History*, Vol. 7, 1976, pp. 96–111.

J. Hilton, *Are Trade Unions Obstructive?* (London: Victor Gollancz, 1935).

R. Hilton (ed.), *The Transition from Feudalism to Capitalism* (London: New Left Books, 1976).

E. J. Hobsbawm, *Labouring Men* (London: Weidenfeld & Nicholson, 1964).

P. Hudson, 'Proto-industrialization: The Case of the West Riding Wool Textile Industry in the 18th and early 19th centuries', *History Workshop*, 12, 1981, pp. 34–61.

J. Hurstfield, 'A route to inefficiency – compulsory contracting', *Low Pay Review*, No. 29, 1987a.

J. Hurstfield, 'The tender trap: the effects of the local government bill', *Low Pay Review*, No. 31, 1987b.

D. T. Jenkins, *The West Riding Wool Textile Industry 1770–1835: A Study of Fixed Capital Formation* (Bath: Pasold Research Fund, 1975).

D. T. Jenkins and K. G. Ponting, *The British Wool Textile Industry 1770–1914* (London: Pasold/Heinemann, 1982).

P. Joyce, *Work, Society and Politics* (London: Methuen, 1980).

C. Littler, 'Internal contract and the transition to modern work systems', in D. Dunkerley and G. Salaman *The International Yearbook of Organisational Studies* (London: Routledge, 1979).

C. Littler, 'Deskilling and changing structures of control' in S. Wood (ed.), *The Degradation of Work* (London: Hutchinson, 1982).

J. De L. Mann, *The Cloth Industry in the West of England from 1640 to 1880* (Oxford: Clarendon Press, 1971).

S. A. Marglin, 'What do bosses do?', *Review of Radical Political Economy*, Vol. 6, No. 2, 1974, pp. 60–112.

K. Marx, *Capital*, Vol. 1 (London: Lawrence & Wishart, 1974).

D. Melossi and M. Pavarini, *The Prison and the Factory: Origins of the Penitentiary System* (London: Macmillan, 1981).

I. Pinchbeck, *Women Workers and the Industrial Revolution* (London: Routledge, 1930).

S. Pollard, *The Genesis of Modern Management* (London: Edward Arnold, 1965).

A. Pollert, *The 'Flexible Firm': A Model in Search of Reality (or a Policy in Search of a Practice)?*, Warwick Papers in Industrial Relations, No. 19 (Warwick: Industrial Relations Research Unit, University of Warwick, 1987).

A. Pollert, 'Dismantling "flexibility" ', *Capital and Class*, No. 34, May, 1988.

G. F. Rainnie, *The Woollen and Worsted Industry: An Economic Analysis* (Oxford: Clarendon Press, 1965).

R. Samuel, 'The workshop of the world', *History Workshop*, No. 3, 1977, pp. 6–72.

E. Schremmer, 'The textile industry in southern Germany 1750–1850', *Textile History*, Vol. 7, 1976, pp. 60–89.

E. M. Sigsworth, *Black Dyke Mills* (Liverpool: Liverpool University Press, 1958).

N. J. Smelser, *Social Change in the Industrial Revolution* (London: Routledge, 1959).

A. J. Taylor, 'The sub/contract system in the British coal industry' in L. S. Presnell (ed.), *Studies in the Industrial Revolution* (London: Athlone Press, 1960).

E. P. Thompson, *The Making of the English Working Class* (Harmondsworth: Penguin, 1974).

A. Ure, *The Philosophy of Manufactures* (New York: Kelley, 1967).

M. Weber, *The Theory of Social and Economic Organisation* (New York: Free Press, 1964).

Wool Textile EDC, *Progress Report 1980* (London: NEDO, 1980).

Index